Guinness Ferguson Mary Catharine

The Story of the Irish Before the Conquest From the Mythical Period to the Invasion Under Strongbow

Guinness Ferguson Mary Catharine

The Story of the Irish Before the Conquest From the Mythical Period to the Invasion Under Strongbow

ISBN/EAN: 9783744738873

Printed in Europe, USA, Canada, Australia, Japan

Cover: Foto ©ninafisch / pixelio.de

More available books at **www.hansebooks.com**

THE STORY OF THE IRISH

BEFORE THE CONQUEST.

FROM THE MYTHICAL PERIOD TO THE INVASION
UNDER STRONGBOW.

BY

M. C. FERGUSON.

LONDON:
BELL AND DALDY, YORK STREET,
COVENT GARDEN.
1868.

PREFACE.

We are told, in the *Senchus Mór*, that, when Saint Patrick had completed the arrangement of that Digest of the Laws of the Gael of Ireland, his coadjutor, Dubtach, who was a Bard as well as a Brehon, "put a *thread of poetry* round it." So, the writer of this little Digest of the Irish Historical Story has endeavoured to intertwine, with the trite detail of names and successions already often chronicled, whatever more interesting incidents can be drawn from the new sources of heroic and picturesque material laid open to the English reader by the labours of lately-deceased, and of living, Irish scholars. If it be objected that a somewhat too favourable view is taken of a rude age and savage manners, it may with truth be said that any errors of sympathy are more than counterbalanced by the undue contempts of which, for many ages, all native Irish historic and legendary material has been the object. And the writer believes that, in forming an estimate of any national character, it is better to err, if at all, on the side of sympathy and respect.

The Irish tradition, however rude, is the intellectual food which has nourished in a long series of generations the only literary life that has subsisted amongst them. To the philosophic historian, no less than to the poet and romance-writer, it is a material full of interest. But the principal object to be hoped for in these pages would be achieved, if the work should happily influence refined and candid minds towards a more tolerant and sympathizing view of the mental tastes and acquisitions of several millions of their countrymen.

20 *North Great Georges Street, Dublin.*
December, 1867.

TABLE OF CONTENTS.

CHAPTER I.
THE MYTHICAL PERIOD.

                                                                                             PAGE

Aborigines preyed on by African pirates.—Colony of Partholan.—Colony of Nemed.—Siege of Tor Conaing.—Battle of the White Strand.—Arrival of the Firbolgs.—Their works in stone.—Arrival of the Tuath De Danaans.—Battles of Moyture.—Characteristic differences in Arms.—Arrival of the Milesian Scoti.—Chivalrous conduct of the Scoti.—Battle of Tailti.—The Scoti conquer the island.—Its distribution.—The laws and social polity of the conquerors.—The remains of these races.—Their influence on the West of Europe . 1

CHAPTER II.
THE HEROIC PERIOD.

The alternate sovereignty of Kimbay and his brothers.—Macha's claim to succeed her father.—Her conquests.—Foundation of Emania.—Cova's usurpation.—Story of Lavra Maen and Moria.—Conor MacNessa reigning at Emania.—The Knights of the Red Branch.—The abdication of Fergus MacRoy.—Maev, Queen of Connaught.—Story of the sons of Usnach.—Story of the *Tain-bo-Cuailgné*.—The " Pillow Conversation " of Aillil and Maev.—The " Boy Feats " of Cuchullin.—How he got his name.—How he took arms.—His heroic conduct

in the *Tain-bo.*—His courtship of Eimer.—The story of
Blanaid.—Cuchullin's combat with his unknown son.—Story
of Atharne.—Story of Mesgedra and Conall Carnach.—Chivalrous traits in both characters.—Death of Conor MacNessa.
—Story of the healing of Conall Carnach.—Chivalrous conduct of Beiilcu.—Deaths of Conall, Fergus MacRoy, and
Maev 23

CHAPTER III.

THE ATACOTTIC PERIOD.

Reigns of Conari Mór and Crifian.—Revolt of the Atacotti (*Aitheach
Tuatha*), and massacre of the nobles.—Usurpation of Carbri
Cat-head.—Resignation of the crown by his son Morann to
the exiled legitimate heir.—Restoration of the noble *caste* in
the person of Feredach.—Second expulsion of the nobles.—
Second restoration in the person of Tuathal the Acceptable.
—Crime of Eochy, King of Leinster, against Tuathal's
daughters, leading to the imposition of the Boarian tribute,
or *Boru* of Leinster.—Rise of the Northern and Southern
Dynasties.—Con Hundred-Battle and Moh Nuad divide the
island.—Lea Con and Lea Moha.—Battle of Moy Lena.—
Chivalrous trait of Goll MacMorna.—Ollioll Olum sovereign
of Lea Moha.—His descendants 88

CHAPTER IV.

THE OSSIANIC PERIOD.

The dream of Eatach.—Battle of Moy Mucrivé.—Lugaid Laga and
the three Ferguses.—The Battle of Crinna.—Reign of Cormac
MacArt.—Story of Cormac and Ethni.—The *Fianna*, or
Militia.—Finn MacCumhal.—Story of Dermid and Grania.
—The death of Dermid.—Oisin.—The Ossianic Poems.—
King Cormac's water-mill.—His retirement at Cletty.—The
burial of King Cormac.—Battle of Gavra.—Banishment of
the Three Collas.—Their return, and failure to provoke King
Muredach to avenge his father's death.—They destroy
Emania.—Descendants of the three Collas.—Crime, and dis-
appointed ambition of Mongfinn.— Retrospect. — Pictish

Table of Contents. vii

origins.—The sons of Umor, and the Firbolgs in the West.—Niall of the Nine Hostages.—His expedition to Alba (Scotland) 100

CHAPTER V.

THE PATRICIAN PERIOD.

Niall's expedition to Armorica.—Captivity of Patrick.—His occupations and thoughts.—His escape.—Niall's expedition on the Loire, and death there.—His descendants, the Northern and Southern Hy-Niall.—King Dathi.—His expedition into Gaul.—Killed by lightning.—His body carried home and interred at Cruachan.—Patrick's return as Apostle of the Irish.—His Easter eve at Slane.—He preaches before King Laery at Tara.—Conversion of Laery's daughters, Ethna and Felimia.—Revision of the Laws, and compilation of the *Senchus Mór*.—King Laery killed "by the Wind and Sun."—Patrick overthrows Crom Cruach and his twelve sub-gods.—Baptizes Ængus, King of Munster.—Diffuses the Gospel throughout Ireland.—Dies at Saul, and is buried at Down Patrick.—The clan system in the early Irish monasteries.—The three orders of the holy men of Ireland.—The burial of Owen Bel, King of Connaught.—Succeeded by Kellach.—Murder of Kellach.—Avenged by his brother Cucongelt.—Final settlement of the Dalriads in Scotland.—Saint Brigid.—Saint Kieran.—Saint Finnian of Clonard.—Saint Finnian of Moville.—Passion for monastic seclusion.—Story of Enda and Saint Fanchea.—Monastic remains of Aran.—Clonmacnoise founded by Saint Kieran.—Murkertach MacErca.—Dermid MacKervil.—Remains at Clonmacnoise.—Saint Kevin.—Glendalough.—Saint Brendan of Clonfert.—His Legend 132

CHAPTER VI.

THE COLUMBAN PERIOD.

Saint Columba.—His noble birth.—A pupil of Saint Finnian.—Companion of Kieran.—Kieran's jealousy rebuked.—Columba's copy of Finnian's Psalter.—King Dermid's judgment in favour of Finnian's copyright.—Leads to the Battle of Cuildrevné.—The MS. still in existence.—Formerly the battle-standard of the O'Donnells.—The bell of Patrick the battle-standard of the Kinel-Owen.—The crozier of Grellan the battle-standard of the O'Kellys.—Story of the emigrants of the Clan Colla and Saint Grellan.—Poem ascribed to Columba.—He goes into exile to I-colm-kill (Iona), in penance for his part in the battle of Cuildrevné.—The Columban Rule.—Their time of celebrating Easter.—The existing MSS. ascribed to Columba.—His metrical dialogue with Cormac.—He returns to Ireland to attend the Synod of Drumceat.—Objects of King Aedh in convening that assembly.—The exactions of the Bards.—Story of King Guary and Sancan, and the quest for the *Tain*.—Columba intercedes for the Bards, and aids the Dalriad king Aidan in establishing his independence.—His death. 176

CHAPTER VII.

THE SCHOLASTIC PERIOD.

Intellectual progress of the Irish between the Convention of Drumceat and the arrival of the Danes.—Comparative paucity of details in the local annals.—Ampler information from continental notices.—Defeat and death of King Aedh at Dunbolg.—His son Maelcova resigns the crown to become a cleric.—Sweeny Menn Ard-Righ.—Assassinated by Congal Claen at the instigation of Donall.—Dream of King Donall.—His feast at Dun-na-n'geadh.—Rebellion of Congal Claen and battle of Moyrath.—Story of Cuanna, who gives his death wound to Congal Claen.—Donall's favour to the church.—He founds the Abbey of Cong.—St. Fechin's church and mill at Fore.—His ecclesiastic establishment on High Island.—Buidhe Chonnaill, "yellow plague."—Other epidemies.—St. Adamnan visits Ireland.—His account of the Holy Places, from the narrative of the pilgrim-bishop Arculf.—Expedition of Egfrid, King of Northumbria, to ravage the coasts of Leinster.—St. Adamnan visits York and obtains the release of Irish captives.—Story of Kenfalla.—Great schools of learning in Ireland.—Armagh.—Prince Aldfrid's itinerary.—Testimony of the Venerable Bede to the learning and hospitality of the Irish.—Poem of Donatus, Bishop of Fiesole, illustrating the state of Ireland in his day.—

Testimony of Eric of Auxerre.—Sweeny of Clonmacnoise assists at the foundation of Oxford.—His bell in the Museum of the Royal Irish Academy.—Irish " wisdom sellers " at the court of Charlemagne.—School of Lismore.—St. Carthagh.— School of Bangor.—St. Columbanus.—His foundations in Burgundy and Italy.—His letters.—Pre-eminence of Ireland as the seat of scholastic education, even after the Danish inroads.—Testimony of the author of the life of Sulgen. —Opinion of Camden. 202

CHAPTER VIII.

THE DANISH PERIOD.

Invasions of the Northmen.—Rise of the Southern Hy-Niall.— Generous devotion and death of King Niall Caillé.—Story of Turgesius.—Tyranny of the Danes.—Their foundation of the seaport towns, and progress in commerce.—Norse influence on the local nomenclature.—Intermarriages between the Northmen and Irish.—St. Olaf.—Norse cruelties in the propagation of the faith contrasted with the mild course of the gospel in Ireland.—Ancient tumuli on the Boyne rifled by the Danes.—King Malachy I. desires to make a pilgrimage to Rome.—King Aedh Finnliath.—King Flann of the Shannon.—Story of his daughter Gormley.—Cormac MacCulinan, King-archbishop of Cashel. — His church on the Rock of Cashel.—His Glossary.—His Psalter.—Rivalry between the Eugenian and Dalcassian Septs of Munster.— State of Munster.—Cormac instigated to war with Leinster by the Abbot Flaherty.—Makes his will.—Battle of Ballaghmoone and death of Cormac.—Honourable conduct of King Flann.—Penance of Flaherty.—Afterwards King of Cashel.— Succeeded by Lorcan, father of Kennedy, father of Brian Boru.—Kennedy admits the claim of alternate succession, according to the will of Ollioll Olum, and yields the throne of Cashel to Callaghan.—Stratagem of the Danish chieftain Sitric.—Callaghan taken prisoner.—Kennedy marches the Munster troops to his rescue.—Gallant conduct of Falvy Finn.—Death of King Flann.—Niall " Black-knee."—Donogh. —Murkertach " Pell-Cloak." — His circuit of Ireland.

—Callaghan's second imprisonment.—Donall O'Neill, son of Murkertach, Prince of Aileach, becomes Ard-Righ.—Surnames introduced.—The great Sept of O'Neill descendants of Donall 229

CHAPTER IX.
THE DALCASSIAN PERIOD.

Reign of Malachy II.—Defeats the Danes at Tara, and at Dublin. —His proclamation.—Rivalry with Brian Boru.—Rise of the Dalcassian tribe under the leadership of the sons of Kennedy. —Struggles of Mahon and Brian with the Danes.—Interview of these princes.—Assembly of the Dal-Gais.—Battle of Sulcoit.—Sack of Limerick.—Song of triumph for Mahon.— His murder.—Brian avenges his death.—Rules Munster from Kincora.—Battle of Glenmama.—Alliances of Brian.—Aspires to the sovereignty.—Malachy deserted by the Northern princes.—Submits to Brian.—Generous conduct of the rivals. —Administrative genius of Brian.—His magnificence.—Maelmurra, King of Leinster, insulted at Kincora.—Conspires with the Danes.—Battle of Clontarf.—Brian's army.—Chivalrous conduct of the deposed King Malachy.—Muster of the Northmen at Clontarf.—Brian's address to his army.— Encounter between Plait and Domnall.—Interview between Murrogh, son of Brian, and Dunlang O'Hartigan.—Conflict of Murrogh and Anrud.—Death of Murrogh.—His son Turlogh drowned.—King Brian in his tent.—Is killed by Brodar 255

CHAPTER X.
THE EVE OF THE CONQUEST.

King Brian and his son Murrogh interred at Armagh.—Retreat of the Dal-Gais.—The Eugenian tribes separate from the Dal-Gais.—The men of Ossory demand hostages.—Heroic conduct of the wounded Dalcassians.—The men of Ossory afraid to attack them.—The remnant of the Dal-Gais reach Kincora.— Results of the Battle of Clontarf.—Malachy II. reascends the throne.—Donogh O'Brien.—Flaherty O'Neill.—Makes a pilgrimage to Rome.—Rise of the Leinster family of Mac

Murrogh.—Turlogh O'Brien deposes his uncle Donogh, who retires to Rome and dies there.—Turlogh sends Irish oak to King William Rufus.—Murkertach Mór O'Brien.—Rise of the family of O'Conor in Connaught.—Laxity of ecclesiastical discipline.—Synods held by Celsus, Gillibert, and St. Malachy.—Malachy's conversations with Pope Innocent II. about the state of Ireland.—Pope Adrian IV. an Englishman.—His Bull authorizing the invasion of Ireland by the English King.—Henry Plantagenet unable at the time to avail himself of the donation.—Abduction of Dervorgilla by Dermid MacMurrogh, King of Leinster.—He is deposed.—Seeks the protection of King Henry II., who gives him letters of aid.—Richard De Clare, Earl of Pembroke (Strongbow), embraces his cause.—The sons and grandsons of the beautiful Nesta.—Henry FitzHenry.—Meyler FitzHenry.—FitzGerald. — FitzStephen. — FitzBernard. — De Barry.—Giraldus Cambrensis.—His description of Dermid Mac Murrogh.—Effects of the Conquest 279

Note on the Sources and Nomenclature 294

THE IRISH BEFORE THE CONQUEST.

CHAPTER I.

THE MYTHICAL PERIOD.

No race which has left its impress on the history of our globe has preserved its primitive traditions with the same tender and jealous care as the Celtic, that early swarm from the Japhetic hive which, the bardic traditions tell us, reached Europe long, long before the dawn of authentic history.

Even then, the Celtic story affirms, there wandered through the pine forests of Ierne an aboriginal people; and its shores were the resort of Vikings, not from Scandinavia, but Africa. The traces of a population ignorant of the use of metals and of the practice of agriculture have been found over all the west of Europe. In Gaul and Britain the record of their existence is the bone-cave and the drift-bank, where Nature has sealed up their knives and hatchets of stone, along with the half fossil remains of the elk, the cave bear, and the elephant. In addition to similar evidences in Ireland, bardic tradition tells us that the leader of these *autoch-*

thones, on the arrival of the first Gaelic swarm from the East was named Cical.

Of Cical and his hunter tribes the varied lay began,
And how in Grecian galleys borne Maeonian Partholan,
Sire of great Slangé on a day, with sight of sail and oar,
Amazed the dwellers of the woods by Inverskene's shore.
Where first invasion first brought in the arts of life; and how
Erin untill'd till then, from him received the spade and plough.

And who was Partholan? and how came he to be dignified with Greek associations? the reader will ask. The name, whencesoever derived, is indelibly imprinted in the old local nomenclature of the country. The traveller, taking the direction of Blessington from Dublin, about five miles out of the city, passes a decayed village called Tallaght; and this name *Tam lacht*, signifying a "plague sepulchre," has been, from time immemorial, used in the connection of the Tam-lacht of the people of Partholan. For the constant tradition is, that the whole colony brought into Ireland by this chieftain perished in a great plague, and that a multitude of them were buried in a common tomb at this spot; and tradition also tells us that this plague had pursued Partholan as a punishment for the guilt of parricide, under the sting of remorse for which, he had become a voluntary exile.

Local tradition also had, from immemorial time, given the name of Slangé, son of Partholan, to the highest peak of the Mourne mountains in Down, up to the time when Slieve Donard acquired its present name, from Domangart, a holy person of the sixth century, whose hermitage occupied the site of the cairn of the buried warrior on the mountain summit.

Forgotten Partholan himself lies 'neath his royal mound
On green Moynalty, hushed at eve by drowsy ocean's sound ;
And clangorous song of flocks by night, when through the
  wintry air
The wide-winged wild geese to their pools by Liffey's side
  repair.
But promised Slangé, tombed aloft on that great mountain's
  head,
Which now, since Domangart hath used the chamber of the
  dead
For cleric rites, no longer owns its name of old renown,—
Slieve-Slangé,—but Slieve-Donard sounds, awaits his calling
  down.

However apocryphal the name of Partholan may now appear, we must recognise the voice of a very remote antiquity in favour of the story of the parricide; of the aborigines whom he invaded and civilized; and of the avenging plague before which his race, though not his memory, has been obliterated.

And what of the African Vikings?

They are known in the recollection of those early times under the name of Fomorians. In the glossary of King Cormac of Cashel, compiled not long after the age of Alfred, this word is said to signify "under sea," in the sense of their ships being descried on the horizon, rising, as it were, from beneath the rim of ocean, and indicating their approach from the Atlantic rather than the narrow seas. From whencesoever they came, they were expert navigators, and their famous glass castle upon Tor Inis, or Tory Island, may possibly have been a vitrified fort. Round these walls of glass, and on the strand beneath, was waged, we are told, one of the earliest of the many "Battles of the White Strand," which supply the place of the "tale of Troy divine" in early Irish and Welsh bardic history. A new colony of adventurers, led by Nemed of the same race with Partholan, issuing from the high table-land of central Asia, the cradle of the Aryan families of mankind, had arrived, and subjected to the servile toils of tillage and building, the remnant of the former population. But the galleys of the "under sea" invaders still rose on the horizon, and poured their troops of Fomorian pirates on the thinly-peopled shores. The glass tower of Tor Inis was the great stronghold of the strangers. It was Nemed with his chief warriors who crossed the turbulent straits, and laid siege to the wonderful castle.

Fierce conflicts were waged upon the shore. The combatants in their fury disregarded the rising tide which overwhelmed them, the crew of one ship only of the Nemedians escaping. Amongst those saved were three chieftains of Nemed's blood, who, though now abandoning the country, were destined to re-people Ireland at a subsequent period.

> They fought ere sunrise at Tor Conainn,
>   All day they fought on the wild sea-shore;
> The sun dropp'd downward, they fought amain,
>   The tide rose upward, they fought the more.
> The sands were cover'd, the sea grew red,
>   The warriors fought in the reddening wave;
> That night the sea was the sea-king's bed,
>   The land-king drifted past cliff and wave.
>
> Great was the rage in those ancient days,
>   (We were pagans then) in the land of Eire;
> Like eagles, men vanquish'd the noontide blaze,
>   Their bones were iron, their nerves were wire.

> We are hinds to-day! The Nemedian kings,
> Like elk and bison of old stalk'd forth;
> Their name—the sea king's—for ever clings
> To the "Giant Stepping Stones" round the north.*

We must endeavour to imagine the island during these vicissitudes, under successive conditions of populousness and desertion, rude wealth and sterility, until a new swarm of adventurers come upon the scene, making their entrance also by the common avenue of Greece. These are the Firbolg, exiles from Thrace. They had been slaves, compelled, under the lash of task-masters, to cultivate the terraces on the steep sides, it may be, of Pindus or Hæmus. Each man was provided with a leathern bag, in which he carried up soil to these hanging gardens. Hence, say the Irish traditions, the name of Firbolg, men of the bag. They conspired, rose, and fled together, and a new infusion of Greek characteristics was thus imparted to the Isle of Destiny. Traces of the Firbolgs remain, not only in the names given by them to different localities, which are yet retained, but in the Duns and earthworks which they erected. The western isles of Aran contain, in admirable preservation to this day, the great stone fortresses of Dun Conor and Dun Ængus, built at a subsequent period by chieftains of this race.

Dun Ængus is a marvellous dry-stone erection. On a promontory which slopes gradually upwards from the landward side, and terminates in an abrupt cliff which frowns over the Atlantic, a considerable space of ground has been enclosed by a massive cyclopean wall. This

---

* From *Inisfail*, by AUBREY DE VERE.

consists of three concentric rings of building, each complete in itself, yet in immediate juxtaposition, and well fitted for defence. The sloping landward side is thickly studded with pillar-stones, firmly fixed in the soil, intended, apparently, to act as a kind of *chevaux-de-frise*, and embarrass the advance of an enemy on the only avenue of approach.

It is inaccessible from the sea. The cliff rises grandly above the wild Atlantic waves, which dash themselves against its base, and threaten its total destruction ere long. It has evidently been largely undermined already. Part of the vast edifice has tumbled into the deep water beneath. That which yet stands overhangs the ocean abysses. A more grand and impressive scene can scarcely be imagined. The utter solitude of the spot: the boundless expanse of ocean, dark-heaving and sublime: the old, old, stronghold— more ancient probably than any building now standing in western Europe, counting its age not by hundreds, but by thousands of years—powerfully impress the imagination. The feeling is enhanced by the loneliness of these rarely-visited and inaccessible islets of the far west, which contain at present the huts only of simple peasants, and ruins of the cells and churches of the earliest Christian ecclesiastics. These are touching in their simplicity and antiquity, yet appear insignificant and comparatively recent, when compared with Dun Ængus and Dun Conor, pagan strongholds of Firbolg chiefs.

These erections belong, as we have said, to the latest period of Firbolg history, when the tribe were closely pressed by their conquering kinsmen, and forced from the rich provinces of the south and east, to seek refuge in more remote and inhospitable districts. The Firbolg blood to this day exists to an appreciable extent in Connaught, and the outlying isles of the west. They were a dark-haired and dark-skinned race, small in comparison with their fair-haired foemen, whose superior *physique*, no less than their higher civilization, and knowledge of arts and metals, assured them a speedy supremacy.

For a third invasion remains to be chronicled. The Tuath-De-Danaans, like their kinsmen the Firbolgs, are said to be descended from Nemed through Ibath, his great-grandson, one of the chieftains who, with the ancestor of the Firbolg, escaped from the battle of Tor-Conaing.

It is claimed for this people also, that they came from Greece, but by way of Scandinavia. We may imagine them to have pursued the course of the rivers which flow to the Baltic, unless—as their traditions seem to indicate, and for which some slight probability may be traced in the features of the country between the Don and the Vistula—that part of Europe was then under water, and the western portion, from the Carpathian mountains, virtually an island, and the passage effected, as the Argo is fabled to have performed it, by sea. The present form of our continent would thus result from the gradual elevation of the soil on the low-lying, flat, alluvial plains of Poland and Russia.

Nuad of the Silver Hand was the chieftain of the Tuath-De-Danaans, when they encountered Eochy, the

reigning Firbolg monarch, in the battle of the Southern
Moyturé. The scene of the engagement is supposed to
be identified near Cong. The fugitive king was pursued, overtaken, and slain, at Ballysadare, in the county
of Sligo. His cairn still exists, on the strand there,
and was formerly deemed one of the "Wonders of
Erin." Indeed the whole of this district of Sligo, as
well as the supposed field of Moyturé itself, abounds
with stone monuments—archaic enough to be co-eval
with the scenes and actors of whom we treat. Nuad is
said to have lost his hand in the battle, and to have
used a silver substitute, framed by the skill of Credné
Cerd, that is, the Smith. The mutilation, however,
incapacitated him for the throne, in accordance with a
law which prevailed to a comparatively late period, and
debarred any one who had a personal blemish from
reigning. The story indicates, at least, the mechanical
skill possessed by the Tuath-De-Danaans, which was so
inexplicable to the vanquished Firbolgs, that they considered their conquerors to be necromancers, or demons.

"The Battle of Moyturé" has come down to us
from a period long prior to the twelfth century in the
form of a bardic tale; one of those romantic pieces
which every well-instructed poet was expected to have
in readiness when called on to entertain an assembly
with song or recitation. It is one of a large class of
similar compositions, but distinguished from most
others by affording tangible evidence on a question of
great archæological interest. In our great museums
the visitor may observe two classes of bronze weapons,
one being of broad, short, and comparatively clumsy

proportions; the other slender, elegant, and of the leaf-bladed or classic form. The Tale of the Battle of Moyturé affords an unsuspected proof that, at whatever time it was composed, the popular belief among the Irish was, that weapons of the former class were peculiar to the Firbolgs, and of the latter to the Tuath-De-Danaans. It describes an interview between the scouts of the adverse armies, who encounter one another in a solitude. They plant their shields in the ground, and, from behind these defences, commence their colloquy. Acquiring greater confidence, they then proceed to examine one another's arms, when the distinction we have mentioned is referred to and commented on. Now it is a remarkable fact, that in all the sepulchral mounds of the kindred Belgic tribes of Britain, the broad, trowel-like blades only have been found, while the classic form of weapon is common in North Britain, through which Irish tradition brings the De-Danaan invaders. A belief in the magical powers of these "God Tribes" lingers in the country, where the fairies are still supposed to be their representatives. To them tradition ascribes the bringing in of the *Lia fail*, or stone of destiny, on which the kings were inaugurated at Tara. It is popularly believed to exist at the present time, under the coronation chair of the Sovereigns of the United Kingdom in Westminster Abbey, having been brought thither from Scone, where it had fulfilled a similar purpose for the Scottish monarchs. Fergus, king of Scotland, of the Dalriadic (Irish) dynasty, sent for it from Tara, desiring to be crowned on this stone of destiny, which secured, that a sovereign of the Scotic race should never fail to sit on the throne founded on the *Lia fail*. The prophecy has not hitherto failed in its accomplishment, as Queen Victoria is a true descendant of the Scotic line. Some of our antiquaries, however, maintain that the *Lia fail* still remains at Tara, and point to a standing pillar stone on a mound yet remaining, as the veritable Stone of Destiny.

For the name of the Green Isle itself, we are indebted to this people, Eri being the name of a daughter of their race—forming Erin in the genitive. Ogma, another of the same family, is presumed to have given name to that species of writing—called ogham—formed by notches on the edges of stones: a form of record which certainly was in use about the time of the introduction of Christianity; while to the great Dagda, one of their kings, is ascribed that marvellous tomb on the banks of the Boyne, the mound of New Grange. This amazing and most interesting monument still exists in perfect preservation. It was opened and pillaged by the Danes, in common with its neighbour tumuli of Knowth and Dowth, and many other sepulchral monuments in different parts of the country. The gold ornaments which the ancient Irish buried with their illustrious dead, were, no doubt, an irresistible temptation to the Viking freebooters of the ninth and tenth centuries of our era. This vast mound, covering nearly two acres in extent, and consisting of a conical grass-covered cairn of small stones, and still partly surrounded by a ring of majestic megaliths, is entered by a passage formed of standing stones of considerable size, guarded by a beautifully-carved cill or lintel at the entrance. This passage measures sixty-three feet in length, and leads to a dome-roofed chamber. Almost every stone employed in the construction of this, and of the smaller chambers which open from it, is not only wonderful from its bulk, but is carefully ornamented with carvings in spirals, lozenges, and other rude, but not ungraceful figures. The plan of the sepulchre is analogous in general design to the Egyptian pyramids. The cairn of stones and clay covering the chambers and passage, corresponds in the Celtic tomb with the angular sloping mass of the pyramid. The conception is scarcely less grand, though the mechanical skill and mass of material employed by the eastern tomb-builders, were incomparably greater. Bardic tradition seems to indicate this as possibly the grave of The Dagda and his three sons. This powerful monarch, "The Great Good Fire," is said to have ruled for seventy years. His death is stated to have been the result of a wound received long before at the battle of the Northern Moyturé. His grandsons, called MacColl, MacKeact, and MacGrené, because they are said to have worshipped the hazel-tree (*Coll*), the ploughshare (*Keáct*), and the Sun (*Grian*), had for their respective wives, Banba, Fola, and Eri, from whom our island obtained the names by which it is known to the Bardic historians. The objects of worship ascribed to the husbands of these ladies may indicate an advancing civilization and practice of the arts of agriculture; but a fresh invasion of Erin by another swarm of Celto-Scythic wanderers was impending, and the Tuath-De-Danaan were to be superseded as a dominant race, by the Milesian immigrants, after they had ruled in Ireland for nigh two hundred years.

The Scoti or Gael, according to their traditions, like the previous colonizers of Erin, traced their descent from Magog, son of Japhet. Unlike the Firbolgs and Tuath-De-Danaans, who passed through Greece on their western route, this wave of Celtic immigrants from their common home in Central Asia, claim to have come by way of Scythia, Egypt, and Spain. Under the leadership of Breogan, they won for themselves a footing in Spain, and founded the city of Brigantium, near Corunna, in Galicia. These adventurers, according to their descendants' story (for we must remember we are still in the region of tradition), impelled by famine, which at that time ravaged Spain, resolved to seek fresh fields and pastures new, and as a preliminary step, sent forth Ith, son of Breogan, to visit Ireland. He is said to have seen the island like a cloud on the horizon, from the watch-tower of Brigantium. The solitary vessel of Ith, with its crew of one hundred and fifty men, landed in the north of Ireland. He found himself able to converse with the people of the country in their common Gaelic tongue. He informed them that he had landed from stress of weather only, without any intention of settling in the country, but hearing that the three grandsons of the Dagda, of whom we have already spoken, were quarrelling among themselves and desired his services as umpire, he advanced to meet them, and having made his award, reproved them for their strife, praising the fruitfulness of the soil of Erin, and its happy temperature.

Ith had set out on his return to his ship, when the Tuath-De-Danaan kings, alarmed by his praises of their country, which they thought indicated a probable return to their shores with a larger armament, followed, and gave him battle on the shores of Lough Foyle. Ith placed himself in the rear of his little army, and bravely protected their retreat to the ship. He was, however, mortally wounded in the fight, but his people carried his corpse to Spain, where his kinsmen, the sons of Miled, the grandson of Breogan, excited by the outrage, resolved to avenge his death.

The Milesians, with a fleet of thirty ships, each ship carrying thirty warriors, their wives, and attendants; eight of the leaders being sons of Miled, neared the Irish coast. The magical lore of the Tuath-De-Danaans availed to raise a mist, and the spell-bound voyagers were compelled to sail round the island before they were able to land. This accomplished, they marched on Tara, and there encountered the three sovereigns, attended by their magicians. They demanded quiet possession of the country, or battle. MacColl, MacKeact, and MacGrené, unprepared for either alternative, offered to abide by the decision of Amergin, one of the sons of Miled, who pronounced that the Milesians should again put to sea, for a distance of nine waves or *tonns*, and then attempt a landing on Erin. Should the Tuath-De-Danaans fail in preventing this, they were bound by the verdict of Amergin to yield the sovereignty of Ireland to the invaders. The Gael were no sooner on the ocean than their fleet was scattered by a terrific storm raised by the magical arts of the Tuath-De-Danaans. The greater number of their ships were wrecked, and their leaders perished in the waves. Eber and Eremon, surviving sons of Miled, however, effected a landing, and in an engagement at Tailti (supposed to be Teltown in Meath), completely subdued the Tuath-De-Danaan princes, who perished with their wives, Eri, Banba, and Fola. Two chieftains of the victorious Gael fell in the pursuit, whose deaths we record, as they gave names to districts long celebrated in Irish heroic story; Cuailgné (now Cooley), in Louth, and the mountainous tract of Slieve Fuad (now the Fews), in the county of Armagh. Such is the story of the Milesian or Scotic immigration; obviously not so old, in its present form, as the events which it purports to relate, but still a tale of very high antiquity; and characterized by one of the earliest traits of that chivalrous spirit which has so strongly marked the Romantic school of European literature.

The victorious leaders at once proceeded to partition the island. Munster was assigned to Eber, Leinster and Connaught to Eremon, while Ulster was given to Eber, son of Ir, son of Miled, who had survived the shipwreck in which his father was drowned. Lugaid, son of Ith the pioneer of the Milesians, had a territory in Munster assigned to him. It is from these successful adventurers that most of our native Irish families claim to trace their descent. But it is singular that while these Milesian representatives abound, and families with Firbolgic ancestors are not unknown, no race, clan, or family, existing at the present time are reputed to have Tuath-De-Danaan blood in their veins.

Among the most prominent Milesian kings we may mention Tiernmas, of the race of Eremon. He is said to have introduced the public worship of idols. Crom Cruach, a hideous idol, surrounded by twelve smaller divinities, was worshipped with cruel rites on the plain of Moy Slaght, in that part of the ancient territory of Breffny which now constitutes the county of Cavan. Tiernmas was also the introducer of those parti-coloured garments now represented by the tartan of the Scottish Gael. The dress of a slave was limited by him to one colour. A peasant was permitted to have two; a soldier or a noble, three; while four colours were allotted to the keeper of a house of hospitality; five to a chieftain, and six might adorn the robes of a king or a queen. It is recorded that this sovereign possessed among his household a refiner of gold, and we may not improbably trace to this period some part of that excellence in the workmanship in the precious metals for which the Irish were so long celebrated, and of which such numerous and varied specimens exist in the museum of the Royal Irish Academy. The manufacture of silver shields, designed as gifts to subordinate chieftains, and the casting of silver coin, are recorded in the reigns of successors of this monarch.

But a far more advanced state of progress is evinced by the legislation of King Olav Fola, a prince of the race of Ir, who instituted the Convention of Tara. This national parliament was held every third year, and to it were summoned the classes illustrious in rank and learning. The monarch entertained all comers for six days, endeavouring, in the exercise of this frank hospitality, to promote good feeling and friendly relations among his subordinate chieftains, bards, and sages. An inspection of national records, whose accuracy was guarded with the most jealous care, is said to have been one duty performed by the *Feis* of Tara, indicating that the pagan Irish possessed the art of writing. Nor is it to be supposed that a people, with whom the transmission of property, and indeed their entire social system, depended on their genealogical accuracy, would fail to guard, by every possible means, against the intrusion of error or corruption into the pedigrees, which were the title-deeds of every proprietor. The invariable custom of naming the father, grandfather, and even more remote ancestor, of each individual who is the subject of the bard or senachie's pen, shows how important family descent was held by the Gael. Their usage of gavelkind, too, while it divided the property of a deceased parent equally among all his sons, and resulted in that minute subdivision which has been, on the whole, injurious to the progress of civilization and centralization, yet promoted the free development of the individual, and that consciousness of equality which has borne fruit in the courteous consideration for others, resulting from self-respect, which to our own day is so striking in the Celtic races. Michelet, in speaking of this law of equality and equitable division, which characterized the Celts of France as well as those of Ireland and Scotland, observes: "As this law of precious equality has been the ruin of these races, let it be their glory also, and secure to them at least the pity and respect of the nations to whom they so early showed so fine an ideal."

While the Norman genius developed the feudal system, the Celtic developed that of the clan, which was formed on the family type. Their kings were head of the family, and held in patriarchal fashion their council-courts in the open air, with the advice and assent of their clansmen, who in the lands belonging to the tribe had their equal and indefeasible rights; nor could the sovereign resort to war without their aid and concurrence. The sovereignty itself was elective in person, though hereditary in blood. When vacant, it was to descend, according to their law of Tanistry, to " the oldest and most worthy man of the same name and blood." The *Tanist*, or heir-apparent, was generally, but not necessarily, the oldest son of the reigning monarch, while the younger members of the family were designated *Roydamna*, or "king-material." The Tanist was generally named at the time when the monarch was elected. To this law of Tanistry may be ascribed, in part, those violent deaths which closed the career of so many Irish kings. This, with that tendency to subdivision which split the country into several petty states, each with its separate ruler, who rendered very equivocal allegiance to the *Ard Righ*, or supreme monarch, resulted in that turbulence and incessant party strife which, to so great an extent, form the subject of the Irish and other early West-European annals.

The professions of Druid, Bard, and Brehon were, in the main, hereditary. The former combined the offices of priest and physician; the Bards were the poets and historians; while the Brehons transmitted and administered that code of laws which is known by their name, and which, in its modes of procedure, is found to bear an unexpected resemblance in many points to the Common Law of England, both being probably to a great extent sprung from the same primitive original.

The custom of fosterage was general, families of rank undertaking the nursing and training in manly exercises of the children of their chiefs. The mutual attachment which sprang up between the foster parents, brothers and sisters, and the scion of noble race who had passed his childhood with them, was one of the strongest feelings of the Irish heart, and led to innumerable instances of devotion which are scarcely intelligible to us at the present day.

But it may be inquired, what tangible remains still exist of these ancient times? They are not few nor unsuggestive. In addition to the bardic traditions which have so far occupied us, we possess in the Celtic tongue itself, the oldest spoken language in Europe, a means whereby we can "repeople the past." Its importance, in a philological point of view, is second only to that of Sanscrit, a kindred tongue; for we must not forget that the Hindoos are a primitive emanation of that Aryan race, moving southwards from their cradle in central Asia, of whom the Celts are the earliest western offshoots. Sanscrit ceased to be a spoken language some 300 years before the Christian era, very much about the period to which we have now brought the history of the Celts of Ireland. But the valuable knowledge to be gained from the Irish tongue is not lost to us, for its written literature exists to our day, and is now, for the first time, diligently studied by competent scholars. Few, indeed, are the men qualified to explore the mine of wealth which belongs to us in the Western Gaelic language. Its greatest Irish interpreters have recently been removed by death. But other labourers in this rich harvest daily arise amongst us. German and French scholars are now pioneering the way for Continental inquiry, and even taking up their abode in Irish-speaking districts to familiarize themselves with the use of this new key to philological and ethnological knowledge. Let us hope that among ourselves prejudices, ignorances, and apathetic indifference to Irish subjects may pass away, and in their stead the desire to do noble work for home and their country inspire in the breasts of Irishmen strenuous efforts to learn more and do more for the honour of their native land.

In Ireland, also, to a greater extent than elsewhere, existing remains, such as raths, forts, duns, cashels, cairns, and cromlechs, abound on all sides, to instruct the antiquarian inquirer. Our national museums and libraries, too, are rich in objects of interest illustrating this early period:—stone, bronze, and iron weapons, gold and silver ornaments, specimens of work in metals, together with manuscripts of great importance, and among these the most exquisite examples which Europe can show of illuminated art. On Irish soil may yet be examined the very oldest erections of western Europe, from the rude cranogues, or lacustrine habitations, built on piles artificially planted in shallow akes, to the earthern forts and stone cyclopean duns, of the pagan period, such as we have already described; the frequent cromlech, also, of unhewn stones, sometimes of enormous bulk; the tumulus, with its central stone chamber, often adorned with hieroglyphical carvings; pillar-stones with ogham inscriptions; Christian churches, cells, stone huts, and graceful round towers; and sculptured crosses, all works of a primitive time, and characteristic of a pure, unmixed, and isolated race.

And not on Irish soil only have the Gael of Ireland left their traces. From the sixth century of the Christian era, Irish missionaries have been the evangelizers of Scotland and of France; have laboured in the spiritual harvest, in England, Germany, Switzerland, Scandinavia, and Italy. The Irish saint, Columba, was the founder of the monastic establishment on Hy, or Iona; "that illustrious island, once the luminary of the Caledonian regions, whence savage tribes and roving barbarians derived the benefits of civilization—the blessings of religion." From Iona went forth Saint Aidan, the converter of the Northumbrian kingdom of his day, and founder of Lindisfarne. Saint Columbanus, another Irishman, evangelized eastern France. His disciple, Saint Gall, instructed the Swiss in the truths of Christianity. Columbanus established not only the early seats of piety and learning at Luxeuil and elsewhere, in Burgundy, but the Irish monastery also of Bobbio, in Italy. It would be tedious to extend this enumeration of illustrious names; the deeds of these, and other benefactors of the world, will occupy us in due time, when we have first considered that earlier and most picturesque period of Irish story, whose pagan traditions, with "tramp of heroes in them," fill and delight the imagination.

These enchanting themes, partly true, partly fabulous, but wholly heroic, poetic, noble, and *naive*, will form the subject of succeeding chapters. The race whose deeds we would chronicle, have been named by the classic writers, Celts. They did not so designate themselves; both in Ireland and Scotland they called themselves Gael, and have ever been distinguished by a strong sentiment of nationality. We shall take leave of them for the present with this "Salutation:" *

Hail to our Celtic brethren, wherever they may be,
In the far woods of Oregon, or o'er the Atlantic sea—
Whether they guard the banner of St. George in Indian vales,
Or spread beneath the nightless north experimental sails,
    One in name and in fame
    Are the sea-divided Gaels.

Tho' fallen the state of Erin, and changed the Scottish land,
Tho' small the power of Mona, tho' unwaked Llewellyn's band;
Tho' Ambrose Merlin's prophecies degenerate to tales,
And the cloisters of Iona are bemoaned by northern gales,
    One in name and in fame
    Are the sea-divided Gaels.

In northern Spain and Brittany our brethren also dwell,
Oh! brave are the traditions of their fathers that they tell;
The eagle and the crescent in the dawn of history pales,
Before their fire that seldom flags, and never wholly fails.
    One in name and in fame
    Are the sea-divided Gaels.

---

* By T. D. M'GEE.

A greeting and a promise unto them all we send—
Their character our charter is, their glory is our end—
Their friend shall be our friend, our foe whoe'er assails
The past or future honours of the far-dispersed Gaels.
        One in name and in fame
        Are the sea-divided Gaels.

CHAPTER II.

THE HEROIC PERIOD.

We have sketched the mythical period of Irish story as far as the reign of Olav Fola. This wise lawgiver and ruler was of the race of Ir, that son of Miled or Milesius, who perished in the storm evoked by the magical arts of the Tuath-De-Danaans. It will be remembered that, according to the decision of Amergin, the invaders had again put to sea, and retired to the distance of "nine waves" from the Irish coast, when the storm evoked by the magical incantations of the De-Danaan Druids assailed them. Their fleet was dispersed, and many suffered shipwreck when the elements thus fought against them.

Ir, we are told, was buried on the Skellig rocks, off the coast of Kerry. There the cairn which bears his name—probably one of the oldest sepulchral monuments in the western world—may be seen to this day. His posterity, in common with the descendants of his more fortunate brothers Eber and Eremon, gave kings to Ireland. From these three sons of Miled, and their cousin Lugaid, son of Ith, the great Irish families trace their pedigrees. From Lugaid claim to descend the O'Driscolls, and other families in the south of Ireland.

Eber is the progenitor claimed by the Munster Clans, the MacCarthy's, O'Briens, &c. From Eremon descend, as they suppose, the O'Donnells, O'Neills, O'Connors, MacMurroghs, and other great races in Ulster, Connaught, and Leinster: while the Mageniscs and their kindred who ruled in that part of Ulster constituting the present counties of Antrim and Down, then called *Uladh* or Ulidia, derive their genealogy from Ir. It is sometimes significantly asked, where are the descendants of the captains and soldiery, if the existing population are all sprung from the kings? Obviously at some point of the pedigree it departs from the truth: but it is equally clear that that point is very high up in the series.

The tribes descended from Ir contributed many heroes whose deeds have a foremost place in ancient story. Kimbay, in whose reign the palace fortress of Emania was founded—an event which is assumed in the annals of Tigernach as the starting-point of authentic Irish history—was a monarch of this race. So also was his wife Macha, who caused the great fort to be erected. The earthworks of Emania exist at the present day.

At this period, about 400 years before Christ, three princes, Hugh Roe, or Hugh the Red, Dithorba, and Kimbay, the sons of three brothers, claimed equal right to the throne. A compact was made by which it was decided that they should rule alternately for seven years. This agreement was confirmed by the guarantee of seven Druids, seven Poets, and seven Champions; "the seven Druids to crush them by their incantations, the seven

Poets to lacerate them by their satires, the seven young Champions to slay and burn them, should the proper man of them not receive the sovereignty at the end of each seventh year." This compact prevailed till each had reigned three times in his turn. Hugh Roe was drowned in the cataract of the Erne at Ballyshannon, where the falls at Assaroe still preserve his name.

His daughter Macha, the red-haired, claimed her turn of the sovereignty in his stead, but Dithorba and Kimbay refused to recognize any claim of succession in a woman. Macha, so far from acquiescing in this decision, raised an army, and defeated her opponents in battle. Dithorba was slain, and his sons exiled. Macha would not acknowledge their claims to the succession, and founded her own rights from henceforth, on the victory she had won. She married Kimbay, and so disposed of all competitors except the exiled princes, sons of Dithorba, whom she again defeated in battle, enslaved, and compelled to erect for her the fort of Emania. She marked out its site, says the tale, with her golden brooch, from whence one fanciful derivation of its name *Eo-muin*, a pin of the neck. After a lapse of more than two thousand years, the remains of this noble fort—for part of it has been destroyed by neighbouring farmers, who have used the soil for agricultural purposes—still exist near Armagh. Navan fort, as it is at present corruptly called, covers upwards of eleven acres of land. This is enclosed by a rampart of earth, and deep fosse and dry ditch. On the summit of the elevated and fortified ground stands a smaller circular fort. Another may also be traced on a slope of the hill, being both protected by the great rampart. The spot well repays a visit. From its elevated position an extensive prospect of the fine country around Armagh, stretching away to the Fews mountains, may be obtained. Here we stand on a fortress of the Celt, which has had a history for upwards of two thousand years. The adjoining townland of Creeve Roe yet preserves the name, and designates the site, of the "House of the Red Branch," a species of military college in which the Ulster warriors were wont to assemble in those old heroic days, and were there trained to deeds of prowess and daring.

Macha survived her husband Kimbay seven years, ruling Ireland in undisputed sovereignty, till she was slain by Rectaid. Her death was avenged by her foster son, Ugainé Mór, or The Great, of the race of Eremon, whose long and prosperous reign made his name illustrious in the native annals, and, if we may credit their testimony, known as a levier of tribute in districts of Britain, and even of the continent of Europe. Literature was cultivated in his time, and his sons were "full of learning;" one of them was the "author of many ancient bard-maxims." Ugainé endeavoured to secure the throne to his own family, exacting from his subjects an oath, "by the sun and moon, the sea, the dew, and colours, and all the elements visible and invisible," that the sovereignty of Erin should not be taken from his descendants for ever. For many generations his offspring, though stained with the blood of kindred, held the supreme authority; but after the lapse of about three hundred years, the races of Ir and Eber again became paramount.

Leary Lorc and Cova, sons of Ugainé Mór by Kesair, a Gallic princess, succeeded him; the latter obtained the sovereignty by the murder of the elder brother and his descendants, which he accomplished by treachery of a very base kind. Cova, who resided at Dinree on the Barrow, feigned sickness, and was visited by his royal brother. Leary received his death-blow from Cova's dagger, as he leaned over the pretended sick man, who consummated his cruelty by the murder of Leary's family: the only member spared was the grandson of the late King, Maen, who, being dumb, was incapable of reigning.

Maen passed his childhood at Dinree, under the guardianship of Ferkertné the poet, and Craftiné the harper, of his grand-uncle Cova. As he grew into manhood he gave promise of great personal beauty and symmetry. In a moment of excessive indignation at an insult offered to him by a companion, Maen recovered his power of utterance. "Lavra Maen!"— (Maen speaks)—was the exclamation of those around him, and the name clung to him ever after. Meantime the monarch at Tara heard of the wondrous event, and summoned Lavra Maen to appear before him. His jealousy having been increased by hearing from Ferkertné and Craftiné that the prince was the most munificent man in Erin, Cova banished them from his dominions.

"The loss will be greater to you than to us," said the harper.

"Depart out of Erin," said the monarch.

"If we can find no refuge in Erin we will," said they. The exiles repaired to Munster, and received at the court of the provincial king the customary hospitality, no questions being asked. At length the king inquired into their story, and hearing that they had been expelled by the Ard Righ, made them welcome to his care and protection. The king had a beautiful daughter whom he guarded with such jealous care that no opportunity of private conversation with the fair Moria could be found by Lavra Maen, who had soon become captivated by her charms. Craftiné, the harper, who was in the confidence of the young prince, according to the romantic legend, took advantage of a grand feast given by the king, and so delighted the monarch and his guests by his music, that the lovers were able to leave the room unperceived. As soon as Craftiné thought them out of hearing, he played on his harp an air of so entrancing a nature that the king and his guests were soothed into a profound slumber; and thus the young lovers had time to exchange vows of mutual affection, and resume their seats at the feast, before their absence had been observed. The queen, remarking the change in her daughter's manner, quickly divined the cause. Moria confessed her attachment to Maen; and his suit finding favour in the eyes of her parents, the lovers were married, and Lavra Maen, at the head of troops furnished by his father-in-law, attacked and captured Dinree.

Cova, roused to action, marched from Tara, and Lavra Maen, unable to cope with him, set sail for Gaul, having sent Moria, under the escort of Craftiné the harper, to her father's court. His faithful wife did not forget the exile. She sent the harper with valuable jewels to her husband in France. Craftiné performed his mission, played an enchanting fairy melody on his harp, and sang to it an impassioned lay which Moria had composed to her hero. The Gaulish king, touched by the grief of the young lovers, assisted Lavra Maen with an auxiliary force, and ships to transport them to Ireland. Maen landed at Wexford, and marched on Dinree. He surprised and defeated Cova, and took Dinree by storm. A Druid who was in the fortress asked who had made the attack: "The mariner," cried a voice from without. "Does the mariner speak?" here joined, and from this circumstance the name of Lavra Loingsech (the mariner speaks) has clung to Maen. This monarch—for by the death of the usurping Cova, Maen succeeded to his rightful inheritance as heir of Ugainé Mór—is claimed as the ancestor of all the true Lagenian, or Leinster families of the race of Eremon, with the exception of the O'Nolans, who are descended from Cova. The province of Laighen Leinster owes its name to him, being so called from the *Laighné* or Spears, with broad heads, which Maen introduced. A story similar to that of King Midas is told of this monarch. His ears, it was whispered, resembled those of a horse; the barber, who became aware of the fact, had his life spared only on promise of inviolable secrecy. He whispered his tale to a willow. The willow was cut down and carved into a harp, and the instrument murmured forth the secret, "Lavra Loingsech has a horse's ears."

Passing over many reigns of the descendants of the great Ugainé, which were not marked by any memorable events, we approach the Christian era, which may be taken as the culminating point of Irish heroic story. At that period Conor MacNessa was reigning over Ulster, at Emania, surrounded by the heroes of Creeve Roe, the gallant knights of the Red Branch, Fergus, son of Roy his step-father, Naisi, Ardan, and Ainlé, sons of Usnach, Conall Carnach, Cuchullin (pronounced *Ku-Kullin*), and many other champions, of whom we shall speak at greater length presently. Maev of Cruachan, the Semiramis of Irish history, was at the same time ruling Connaught from her fort of Rath Croghan, while her throne was defended by her husband Ailill, Keth, son of Magach, Beälcú (pronounced *Bayal-Ku*), and other Connacian heroes whose histories we must not anticipate.

We return, therefore, to Fathna the Wise, father of Conor MacNessa. This monarch, of the race of Ir, fell by the hand of Eochy Feliah, a prince descended from Eremon. Fathna left a young and beautiful widow, Nessa, who in due time was wooed and won, on somewhat singular conditions, by Fergus MacRoy, the then occupant of the throne of Uladh.

The legend has been versified, and to it we refer the reader who may care to know the terms on which this haughty widow consented to submit again to the yoke of matrimony.

THE ABDICATION OF FERGUS MACROY.

Once, ere God was crucified,
I was king o'er Uladh wide:
King, by law of choice and birth,
O'er the fairest realm of earth.

I was head of Rury's race;
Emain was my dwelling-place;
Right and Might were mine; nor less
Stature, strength, and comeliness.

* * * *

Such was I, when, in the dance,
Nessa did bestow a glance,
And my soul that moment took
Captive in a single look.

* * * *

" Lady, in thy smiles to live,
Tell me but the boon to give,
Yea I lay in gift complete
Crown and sceptre at thy feet."

" Not so much the boon I crave :
Hear the wish my soul would have,"
And she cast a loving eye
On her young son standing by.

" Conor is of age to learn ;
Wisdom is a king's concern ;
Conor is of royal race ;
Yet may sit in Fathna's place.

" Therefore, king, if thou wouldst prove
That I have indeed thy love,
On the judgment seat permit
Conor by thy side to sit.

" That by use the youth may draw
Needful knowledge of the Law."
I with answer was not slow,
" Be thou mine, and be it so." *

---

* From *Lays of The Western Gael*, by SAMUEL FERGUSON.

Fergus, happy in the society of the beautiful Nessa, suffers himself to be gradually superseded by his youthful substitute; until Conor has acquired too firm a hold on the popular favour to be dislodged from the sovereignty.

The supreme king of Ireland at this time was Eochy Feliah, the slayer of Fathna the Wise. He restored the pentarchy, thus setting aside the arrangements made about 300 years before by Ugainé Mór. He was the parent of six daughters, of whom Maev was the most distinguished; she had been married to Conor MacNessa, but left him and returned to her father's court, who gave her in marriage to Tinne, one of the provincial kings he had appointed in Connaught. He re-edified the rath of Cruachan, employing for the purpose a fierce tribe of Firbolgic origin, the *Gowanree*, who were compelled to labour unremittingly at the earthworks, and are said to have completed the dyke in one day. Maev named her residence after her mother, Cruacha; and, on the death of Tinne, ruled Connaught for ten years, with much vigour and ability. She afterwards married Ailill, a Leinster prince, to whom she bore seven sons, who were called the seven Manés, and were distinguished as " Mané the motherlike, Mané the fatherlike, Mané who resembled both, Mané of little valour, Mané of great valour, Mané the silent, and Mané of the boastful words."

But before we continue the history of Queen Maev, we must advert to certain causes which in the meantime had induced the ex-king of Uladh to seek an asylum at the court of Cruachan. We have already alluded to his abdication in favour of his stepson, Conor. This young prince, as he grew up, tarnished his great qualities by cruelty and treachery. He had educated a beautiful damsel, keeping her secluded from all mankind till she should be of an age to become his wife. Her name, Deirdré, signifying *alarm*, had been bestowed at her birth by the Druid Cathbad, and was prophetic of the long train of conflict and disaster to which her charms gave rise. Notwithstanding the precautions of Conor, she saw and loved Naisi, the son of Usnach. He was sitting in the midst of the plain of Emania, playing on a harp. Sweet was the music of the sons of Usnach—great also was their prowess; they were fleet as hounds in the chase—they slew deer with their speed. As Naisi sat singing on the plain of Emain he perceived a maiden approaching him. She held down her head as she came near him, and would have passed in silence. "Gentle is the damsel who passeth by," said Naisi. Then the maiden looking up, replied, "Damsels may well be gentle when there are no youths." Then Naisi knew it was Deirdré, and great dread fell upon him. "The king of the province is betrothed to thee, oh damsel," he said. "I love him not," she replied; "he is an aged man. I would rather love a youth like thee." "Say not so, oh damsel," said Naisi, "the king is a better spouse than the king's servant." "Thou sayest so," said Deirdré, "that thou mayest avoid me." Then plucking a rose from a briar, she flung it towards him, and said, "Now thou art ever disgraced if thou rejectest me." "Depart from me, I beseech thee, damsel," said Naisi. "If thou dost not take me to be thy wife," said

D

Deirdré, "thou art dishonoured before all the men of thy country after what I have done." Then Naisi said no more, and Deirdré took the harp, and sat beside him playing sweetly. But the other sons of Usnach, rushing forth, came running to the spot where Naisi sat, and Deirdré with him. "Alas!" they cried, "what hast thou done, oh brother? Is not this damsel fated to ruin Ulster?" "I am disgraced before the men of Erin for ever," said Naisi, "if I take her not after that which she hath done." "Evil will come of it," said the brothers. "I care not," said Naisi. "I had rather be in misfortune than in dishonour; we will fly with her to another country." So that night they departed, taking with them three times fifty men of might, and three times fifty women, and three times fifty greyhounds, and three times fifty attendants; and Naisi took Deirdré to be his wife.

After wandering through various parts of Ireland, "from Easroo to Ben Edar, and from Dundelgan to Almain," the fugitives at length took shelter in Scotland, where they found an asylum on the banks of Loch Etive. The loss of three warriors of such repute soon began to be felt by the nobles of Ulster, who found themselves no longer able to make head with their accustomed success against the southern provinces. They therefore urged Conor to abandon his resentment, and recal the fugitives. Conor, with no other intention than that of repossessing himself of Deirdré, feigned compliance. But, to induce Clan Usnach (as the fugitives were called) to trust themselves again in the hands of him whom their leader had so outraged, it was necessary that the message of pardon should be

borne by one on whose warranty of safe conduct the most implicit reliance could be placed. After sounding some of his chief nobles who were of sufficient authority to undertake the mission, among the rest Cuchullin, and finding that any attempt to tamper with them would be unavailing, Conor fixes on Fergus, the son of Roy, as a more likely instrument, and commits the embassy to him. But though he does not so much fear the consequences of compromising the safe conduct of Fergus, as of Cuchullin or the others, he yet does not venture openly to enlist him in the meditated treachery, but proceeds by a stratagem which, in these days, may appear somewhat far-fetched, yet probably was not inconsistent with the manners of that time. Fergus was of the order of the Red Branch, and the brethren of the Red Branch were under vow not to refuse hospitality at one another's hands. Conor, therefore, arranged with Barach, one of his minions, and a brother of the order, to intercept Fergus on his return, by the tender of a three days' banquet, well knowing that the Clan Usnach must in that case proceed to Emania without the presence of their protector. Meanwhile Fergus, arriving in the harbour of Loch Etive, where dwelt Clan Usnach in green hunting booths along the shore, "sends forth the loud cry of a mighty man of chase." Then follows a characteristic passage :—
" Deirdré and Naisi sat together in their tent, and Conor's polished chessboard between them. And Naisi, hearing the cry, said, ' I hear the call of a man of Erin.' ' That was not the call of a man of Erin,' replied Deirdré, ' but the call of a man of Alba.' Then again Fergus

shouted a second time. 'Surely that was the call of a man of Erin,' said Naisi. 'Surely no,' said Deirdré; 'let us play on.' Then again Fergus shouted a third time, and Naisi knew that it was the cry of Fergus, and he said, 'If the son of Roy be in existence, I hear his hunting shout from the loch; go forth, Ardan, my brother, and give our kinsman welcome.' 'Alas!' cried Deirdré, 'I knew the call of Fergus from the first.'" For she has a prophetic dread that foul play is intended them, and this feeling never subsides in her breast from that hour till the catastrophe. Quite different are the feelings of Naisi; he reposes the most unlimited confidence in the safe conduct vouched for by his brother in arms, and, in spite of the remonstrances of Deirdré, embarks with all his retainers for Ireland. Deirdré, on leaving the only secure or happy home she ever expects to enjoy, sings a pathetic farewell to fair Alba, the mountain, cliff, and dun, and her green sheeling on the shores of Glen-Etive.

Barach meets them on their landing, and detains Fergus, who reluctantly assigns his charge to his two sons, Red Buiné Borb and Illan Finn, to conduct them in safety to their journey's end. Deirdré's fears are more and more excited; she has dreams and visions of disasters. She urges Naisi to go to Dunseverick or to Dundelgan (Dundalk, the residence of Cuchullin), and there await the coming up of Fergus. Naisi is inflexible. It would injure the honour of his companion in arms to admit any apprehension of danger while under his pledge of safe conduct. The omens multiply. Deirdré's sense of danger becomes more and more acute.

Still Naisi's reply is, "I fear not; let us proceed."
At length they reach Emania, and are assigned the
house of the Red Branch for their lodging. Calm, and
to all appearance unconscious of any cause for apprehension, Naisi takes his place at the chess-table, and
Deirdré, full of fears, sits opposite. Meanwhile the
king, knowing that Deirdré was again within his reach,
could not rest at the banquet, but sends spies to bring
him word "if her beauty yet lived upon her." The
first messenger, friendly to Clan Usnach, reports that
she is "quite bereft of her own aspect, and is lovely
and desirable no longer." This allays Conor's passion
for a time; but growing heated with wine, he shortly
after sends another messenger, who brings back the
intelligence, that not only is Deirdré "the fairest
woman on the ridge of the world," but that he himself
has been wounded by Naisi, who had resented his
gazing in at the window of the Red Branch, by flinging
a chessman at his head, and dashing out one of his eyes.
This was all that Conor wanted; he starts up in pretended indignation at the violence done his servant,
calls his body-guard, and attacks the Red Branch.
The defence now devolves on the sons of Fergus. Clan
Usnach scorn to evince alarm, or interfere in any way
with the duties of their protectors. But Deirdré cannot
conceal her consciousness that they are betrayed.
"Ah me!" she cries, hearing the soldiery of Conor at
the gates, "I knew that Fergus was a traitor." "If
Fergus hath betrayed you," replied Red Buiné Borb,
"yet will not I betray you." And he issues out and
slays his "thrice fifty men of might." But when Conor

offers him Slieve Fuad for a bribe, he holds back his hand from the slaughter, and goes his way. Then calls Deirdré, "Traitor father, traitor son!" "No," replies Illan Finn, "though Red Buiné Borb be a traitor, yet will not I be a traitor. While liveth this small straight sword in my hand I will not forsake Clan Usnach!" Then Illan Finn, encountering Fiachra, the son of Conor, armed with Ocean, Flight, and Victory, the royal shield, spear, and sword, they fight "a fair fight, stout and manly, bitter and bloody, savage and hot, and vehement and terrible," until the waves round the blue rim of Ocean roared, for it was the nature of Conor's shield that it ever resounded as with the noise of stormy waters when he who bore it was in danger. Summoned by which signal, one of King Conor's nobles, coming behind Illan Finn, thrusts him through. "The weakness of death then fell darkly upon Illan, and he threw his arms into the mansion, and called to Naisi to fight manfully, and expired." Clan Usnach at length deign to lay aside their chess-tables, and stand to their arms. Ardan first sallies out, and slays his "three hundred men of might;" then Ainlé, who makes twice that havoc; and last, Naisi himself; and "till the sands of the sea, the dewdrops of the meadows, the leaves of the forest, or the stars of heaven, be counted, it is not possible to tell the number of heads, and hands, and lopped limbs of heroes that there lay bare and red from the hands of Naisi and his brothers on that plain." Then Naisi came again into the Red Branch to Deirdró; and she encouraged him, and said, "We will yet escape; fight manfully, and fear not." Then the sons of Usnach made a phalanx of their shields, and spread the links of their joined bucklers round Deirdré, and bounding forth like three eagles, swept down upon the troops of Conor, making great havoc of the people. But when Cathbad, the Druid, saw that the sons of Usnach were bent on the destruction of Conor himself, he had recourse to his arts of magic, and he cast an enchantment over them, so that their arms fell from their hands, and they were taken by the men of Ulster; for the spell was like a sea of thick gums about them, and their limbs were clogged in it, that they could not move. The sons of Usnach were then put to death, and Deirdré, standing over the grave, sang their funeral song.

> The lions of the hill are gone,
> And I am left alone—alone.
> Dig the grave both wide and deep,
> For I am sick, and fain would sleep!
>
> The falcons of the wood are flown,
> And I am left alone—alone.
> Dig the grave both deep and wide,
> And let us slumber side by side.
>
> The dragons of the rock are sleeping,
> Sleep that wakes not for our weeping.
> Dig the grave, and make it ready,
> Lay me on my true-love's body.
>
> Lay their spears and bucklers bright
> By the warriors' sides aright;
> Many a day the three before me
> On their linked bucklers bore me.

Lay upon the low grave floor,
'Neath each head, the blue claymore:
Many a time the noble three
Reddened these blue blades for me.

Lay the collars, as is meet,
Of their greyhounds at their feet;
Many a time for me have they
Brought the tall red deer to bay.

In the falcon's jesses throw
Hook and arrow, line and bow;
Never again, by stream or plain,
Shall the gentle woodsmen go.

Sweet companions ye were ever—
Harsh to me, your sister, never;
Woods and wilds and misty valleys
Were with you as good 's a palace.

Oh! to hear my true-love singing,
Sweet as sound of trumpets ringing;
Like the sway of Ocean swelling
Rolled his deep voice round our dwelling.

Oh! to hear the echoes pealing
Round our green and fairy sheeling,
When the three, with soaring chorus,
Passed the silent skylark o'er us.

Echo now, sleep morn and even—
Lark alone enchant the heaven!—
Ardan's lips are scant of breath,
Naisi's tongue is cold in death.

Stag, exult on glen and mountain—
Salmon, leap from loch to fountain—
Heron, in the free air warm ye—
Usnach's sons no more will harm ye.

> Erin's stay no more you are.
> Rulers of the ridge of war!
> Never more 'twill be your fate
> To keep the beam of battle straight!
>
> Wo is me! by fraud and wrong,
> Traitors false and tyrants strong,
> Fell Clan Usnach, bought and sold,
> For Barach's feast and Conor's gold!
>
> Wo to Emain, roof and wall!
> Wo to Red Branch, hearth and hall!
> Tenfold wo and black dishonour
> To the foul and false Clan Conor!
>
> Dig the grave both wide and deep,
> Sick I am, and fain would sleep.
> Dig the grave and make it ready,
> Lay me on my true-love's body!

So saying, she flung herself into the grave, and expired.

Fergus, at the feast, heard the fury of the elements and dash of waves, which warned him that the wearer of the magic shield of Conor was in grievous bodily peril:

> Rang the disk where wizard hammers, mingling in the wavy field
> Tempest wail and breaker clamours, forged the wondrous Ocean shield,
> Answering to whose stormy noises, oft as clanged by deadly blows,
> All the echoing kindred voices of the seas of Erin rose.
>
> Moaned each sea-chafed promontory; soared and wailed white Cleena's wave,
> Rose the surge of Inver Rory, and through column'd chasm and cave

Reaching deep with roll of anger, till Dunseverick's dungeons reel'd,
Roared responsive to the clangour struck from Conor's magic shield.

You—remember—red wine quaffing, in Dunseverick's halls of glee,
Heard the moaning, heard the chafing, heard the thundering from the sea.
Knew that peril compassed Conor, came, and on Emania's plain
Found his fraud and your dishonour,—Deirdré ravished, Illan slain.

Indignant at the violation of his safe conduct, Fergus, having chastised the treachery of Conor, retires into exile, accompanied by Cormac Conlingas, son of Conor, and by three thousand warriors of Uladh. They received a hospitable welcome at Cruachan from Maev and her husband, Ailill, whence they afterwards made many hostile incursions into Ulster, taking part among others in the famous fray called in Irish tradition the Tain Bo Cuailgné, or cattle spoil of Cuailgné (a district in Louth), which originated in a dispute between Ailill and Maev. This we shall give in the quaint and humorous language of the unpublished MS. translation of the great Irish epic:—

"On one occasion that Ailill and Maev had arisen from their royal bed in Cruachan of Rath Conrach, a pillow-conversation was carried on between them:—

"'It is a true saying, O woman,' said Ailill, 'that a good man's wife is a happy creature.'

"'Why do you say so?' said Maev.

"'The reason that I say so,' said Ailill, 'is because you are happier this day than the day I espoused you.'

"'I was happy before I knew you,' said Maev.

"'It was a happiness of which we never heard,' said Ailill; 'we only heard of your being in the dependent position of a woman, whilst your nearest enemies stole and plundered, and carried off your property.'

"'Not so, was I,' said Maev; 'but my father was arch-king of Erin, that is Eochy Fiedlech, son of Finn, son of Finnoman, son of Finneon, son of Finnlag (&c.). He had six daughters of daughters; viz., Derbrin, Eithne, and Ele; Clothra, Mugain, Maev, myself, who was the most noble and illustrious of them: I was the best for gifts and presents of them. I was the best for battle and fight and combat of them. It was I that had fifteen hundred noble mercenaries, soldiers; sons of foreign chiefs; and as many more of the sons of my own landholders; and there were ten (men) with every soldier of them, and eight with every soldier, and seven with every soldier, and six with every soldier, and five with every soldier, and three with every soldier, and two with every soldier, and a soldier with every soldier. These I had for my ordinary household,' said Maev; 'and for that it was, that my father gave me a province of the provinces of Erin; viz., the province of Cruachan, where I am called Maev of Cruachan. And I was sought in marriage by Finn, son of Ross Ruadh, King of Laighin, and by Cairpri Nia Fear, the son of the King of Teamair, and by Conor, son of Fachna Fathach. And

I was sought by Eochy, son of Luchta; and I did not
go, because it was I that demanded the extraordinary
dowry, such as no woman ever before sought from the
men of Erin; viz., a man without parsimoniousness,
without jealousy, without fear. If the man who would
have me, were parsimonious, we were not fit to be united
in one, because I am good at bestowing gifts and presents; and it would be a reproach to my husband that
I were better in gifts than he; and it would be no
reproach now, if we were equally good, provided that
we were both good. If my husband were timid, we
were not the more fit to unite, because I go in battles
and fights, and combats, by myself alone; and it would
be a reproach to my husband that his wife were more
active than himself; and it is no reproach if we are
equally active, but that we are active both of us. If
the man who had me were jealous, we were not matched
either, because I was never without having a man in
the shadow of another. I have found that man; viz.,
you; viz., Ailill, the son of Ross Ruadh, of the men
of Laighin. You were not parsimonious; you were
not jealous; you were not timid. I gave you an
engagement and dowry, the best that is desired of
woman; viz., the array of twelve men, of clothes; a
chariot, with thrice seven *cumhals*; the breadth of your
face of red gold; the span of your left wrist of carved
silver. Should any one work reproach, or injury, or
incantation on you, you are not entitled to *Diré** or
Enoclann † for it, but what comes to me,' said Macv,

* Dire was a fine for any bodily injury.
† Eneclann was a fine for satire, or reproachful words, &c.

'because a man in attendance on a woman is what you are.'

"'Such was not my state,' said Ailill, 'but I had two brothers, one the king of Temar, and the other king of Laighin. I left them the sovereignty because of their seniority. And you were not better for gifts and presents than I was. I have not heard of a province of Erin in woman-keeping but this province alone. I came then, and I assumed sovereignty here in succession to my mother; for Máta of Murisg, the daughter of Mágach, was my mother, and what better queen need I desire to have than you, since you happen to be the daughter of the arch-king of Erin.'

"'It happens, however,' said Macv, 'that my goodness is greater than yours.'

"'I wonder at that,' said Ailill, 'since there is no one that has more jewels, and wealth, and riches than I have—and I know there is not.'"

Ailill and Macv then commenced a comparison of their goods and effects—for women at this time had their dowries secured to them, and did not lose by marriage their separate rights of property. Their jewels, their garments, their flocks were compared, and found to be of equal value and excellence, with one notable exception only. "There was a particularly splendid bull of Ailill's cows, and he was the calf of one of Macv's cows, and Finnbennach (White-horn) was his name; but he deemed it not honourable to be in a woman's dependence, and he passed over to the king's cows." The queen was indignant, but hearing that Daré, son of Factna, of Cuailgné, was the possessor of a brown bull, a still finer animal than the white-horned deserter of her drove, she despatched her courier, MacRoth, to Daré, requesting of him the loan of the Donn Cuailgné (the Brown one of Quelny) for a year, and promising to restore him with fifty heifers to boot, a chariot worth sixty-three cows, and other marks of her friendship and high consideration.

Daré courteously complied with the request of Macv, and prepared an entertainment for her envoys. During the progress of the feast, some surly Connacian, in reply to an observation on the happy termination of their mission, observed, that it was as well that the Ultonians had agreed to send with them the Donn Cuailgné, as, if he had been refused, they would have carried him back with them by force. This unprovoked insult excited the just indignation of Daré. He swore by his " swearing gods," that the Connaught envoys should not now have the bull, either by consent or by force.

The messengers returned to Macv, and the disappointed queen summoned her forces, and called on her friends and allies, and the Ultonian exiles who had found refuge at her court, to join in a foray, the object of which should be the capture of the desired Donn Cuailgné. Fergus MacRoy, and Conor's own son, Cormac Conlingas, who had left Emania on the violation of their safe conduct to the sons of Usnach, brought their contingent to the Connacian army. It was not without much hesitation and many mental pangs, that these noble exiles consented to take part in an expedition directed against their countrymen and former friends. Macv led her armies in person. " A woman, comely, white-faced, long-cheeked, and large; gold-yellow hair on her; a short crimson cloak on her; a gold pin in the cloak over her breast; a straight, carved-backed spear flaming in her hand." Such was the appearance of this royal amazon when leading her hosts to the fray. Ailill and his son Mané, who resembled both parents, are thus described:—

"Two great men with flaming eyes; with golden crowns of blazing gold over them; kingly armour on them; gold-hilted, long swords at their girdles, in bright silver scabbards, with pillows of chequered gold on their outside."

Mané the motherlike, and Mané the fatherlike, as follows:—

"There came to me two soft youths there. They were both alike: curled hair on the one of them; curled yellow hair on the other; two green cloaks wrapped round them; two bright pins of silver in these cloaks over their breasts; two shirts of smooth yellow silk to their skins; white-hilted swords at their sides; two white shields with fastenings of fair silver on them; two fleshy-pointed spears, with bright silver ferules in their hands."

The itinerary of their journey exists, and is a document of much interest, as the halting-places and daily route of the Connaught armies may yet be distinctly traced. Onward they marched, crossing the Shannon at Athcoltna, and after many wanderings amid the unexplored central fastnesses of the present Longford, Leitrim, and Westmeath, arrived on the borders of Ulster without molestation.

And now appears on the stage the heroic figure of Cuchullin.

> When 'mid ford on Uladh's border, young Cuchullin stands alone,
> Maev and all her hosts withstanding:—"Now for love of knightly play,
> Yield the youth his soul's demanding—let the hosts their marchings stay.
> Till the death he craves be given, and upon his burial stone
> Champion praises duly graven, make his name and glory known;
> For in speech-containing token age to ages never gave
> Salutation better spoken than, 'Behold a hero's grave.'"

Cuchullin is the *preux chevalier* of Irish chivalrous story. He possessed every quality of mind and body proper, in the estimation of our ancestors, for a perfect heroic character.

"These were the several and diverse and numerous gifts peculiar to Cuchullin: the gift of form; gift of face; gift of symmetry; gift of swimming; gift of horsemanship; gift of chess-playing and backgammon; gift of battle; gift of fight; gift of combat; gift of vision; gift of eloquence; gift of counsel; gift of blushing; gift of paling; gift of best leading from his own country into a border country."

We must, however, extract from the epic of the *Tain Bo* the picturesque incidents it relates of Cuchullin's childhood (his "Boy-feasts," as they are called), before we give the maturer deeds of his chivalrous manhood. His mother, Dectire, was the sister of Conor Mac-Nessa. His father, Sualtain, was a man of mediocre talents. Their child, Cuchullin, was a hero from his infancy.

"The little boy asked of his mother if he would go to sport on the sporting green of Emain.

"'This is too early for you, my little son,' said his mother, 'until some champion of the champions of Ulster accompany you, or some guardian of Conor's guardians, to undertake your protection and safety from the youths.'

"'I think that too long, O mother,' said the little boy, then; 'and I shall not be arguing, but do thou show me where Emain is.'

"'Far from you,' said his mother, 'is the place where it is. Slieve Fuad is between you and Emain.'

"'I will myself make a guess of the way, alone,' said he.

"The boy set forward, taking with him his implements of pleasure. He took his hurl of brass, and his ball of silver, and his shooting arrows, and he took his top-burned spear of frolic, and he began to shorten his way by them."

The child was rudely handled by the youths who were sporting on the green at Emain. The disturbance reached the ears of Conor—who was playing at chess with Fergus MacRoy—at the moment when the aggrieved stranger had turned to bay, and was chasing five of his opponents. The king caught him by the wrists.

"'My dear little boy,' said Conor, 'I see no cause that you have to attack the boys.'

"'I have great cause,' said the little boy; 'I have

not received the recognition of a stranger—though I have come from remote lands—from the youths on my arrival.'

"'Then now, who art thou?' said Conor.

"'I am Setanta, the son of Sualtain; I am the son of Dectire, thy own sister, and it was not from you I expected to be thus aggrieved.'"

Conor, with some difficulty, makes peace between the youngsters. The education of his little nephew progressed from this period. The next adventure recorded of him is as follows:—

The following year Conor and a few select guests were invited to a feast at the Dun of Culann, the smith, who apologized for limiting his invitations " because it was not lands or tenements he had, but his sledge, and his anvils, and his hands, and his tongs." The king accepts, and on his way to the abode of Culann, observes, with Fergus MacRoy who accompanied him, the feats of his nephew and his companion youths who were sporting on the plain of Emania—

"'Alas! O youths,' said Conor, 'happy the country out of which the little boy that you see has come; if he knew the manly deeds as well as the boyish deeds.'

"'It is not proper to say that,' said Fergus; 'because, in proportion as the little boy grows, so will manly deeds grow with him.'

"'Let the little boy be called unto us, that he may come with us to drink of the feast to which we are going,' said Conor.

"'I shall not go,' said the little boy.

"'Why so?' said Conor.

"'Because the youths have not had enough of play and pleasure, and I shall not leave them until they have had enough of play.'

"'It would be too long for us to be waiting on thee,' said Conor, 'and we shall not either.'

"'Go ye before us,' said the little boy, 'and I shall follow you.'

"'You do not know the way,' said Conor.

"'I shall follow in the track of the company, and of the horses, and of the chariots.'"

So Conor went to the house of Culann, the smith. The king and his company were served and honoured, according to their degrees, their professions, their privileges, their nobility, and their gentle accomplishments. Green, fresh rushes were spread under them. They began to drink and be happy.

Culann asked of Conor :

"'Good, O king, hast thou appointed with any one this night to follow thee to this house ?'

"'I have not appointed indeed,' said Conor, because he forgot the little boy with whom he appointed to follow him.

"'Why so ?' said Conor.

"'I have a good chain-hound,' said Culann, 'and when once his hound-chain is loosened, no stranger dare travel within the same cantred with him, visitor or traveller, and he recognizes no one but myself. He has the power of an hundred in him, of strength.'

"'Let the chain-hound be set loose, that he may protect for us the cantred.' The chain-hound was then se loose from this hound-chain, and he made a quick circuit of the cantred, and returned to the seat where he always kept watch for the mansion. And there he crouched with his head on his paws, and fierce, cruel, churlish, dog-like was he that sat there."

To return to the youths. "They were in Emain until it was time for them to disperse. Each of them went to the house of his own father and mother, nurse, or tutor.

"The little boy now set out on the track of the company, till he came to the smith's house. He occupied himself, to shorten the way, with his implements of pleasure. When he came to the green of the house in which Culann and Conor were, he cast all his implements before him but his ball alone.

"The chain-hound descried the little boy, and howled at him so that the howling of the chain-hound was heard throughout the surrounding territory; and it was not a division of feasting he seemed inclined to make of him, but to swallow him at once into the cavity of his chest, through the capaciousness of his throat and over the cartilage of his breast."

The child contends with, and kills, the formidable dog. The noise of the conflict recalled to Conor the appointment he had made with his nephew, and he exclaims, in great distress of mind—

"' The little boy whom I desired to come after me— the son of my sister—Setanta, the son of Sualtain, is killed by the chain-hound.'

' They arose together, the renowned Ultonians, and although the door of the court was standing wide open, each of them made his nearest way out over the battlements of the Dun.

"Though readily they all reached, quicker did Fergus reach, and whip the little boy from the ground to the rack of his shoulder, and he brought him into the presence of Conor.

"And Culann came out, and saw his chain-hound in divided fragments. It was a stroke of his heart against his chest to him. He went into the Dun after.

"'I am happy at your coming, little boy,' said Culann, 'on account of your mother and your father, but I am not happy at your coming on your own account.'

"'What have you against the boy?' said Conor.

"'It is not lucky that you have come to me to quaff my ale, and eat my food, for my present hospitality is hospitality cast away, and my life is a lost life. Good was the family-man you have taken from me. He guarded cows and flocks and cattle for me.'

"'Be not angry of it, O master Culann,' said the little boy, 'because I will pronounce a true sentence in this case.'

"'What sentence do you pronounce in it, my boy?" said Conor.

"'If there is a whelp of the seed of this hound in Erin, he shall be reared by me until he is of the efficiency of his father. I shall be a hound to protect his flocks, and his cattle, and his territory during that time.'

"'Well hast thou pronounced thy judgment, my little boy,' said Conor.

" ' We would not ourselves,' said Cathbad (Conor's Druid and Brehon) ' pronounce a better; and why should thy name not be Cu-Chulain (Culann's hound) in consequence.'

" ' Not so,' said the little boy, ' I prefer my own name, Setanta, the son of Sualtain.'

" ' Say you not that, my little boy,' said Cathbad, ' because the men of Erin and Alba will tremble at that name, and the mouths of the men of Erin and of Alba shall be full of that name.'

" ' I like, then, that it be my name,' said the little boy, and it is from this that the famous name of Cuchullin has attached to him."

The noble nature of the young hero displayed itself the ensuing year, under the following circumstances :—

" Cathbad, the Druid, was instructing his pupils by Emain on the north-east, having eight pupils of the science of Druidism with him. One of them asked his tutor, what was the luck and prognostication of that day on which they were. Was it good or was it evil ? Then Cathbad said,—

" ' The little boy who would take arms this day would be noble and illustrious, but would be unhappy and short lived.'

" He—Cuchullin—heard these words, though he was at his sports on the south-west of Emain; and he cast away from him his implements of pleasure, and went to the sleeping-house of Conor.

" ' All happiness to thee, O King of Champions !' said the little boy.

"'That is a salutation of soliciting something from a person,' said Conor; 'what do you ask, my little boy?'

"'To take arms,' said the little boy.

"'Who advised you, my little boy?' said Conor.

"'Cathbad, the Druid,' said the little boy.

"'You shall not be deceived therein, my little boy,' said Conor.

"Conor gave him two spears, and a sword, and a shield. The little boy swung and balanced the arms until he shivered them into crumbs and splinters.

"Conor gave him two other spears, and a shield and sword. He swung, balanced, shook, and bent them until he shivered them into crumbs and splinters.

"There were fourteen suits of arms that Conor had for the service of the youths and princes: (when any one of them took up arms, it was Conor that gave him aggressive accoutrements: he had the gift of valour in consequence:) however, this little boy shivered them all into crumbs and splinters.

"'These indeed are not good weapons, my master Conor,' said the little boy, 'my safety would not come of them.'

"Conor gave his own two spears, and his shield and sword to him. He swung and balanced, shook and bent them, until he brought their points to their shanks; and the arms did not break, and they withstood him.

"'These indeed are good arms,' said the little boy, 'they are my match. Happy the king whose arms and accoutrements these are. Happy the country to which he belongs.'

"Then came Cathbad, the Druid, into the pavilion, and said, 'Has he taken these on?'

"'He has, indeed,' said Conor.

"'It is not the son of your mother I could wish to see take them on this day,' said Cathbad.

"'How now, was it not you that advised him?' said Conor.

"'It was not I, indeed,' said Cathbad.

"'What did you mean, you fairy sprite?' said Conor. 'Is it falsehood you have spoken to us?'

"'Be not you angry now, my master Conor,' said the little boy; 'because it is certain that it was he that advised me. For his pupil asked him what luck there was on the day, and he said, The little boy that would take arms in it, would be the noble and renowned, and would be unhappy, and short-lived too. Glorious fate! though I were but one day and one night in the world, provided that my history and my adventures lived after me!'"

Cuchullin speedily fleshes his maiden sword. He sets off in his chariot to seek adventures, and returns to Emania with the bloody heads of the three sons of Nectain; wild deer bound to his chariot, and captured wild birds fluttering around him.

But the most heroic achievement of the young warrior was his series of single-handed combats with the picked men of the Connacian armies led by Ailill and Macv in person, when he defended the fords, and stopped the onward march of the hosts of the *Tain-bo*, on the borders of Ulster. He held these passes into the threatened province—for the chivalrous custom of the times permitted none to refuse a challenge, nor the host to advance till the result of the single combats should be known—till the Ultonians had time to muster their forces, and arrive to give battle to the armies of Connaught in defence of their land and their cattle.

The *Tain Bo Cuailgné* recounts at great length the combats that ensued, in all of which Cuchullin was victorious.

What, another and another, and he still for combat calls?
Ah! the lot on thee, his brother sworn in arms, Ferdiah, falls,
And the hall with wild applauses sobbed like women ere they wist,
When the champions in the pauses of the deadly combat kiss'd.

The youthful Ferdiah was most reluctant to engage in strife with his former friend and companion Cuchullin, for "with the same tutors they learned the science of feats of bravery and valour; with Scatha, and with Uatha, and with Aifé."

The name of Scatha, the Amazonian instructress of these youths, is still preserved in *Dun Sciath* in the island of Skye, where "great Cuchullin's name and glory" yet linger. The Coolin mountains, named after him—those "thunder-smitten, jagged Cuchullin peaks of Skye," the grandest mountain range in Great Britain—attract to that remote island of the Hebrides, worshippers of the sublime and beautiful in nature, whose enjoyments would be largely enhanced if they knew the heroic legends which are connected with the glorious scenes they have travelled so far to witness. Cuchullin is one of the foremost characters in Macpherson's *Ossian*, but the quasi-translator of Gaelic poems places him more than two centuries later than the period at which he really lived. The tendency of the public mind at present is somewhat unjust to Macpherson. The repugnance naturally felt at any literary falsification blinds many to the poetry and beauty of his adaptations of the Gaelic legends, which are associated with the name of Ossian. With the exception of his alteration of names and localities, framed in order to connect the traditions of the ancient poet with Scotland, rather than with Ireland, he took few liberties with his originals that were not fully warranted by the character of the material with which he had to deal. If he had honestly claimed for himself the authorship of the book, and acknowledged himself an adapter, rather than a translator, he would be entitled to high approval; for amidst much that is turgid and bombastic, there is grandeur, and pathos, and sublimity, in the *Ossian* of Macpherson.

But to return to Ferdiah. His aversion to contend with his former companion in arms, is at last overcome by the satirists of Maev: "Ferdiah came with them for the sake of his honour, for he preferred to fall by the shafts of valour, gallantry, and bravery, rather than by the shafts of satire, censure, and reproach."

The eventful morning of combat is about to dawn.

"Ferdiah's horses were harnessed, and his chariot was yoked, and he went forward to the ford of battle. And the day with its full lights had now come.

"' Good, my servant,' said Ferdiah; ' spread for me the cushions and skins of my chariot under me, here, until I take my deep rest and sleep, here, because I slept not the end of the night for anxiety about the combat and battle.'

"The servant unharnessed the horses. He spread the cushions and skins of the chariot under him.

"Cuchullin arose not at all until the day with all its lights came, because that the men of Erin should not say that it was fear or dread that induced him, if he had arisen. And when day with all its lights came, he commanded his charioteer that he should harness his horses and yoke his chariot.

"'Good, my servant,' said Cuchullin; 'harness our horses for us, and yoke our chariot, for he is an early-rising champion who comes to meet us to-day, Ferdiah MacDaman MicDaré.'

"'The horses are harnessed, the chariot is yoked; step you into it, and it will not disparage your valour.'

"And then the strokeful, featful, battle-winning, red-sworded hero, Cuchullin Mac Sualtáin, sprang into his chariot."

The heroes meet at the ford, and exchange greetings, not unmixed with reminiscences of their happy boyish days.

"'Too long have we remained this way now,' said Ferdiah; 'and what arms shall we fight with to-day?'

"'Thine is the choice of arms till night, this day,' said Cuchullin; 'for it is you that first reached the ford.'

"'Do you remember at all,' said Ferdiah, 'the

missive weapons we were used to practise with Scatha, and with Uatha, and with Aifé?'

"'I remember, indeed,' said Cuchullin.

"'If you remember, let us resort to them.'"

Night arrives without any decisive advantage on either side.

"'Let us desist now for the present, O Cuchullin,' said Ferdiah.

"'Let us, indeed, desist, if the time has come,' said Cuchullin.

"They stopped. They threw their arms away from them into the hands of their charioteers. Each of them approached the other, and each put his hands round the other's neck and gave him three kisses.

"Their horses were in the same paddock that night, and their charioteers at the same fire. And their charioteers spread beds of green rushes for them, with wounded-men pillows to them.

"Their professors of healing and curing came to heal and cure them, and they put herbs of healing and curing into their cuts, and their wounds, and their clefts, and all their wounds. Every herb and every plant of healing and curing that was put to the cuts, and wounds, and clefts, and all the wounds of Cuchullin, he would send an equal division of them from him westwards over the ford to Ferdiah.

"Every kind of food, and of palatable pleasant intoxicating drink that was sent by the men of Erin to Ferdiah, he would send a fair moiety of them over the ford northward to Cuchullin."

Day after day the combat is renewed; great wounds

are given and received. At last Ferdiah falls. 'Cuchullin laid Ferdiah down there, and a cloud, and a faint, and a weakness fell on Cuchullin.' The hero, exhausted by his wounds and long-continued strife, and still more by the distress of mind caused by the death of his loved friend, lies long on his bed of sickness, and is unable to take part in the impending battle between the Ultonians and the now retreating forces of Ailill and Maev. His father visits him, and is thus quaintly described in the poem :—

"For thus was Sualtain. He was not a bad champion, and he was not a good champion, but he happened to be a big, good sort of person."

Cuchullin sends him to rouse the Ultonians. He performs his embassy in the following manner :—

"'You have been plundered by Ailill and Maev,' said Sualtain; 'your women, and your children, and your youths, your horses, and your studs, your flocks, your herds, and your cattle have been carried away. Cuchullin is alone detaining and delaying the four great provinces of Erin, in the gaps and the passes of the country of Conaille Murthevné. * * * And if you do not immediately avenge this, it will not be avenged to the end of time and life.'"

Conor musters his hosts, but Ailill and Maev are already on their way to Connaught; the original cause of the war, the *Donn Cuailgné* himself, being captured, and led towards the pastures of Cruachan.

MacRoth, the herald of Connaught, is left to watch for the foe, who might be expected to harass their retreat.

"MacRoth went forward to reconnoitre the great

wide-spreading plain of Meath. MacRoth was not long doing so when he heard something—the sound, and the tramp, and the clamour, and the noise.

"There was nothing that he could think it to be, unless it was the falling of the firmament on the face of the earth ; or unless it were the salmon-abounding blue ocean that flowed over the face of the world ; or unless it was the earth severed from its earthly motion ; or unless it was the forests that fell each tree into the catches and forks and branches of the other."

The Ultonian hosts advance. The armies pass that night on the plains of Slewen. At dawn of day the battle begins. The disabled Cuchullin, longing, but unable, to take part in the conflict, charges his charioteer to give him tidings of the fight.

"Leagh had not remained long looking till he saw the men of Erin all arising together, snatching up their shields, and their spears, and their swords, and their helmets, and pressing, each party the other, forward to the battle.

"The men of Erin began, each of them, to hew, and to cut down, to partition, to disjoint, to slaughter, and to destroy each other for a long time.

"' How is the battle fought now, my master Leagh ?' said Cuchullin.

"' Manfully is it fought,' said Leagh. ' For though I were to take my chariot, and Eu, Conall's charioteer, were to take his, and though we were to drive in our two noble chariots to meet each other through the array of their arms, neither shoe, nor wheel, nor seat, nor shaft of them could pass through, for the tightness, and for the firmness, and for the fastness with which their arms are grasped in the hands of the warriors at this moment.'

"'Alas, that I am not of strength to be among them!' said Cuchullin; 'for if I were of strength my breach would be conspicuous there to-day.'

"'Hush now, my Hound,' said Leagh. 'It is no disgrace to your valour—it is no reproach to your honour. You have done bravely before now. You shall do so again.'"

Cuchullin cannot be kept back even by the entreaties of his attendant. His wounds are too fresh to permit him to take an active part in the combat, but he meets his ancient master and friend, Fergus MacRoy, and adjures him, by his former promise to that effect, no longer to take part against his countrymen of Ulster, nor to avenge on them the wrongs he had sustained from his step-son, Conor. Fergus, thus appealed to, retires, and the Connacians accept his retreat as a signal for leaving the field. They send on before them the Bull which was the original cause of their foray, and—under the guardianship of Maev, who courageously protects the rear of her defeated army—retire towards Cruachan. The finale—as regards the Donn Cuailgné—is highly grotesque. "When he saw the beautiful unknown country" (the rich pasture land of Roscommon) "he gave his three rounds of roars aloud. But the Finnbennach of Ai heard him." This was the Bull that had gone over from Maev's cows because "he deemed it not honourable to be in a woman's dependence," and he allowed no other beast "to dare to raise a roar higher than a lowing within the four fords of Ai." So he raised his head on high, and came forward to Cruachan to meet the Donn Cuailgné.

The Battle of the Bulls was as furious as had been that of the Connacians and Ultonians, on their account. After a terrible encounter, in which no one ventured to intervene, the men of Erin "saw the Donn Cuailgné coming past Cruachan, coming from the west, and carrying the Finnbennach on his peaks and on his horns."

Having shaken off his defeated antagonist, the Bull "turned his face to the north, and recognized the country of Cuailgné, and went towards it."

Let us hope, notwithstanding the tragical end assigned to him in the romance, where he dashes out his brains in charging at a rock, that in his native plains of Louth he found fresh fields and pastures new, and that the readers who have followed his adventures in the *Tain bo Cuailgné* shall be sharers in the blessing invoked at the close of the poem 'on every one who shall faithfully study the *Tain.*'

Cuchullin also plays the part of hero in tales of love and courtship which still exist among the unpublished Irish MSS. in our libraries. His wooing of Eimer, the beautiful daughter of Forgall Monach, a personage who held a court of general hospitality at Lusk, near Dublin, has many romantic circumstances attending it. Having heard of the charms and accomplishments of the Lady Eimer, Cuchullin, accompanied by his faithful Leagh, set out from Emania, and discovered, on reaching her father's abode, the lady he sought, in the companionship of others of her sex and station, pursuing her customary sports and occupations. Eimer was no less gifted than Cuchullin himself. Hers, we are told, were " the gift of beauty of person, the gift of voice, the gift of music, the gift of embroidery and all needlework, the gift of wisdom, and the gift of virtuous chastity." Her discretion was not inferior to her accomplishments. She declined to listen to the addresses of Cuchullin, alleging that she was but a younger daughter. She enlarged on the virtues and charms of her elder sister, and suggested that he should seek her father's sanction, and become a suitor to that lady.

Forgall was not disposed to part with either of his daughters. In the guise of a stranger he presented himself at the court of Conor; praised the varied feats and accomplishments which were exhibited in honour of the stranger's visit to Emania, by the knights of the Red Branch, including Cuchullin himself, and suggested to Conor that his young warriors should complete their military education under the tuition of Scatha, on the island of Skye. It was thus that Cuchullin became the pupil of this remarkable instructress, to whom he so often referred in after-life. His sojourn in the Hebrides perfected him in all knightly and manly exercises, and kept him far removed from Erin, which had been the secret object of Forgall in recommending the school of Dun Sciath.

Forgall's project was not so successful as he had hoped. Eimer and Cuchullin found means of exchanging vows of constancy, for by this time the hero had won the fair lady's heart. He remained in Scotland till he had acquired all that Scatha could teach, and then returned to Ireland, to claim the hand of Eimer. On his homeward route he played the part of a Perseus to an Andromeda of Rathlin island, rescuing from certain pirates a damsel exposed on the shore, and destined to be their captive in lieu of tribute which the islanders were unable to pay. Declining any reward for his services in slaying the pirates, Cuchullin hastened to Lusk, but the Lady Eimer was closely guarded in her father's fortress. Cuchullin stormed the fort, and carried her off in triumph, not without the penalty of combats with their pursuers at various fords and passes, in the line of country between Lusk and Armagh.

Another romantic adventure in which Cuchullin was concerned as one of the knights of the Red Branch, was an attack on an island called Mana, where resided a most beautiful damsel named Blanaid. Curoi MacDaré, the leader of the Munster order of chivalry,—the Clan Degaid, as they were called,—was present on this expedition in the disguise of a grey-coated clown, and gave valuable aid to the Ulster champions, on condition that, should he succeed in procuring for them entrance into the fort, he should have his choice of all the jewels it contained. Success being achieved, the clown in the grey garb named Blanaid herself as the jewel he would claim, and on Cuchullin disputing the point with him, Curoi succeeded in carrying her off by stratagem. Cuchullin pursued him towards Munster, but being worsted in an encounter with Curoi,—who inflicted on him the double disgrace of "binding him in five-fold fetter, wrists and ankles, wrists and neck," and cutting off his long love-locks,—he was compelled to return to Ulster, and there await the growing of his hair, as this loss was esteemed disgraceful for a man of Erin.

A year elapsed before Cuchullin's hair had grown, when he again sought Blanaid. He found her on the banks of the stream afterwards called the Finglas or White-brook, in Kerry. Curoi's abode still exists, and preserves his name, on the summit of Cahir-Conree, the grand mountain which towers over Tralee. Blanaid lamented her fate, and implored Cuchullin to return at an appointed time and rescue her, at a signal agreed on between them.

> "But hearken, dear Cuchullin,
> Heed well the words I say,
> Gather thy forces far and wide,
> And on the thirtieth day,
> Encamped in yonder forest,
> Watch well the river clear,
> *When its stream runs white*, with main and might
> Charge, as thou hold'st me dear." *

The scheme which Blanaid had imagined, was to persuade Curoi to build for himself a fortress which should surpass all the royal residences in Erin, and to disperse the Clan Degaid in search of great stones for the erection of this cyclopean structure. At the moment when Curoi was alone, and defenceless, Blanaid overturned into the river, pails of milk which

* From *Goethe*, by E. KENEALY.

she had prepared for the purpose, thus making the concerted signal for the attack of the fortress and capture and death of Curoi. Her treachery did not go unpunished. Ferkertné, the bard of the murdered Curoi, followed her to Ulster. He found her, in company with Conor and Cuchullin, on the promontory of Ken-Barra. He approached her, twined his arms around her, and sprang with her in this fatal embrace over the brow of the cliff, into the wild ocean beneath.

Before taking leave of Curoi MacDaré, we may mention that his descendants still hold a high position in his county of Kerry. O'Connell was a representative of this ancient champion of the Clan Degaid.

The glory and happiness of Cuchullin were clouded in his after-life by a tragical occurrence, arising from a sin of his youth. During his residence in Skye, he loved, and abandoned, the Lady Aifé. She bore him a son, and trained her unconscious child to be the actor in the schemes of vengeance which she nourished against Cuchullin. The young Conloch was educated in all martial exercises, and when fully perfected, sent by his mother to Erin, with injunctions never to tell his name, or refuse to fight a single combat against the most powerful champion.

> "Conloch, haughty, bold, and brave
> Rides upon Ierne's wave,
> Flushed with loud-applauding fame,
> From Dunsciaik's walls he came,
> Came to visit Erin's coast—
> Came to prove her mighty host." *

---

* Translated from the Irish by Miss Brooke.

Conloch returned an insolent answer to the messenger sent by Conor MacNessa, to demand his name and purpose. He encountered, and defeated, several champions sent by the king. At last Cuchullin approaches. Conloch is moved by the yearnings of natural affection, but still declines to tell his name and lineage to the hero, whom he alone knows to be his father. They fight, and Conloch falls. Ere he dies, he reveals the fatal secret, and implores the forgiveness of his parent. The grief of Cuchullin ends only with his life. His death occurred ('tis said in A.D. 2) at the battle of Murthevné, near Dundalk. Here " the manly, beauteous champion fell; it was not the fall of a dastard." His death was avenged by his kinsman Conall Carnach. When the event happened, Conall was beyond sea; but the widowed Eimer sent to acquaint him, and to hasten his return, that he might avenge Cuchullin. This great knight of the Red Branch found the head of the hero used as a hurling-ball. He contended with, and slew those who had so insulted the remains of his friend. Cuchullin's head and right hand are said to have been buried at Tara.

Conall Carnach, this knight of the Red Branch who avenged Cuchullin, was of the race of Ir, son of Miled. He was kinsman also to Fergus MacRoy, through their common ancestor, Rury Mor, king of Ireland—from whom the Clan Rury derive their name. He fills a foremost place in heroic story at this period—the commencement of the Christian era. The courage and daring of these doughty champions made them very formidable antagonists, and their successes tempted them to seek occasion for a display of their prowess. Nor was this overbearing and aggressive disposition confined to the warriors of Ulster. Even the bards of the northern kingdom presumed on the warlike repute of its heroes, to insult and oppress the less powerful chieftains of other districts. It is recorded of Atharné, a poet at the court of Conor, that he set out on a tour of visits to the other provincial kings, with the sole object of "picking a quarrel" on behalf of the Ultonians with their weaker neighbours. With this object he insolently demanded the most costly gifts, which were yielded to him for the sake of peace. Eochy, king of mid-Erin, actually bestowed on Atharné his one remaining eye, which the audacious poet demanded of the already mutilated prince, little expecting his request to be granted, but intending to fix a quarrel, should it be refused. Loch Derg (on the Shannon) is said in the legend to have derived its name (the Lake of the Red Eye) from this circumstance. In Leinster, Atharné demanded the gift of one hundred and fifty ladies, seven hundred white cows with red ears, and other cattle. His unreasonable petition was accorded with such ready alacrity that it aroused the poet's suspicions. He therefore sent to Conor, asking from him an escort of Ultonians, who should meet him at the boundary of the respective kingdoms, and repel any attempt at the forced restitution which he anticipated at the hands of his Leinster escort, the moment they should be at liberty to attack him without infringing the laws of hospitality. These laws, which it would have been deemed dishonourable to violate, protected Atharné and his ill-gotten gains while in the territory of the men of Leinster. It was at the ford of the Liffey at Dubhlinn, the *black pool* which gives its name to Dublin, that a causeway of hurdles was thrown across the river for the transport of the flocks, from which the Irish capital obtained its name of *Ath Cliath*, meaning "Hurdle-ford." Here—for the Liffey was at this time the boundary between Leinster and Ulster—as Atharné had anticipated, his late hosts, the instant he had passed out of their country, seized upon their women and cattle. A battle ensued, in which the Ultonians succeeded in forcing their retreat to the Hill of Howth, and carrying the cattle with them. From the summit of Ben Edar, the poet cursed the land he had left, and a blight fell on all things in Leinster, which lasted till the outraged Atharné was persuaded to remove his malignant infliction.

> "Sing while you may, nor grieve to know
> The song you sing shall also die:
> Atharna's lay has perished so,
> Though once it thrilled this sky
> Above us, from his rocky chair,
> There, where Ben Edar's landward crest
> O'er eastern Bregia bends, to where
> Dun Almon crowns the west:
> And all that felt the fretted air
> Throughout the song-distempered clime
> Did droop, till suppliant Leinster's prayer
> Appeased the vengeful rhyme."*

---

* From *The Cromlech on Howth*, by S. FERGUSON.

While the Ultonians, with Atharné, were encamped at Howth, Conall Carnach made various onslaughts on the Leinster men, urged by a desire to revenge the deaths of his brothers, who had been slain during the siege. He overtook and encountered Mesgedra, the King of Leinster, vanquished him in single combat, cut off his head, and carried the bleeding trophy with him in his chariot. He had not travelled far when he met Mesgedra's queen, Būana, returning with an escort of fifty ladies, from a visit to Meath. "Thou art commanded to come with me," said Conall, addressing her.

"Who has commanded me?" replied the queen.

"Mesgedra," rejoined Conall.

"Hast thou brought me any token from him?" asked the queen.

"I have brought his chariots and horses," said Conall.

"He makes many presents?" said the lady.

"Come into my chariot: his head is here too," rejoined the champion.

"Give me liberty to lament for my husband," said the bereaved woman, and then she shrieked aloud her grief and sorrow with such intensity that her heart broke, and she fell dead from her chariot.

The MS. story of the siege of Howth (*Talland Etair*), from which we glean these incidents, contains, in the midst of much that is barbarous and revolting, some traits of generous sentiment worthy of being called chivalrous, and well deserving the attention of inquirers into the sources of mediæval romantic literature.

Mesgedra, with a single squire, flying from the

pursuit of the Ultonians, reaches the ford of Clane. Here they halt to snatch a moment's repose. "I shall sleep awhile," said the charioteer, "and thou canst sleep afterwards."—"It is agreeable to me," said the king, yielding the privilege of first refreshment to his humbler companion. The charioteer sleeps, and Mesgedra, looking at the river, is aware of a large nut floating towards him. He divides the kernel, keeping one half for the charioteer, and eats the other. At this moment the charioteer awakens from "an evil vision." "Is it a nut thou didst eat?" he demands: "hast thou left half for me?"—"Catch the horses, *gilla*," said the king. Then the charioteer resenting the king's supposed ungenerous greediness, exclaims, "He who would eat a little behind the back of a hungry comrade would eat much," and in rash rage drew his sword, and smote off Mesgedra's hand. "Evil is the deed," said Mesgedra. "Open my hand: the half of the nut is there." When the charioteer saw that it was so, "he turned the sword against himself, so that it went out through his back." At this moment Conall approaches from the opposite side of the ford: "I am here," said Mesgedra. "What then?" said Conall. "What more," said Mesgedra, "save to assail him of whom the debt is due, whatever be the strait he may be in."—"Prepare," said Conall. "It is not true valour," said Mesgedra, "for you to fight with a one-handed man."—"So it shall be with me also," said Conall: "my hand shall be bound to my side," said Conall. Conall's hand was triple-bound to his side. They fought. The river was red from them:

in the end Conall was the stronger. "Lo now, O Conall," said Mesgedra, "I know that thou wilt not depart until thou bearest with thee this head: bear, then, my head on thy head, and my renown on thy renown." When it is remembered that this was one of the traditionary "prime tales" known by every duly qualified bard for ages prior to the twelfth century (for it is one of those enumerated in the *Book of Leinster*, and the *Book of Leinster* was compiled for Dermid MacMurrogh in his youth), it will not appear necessary, in the absence of evidence, to assume that the Arthurian legend and the cycle of Armoric romance could not have originated among the Celtic populations.

Conall buried Büana, and the head of her husband with her, having previously, in compliance with a barbarous custom, extracted the brains, which were mixed with lime, and made into a ball. This ball was deposited in the House of the Red Branch, at Emania, and was destined to play an important part afterwards; for a prophecy existed that Mesgedra would avenge himself on the Ulstermen.

On one occasion, Keth MacMagach, a Connaught hero, and nephew of Maev of Cruachan, passing disguised near Emania, observed two fools of Conor's court playing on the green with the fatal ball, which they had purloined from the trophy-house of Creeve Roe. Keth, aware of the prediction, possessed himself of it, and always carried it in his girdle, awaiting an opportunity of using it against Conor. This he obtained by a characteristic stratagem, on a subsequent encounter between the Connacians and the Ultonians, in which Conor himself commandeth the northern forces.

Conor was vain of his personal symmetry and beauty: "For there was not upon earth the shape of a person like the shape of Conchobhar (Conor), namely, in form, and face, and countenance; in size, and symmetry, and proportion; in eyes, and hair, and whiteness; in wisdom, and prudence, and eloquence; in costume, and nobleness, and mien; in arms, and amplitude, and dignity; in accomplishment, and valour, and family descent."

The golden colour of Conor's hair is also recorded. The wound in his head, received in the manner about to be mentioned, was, according to the story, "stitched with thread of gold, because the colour of Conchobhar's hair was the same as the colour of the gold." Thus gifted, and not unwilling to display his gifts, Conor unsuspectingly acceded to a request made by some of the Connacian ladies that he should approach them between the armies, so that they might judge whether fame had reported truly of his personal dignity and martial bearing.

Keth disguised himself in female attire, and with his sling and Mesgedra's brain-ball, stationed himself among the women who awaited the approach of the handsome king. Conor came within reach of the missile. Keth cast the fatal ball from his sling, and imbedded it deeply in the head of the monarch.

Conor's physicians hesitated to remove the ball, but succeeded in restoring him to the use of his faculties, and permitted him soon to resume his former habits, only cautioning him against any violent exertion or emotion, especially against indulgence in anger. On this circumstance of the tradition, and the supposed synchronism of Conor's death with the time of Our Lord's crucifixion, has been founded a Christian legend of singular but picturesque wildness. Conor, startled by the supernatural darkness which accompanied the Passion of Our Lord, inquires from his Druids of its cause. They reply, "that Jesus Christ, the Son of the living God, was at that moment suffering at the hands of the Jews." "What crime has he committed?" said Conor. "None," replied they. "Then they are slaying him being innocent?" asked Conor. "It is so," said the Druids. Thereupon Conor, bursting into uncontrollable fury, drew his sword, rushed into an adjoining wood, and began to hew and hack the trees, supposing them in his frenzy to be the obnoxious Jews: and the legend preserves, in archaic but characteristic language, the rhapsody, or *rhetoric*, as it is called, pronounced by him on that occasion.

"Good now," said Conchobhar; "it is a pity that he (Christ) did not appeal to a valiant high-king, which would bring me in the shape of a hardy champion, my lips quivering, until the great valour of a soldier should be witnessed dealing a breach of battle between two hosts. Bitter the slaughter by which there would be propitiated free relief. With Christ should my assistance be. A wild shout has sprung at large : a full Lord, a full loss is lamented ; the crucifixion of a king, the greatest body, who was an illustrious, admirable king. I would complain of the deed to the faithful host of noble feats, whose vigilant, beautiful aid should be with the merciful God to relieve Him. Beautiful the overthrowing which I would give. Beautiful the combat which I would wage for Christ, who is being defiled. I would not rest, though my body of clay had been tormented by them. . . . It crushes my heart to hear the voice of wailing for my God, and that this arm does not come to reach with true relief to arrest the sorrow of death—because I am told that it is dangerous for me to ride in chariots—without avenging the Creator." In the midst of these excitements, the ball started from its place, where it had remained imbedded in his skull, and Conor fell dead on the spot. Another tradition ascribes to the visit of Altus, a Roman centurion sent to demand tribute of Conor, his knowledge of the incarnation and mission of Christ.

To return to Conall Carnach.

His haughty and overbearing character displayed itself at a feast given by a Leinster prince, MacDatho, to the Connaught men and Ultonians. MacDatho was possessed of a noble hound, which was envied by Conor MacNessa as well as by Ailill and Maev. Afraid to offend these rival sovereigns by yielding the hound to either, MacDatho invited them all to a great feast. His hospitable board was graced by a famous pig. But who was to carve this dainty dish? Keth Mac-Magach and Conall Carnach contended for the honour. At last it was conceded to the Ulster hero, who helped his countrymen to the dainty morsels, tossing over the forelegs of the pig to the Connaught guests. Of course bloodshed resulted, and the poor hound fell victim to their swords. We turn from this ignoble strife to a more gallant combat between Conall and Keth, in which the latter lost his life, and Conall was all but mortally wounded. The scene was Slieve Fuad, now the Fews; the time, winter; and Conall, though the victor, alone and bleeding amid the drifting snowstorm, was captured by the Connacian hero, Beälcu, who restored him to health that he might afterwards avenge Keth in single combat with Conall. The circumstances, with some deviations from the rude original, have been amplified into a dramatic ballad commemorative of this primitive instance of chivalrous generosity.

The Healing of Conall Carnach.

O'er Slieve Few, with noiseless tramping through the heavy drifted snow,
Beälcu Connacia's champion, in his chariot tracks the foe;
And anon far off discerneth, in the mountain hollow white,
Slinger Keth and Conall Carnach mingling, hand to hand, in fight.

Swift the charioteer his coursers urged across the wintry glade:
Hoarse the cry of Keth and hoarser seemed to come demanding aid;
But through wreath and swollen runnel, ere the car could reach anigh,
Keth lay dead, and mighty Conall bleeding lay at point to die.

Whom beholding spent and pallid, Beälcu exulting cried,
"Oh thou ravening wolf of Uladh, where is now thy northern pride?

What can now that crest audacious, what that pale defiant
    brow,
Once the bale-star of Connacia's ravaged fields, avail thee
    now?"

"Taunts are for reviling women," faintly Conall made reply.
"Wouldst thou play the manlier foeman? end my pain and
    let me die!
Neither deem thy blade dishonoured that with Keth's a
    deed it share
For the foremost two of Connaught feat enough and fame to
    spare."

"No; I will not! Bard shall never in Dunseverick hall
    make boast
That to quell one northern riever needed two of Croghan's host;
But because that word thou'st spoken, if but life enough
    remains,
Thou shalt hear the wives of Croghan clap their hands
    above thy chains.

"Yea, if life enough but linger, that the leech may make thee
    whole,
Meet to satiate the anger that beseems a warrior's soul,
Best of leech-craft I'll purvey thee; make thee whole as healing
    can;
And in single combat slay thee, Connaught man to Ulster
    man."

Binding him in five-fold fetter, wrists and ankles, wrists and
    neck,
To his car's uneasy litter, Beälcu upheaved the wreck
Of the broken man and harness; but he started with amaze
When he felt the northern war-mace, what a weight it was
    to raise.

Westward then through Breiffney's borders, with his captive
    and his dead,
Tracked by bands of fierce applauders, wives and shrieking
    widows sped;

And the chained heroic carcass on the fair green of Moy Slaght
Casting down, proclaimed his purpose, and bade Lee, the leech, be brought.

Lee, the gentle-faced physician, from his herb-plot came and said:
"Healing is with God's permission; health for life's enjoyment made;
And though I mine aid refuse not, yet, to speak my purpose plain,
I the healing art abuse not, making life enure to pain.

"But assure me, with the sanction of the mightiest oath ye know,
That in case, in this contention, Conall overcome his foe,
Straight departing from the tourney by what path the chief shall choose,
He is free to take his journey, unmolested, to the Fews.

"Swear me further, while at healing in my charge the hero lies,
None shall through my fences stealing, work him mischief or surprise;
And if God the undertaking but approve, in six months' span
Once again my art shall make him meet to stand before a man."

Crom their God they then attested, Sun and Wind for guarantees,
Conall Carnach unmolested by what exit he might please,
If the victor, should have freedom to depart Conuncia's bounds;
Meantime, no man should intrude him, entering on the hospice grounds.

Then the burthen huge receiving, in his hospice-portal, Lee,
Stiffened limb by limb relieving with the iron fetter-key,
As a crumpled scroll unrolled him, groaning deep, till laid at length,
Wondering gazers might behold him, what a tower he was of strength.

Spake the sons to one another, day by day, of Beälcu—
"Get thee up and spy, my brother, what the leech and North-
 man do."
"Lee at mixing of a potion: Conall, yet in nowise dead,
As on reef of rock the ocean, tosses wildly on his bed."

"Spy again with cautious peeping: what of Lee and Conall
 now?"
"Conall lies profoundly sleeping: Lee beside with placid brow."
"And to-day?"—"To-day he's risen; pallid as his swathing
 sheet,
He has left his chamber's prison, and is walking on his feet."

"And to-day?"—"A ghastly figure, propped upon his spear
 he goes."
"And to-day?"—"A languid vigour through his larger ges-
 ture shows."
"And to-day?"—"The blood renewing mantles all his clear
 cheek through:
Would thy vow had room for rueing, rashly-valiant Beälcu!"

So with herb and healing balsam, ere the second month was
 past,
Life's increases, smooth and wholesome, circling through his
 members vast,
As you've seen a sere oak burgeon under summer showers
 and dew,
Conall, under his chirurgeon, filled and flourished, spread and
 grew.

"I can bear the sight no longer: I have watched him moon
 by moon;
Day by day the chief grows stronger, giant-strong he will be
 soon.
Oh my sire, rash-valiant warrior! but that oaths have built
 the wall,
Soon these feet should leap the barrier, soon this hand thy
 fate forestall."

"Brother, have the wish thou'st uttered: we have sworn, so let it be;
But although our feet be fettered, all the air is left us free.
Dying Keth with vengeful presage did bequeath thee sling and ball,
And the sling may send its message where thy vagrant glances fall.

"Forbaid was a master-slinger; Maev, when in her bath she sank,
Felt the presence of his finger from the further Shannon bank;
For he threw by line and measure, practising a constant cast
Daily in secluded leisure, till he reached the mark at last.

"Keth achieved a warrior's honour, though 'twas mid a woman's band,
When he smote the amorous Conor bowing from his distant stand.
Fit occasion will not fail ye: in the leech's lawn below,
Conall at the fountain daily drinks within an easy throw."

"Wherefore cast ye at the apple, sons of mine, with measured aim?"
"He who in the close would grapple, first the distant foe should maim;
And since Keth, his death-balls casting, rides no more the ridge of war,
We, against our summer hosting, train us for his vacant car."

"Wherefore to the rock repairing, gaze ye forth, my children, tell?"
"'Tis a stag we watch for snaring, that frequents the leech's well."
"I will see this stag, though, truly, small may be my eyes' delight."
And he climbed the rock where fully lay the lawn exposed to sight.

Conall to the green well-margin came at dawn and knelt to drink,
Thinking how a noble virgin by a like green fountain's brink,
Heard his own pure vows one morning, far away and long ago;
All his heart to home was turning, and his tears began to flow.

Clean forgetful of his prison, steep Dunseverick's windy tower,
Seemed to rise in present vision, and his own dear lady's bower.
Round the sheltering knees they gather, little ones of tender years,—
Tell us, mother, of our father—and she answers but with tears.

Twice the big drops plashed the fountain. Then he rose, and turning round,
As across a breast of mountain sweeps a whirlwind, o'er the ground
Raced in athlete feats amazing, swung the war-mace, hurled the spear:
Beälcu, in wonder gazing, felt the pangs of deadly fear.

Had it been a fabled griffin, suppled in a fasting den,
Flashed its wheeling coils to Heaven o'er a wreck of beasts and men,
Hardly had the dreadful prospect bred his soul more dire alarms;
Such the fire of Conall's aspect, such the stridor of his arms.

"This is fear," he said, "that never shook these limbs of mine till now.
Now I idly mourn that ever I indulged the boastful vow.
Yet 'twas righteous wrath impelled me; and a sense of manly shame
From his naked throat withheld me, when 'twas offered to my aim.

"Now I see his strength excelling: whence he buys it: what he pays.
'Tis a God who has his dwelling in the fount, to whom he prays.
Thither comes he weeping, drooping, till the well-God hears his prayer,
Thence departs he, soaring, swooping, as an eagle through the air.

"Oh thou God, by whatsoever sounds of awe thy name we know,
Grant thy servant equal favour with the stranger and the foe!
Equal grace, 'tis all I covet; and if sacrificial blood
Win thy favour, thou shalt have it on thy very well-brink, God!

"What and though I've given pledges not to cross the leech's court?
Not to pass his sheltering hedges, meant I, to his patient's hurt.
Thy dishonour meant I never: never meant I to forswear
Right divine of prayer wherever Power divine invites to prayer.

"Sun that warm'st me, Wind that fann'st me, ye that guarantee the oath,
Make no sign of wrath against me: tenderly ye touch me both;
Yea then, through his fences stealing ere to-morrow's sun shall rise,
Well-God! on thy margin kneeling I will offer sacrifice."

"Brother, rise, the skies are ruddy: if we yet would save our sire,
Rests a deed courageous, bloody, wondering ages shall admire:

Hie thee to the spy-rock's summit: ready there thou'lt find
    the sling.
Ready there the leaden plummet; and at dawn he seeks the
    spring."

Ruddy dawn had changed to amber: radiant as the yellow
    day
Conall, issuing from his chamber, to the fountain took his
    way:
There, athwart the welling water, like a fallen pillar, spread,
Smitten by the bolt of slaughter, lay Connacia's champion,
    dead.

Call the hosts! convene the judges! cite the dead man's chil-
    dren both!—
—Said the judges, "He gave pledges; Sun and Wind; and
    broke the oath,
And they slew him: so we've written: let his sons attend
    our words."—
"Both, by sudden frenzy smitten, fell at sunrise on their
    swords."

Then the judges—"Ye who punish man's prevaricating vow,
Needs not further to admonish: contrite to your will we bow,
All our points of promise keeping: safely let the chief go
    forth."
Conall to his chariot leaping, turned his coursers to the
    North:

In the Sun that swept the valleys, in the Winds' encircling
    flight,
Recognizing holy allies, guardians of the Truth and Right;
While, before his face, resplendant with a firm faith's candid
    ray,
Dazzled troops of foes attendant, bowed before him on his way.

But the calm physician, viewing where the white neck joined
    the car,
Said, "It is a slinger's doing: Sun nor Wind was actor here.

Yet till God vouchsafe more certain knowledge of his sovereign
    will,
Better deem the mystic curtain hides their wonted demon's
    still.

" Better so, perchance, than living in a clearer light, like me,
But believing where perceiving, bound in what I hear and
    see ;
Force and change in constant sequence, changing atoms,
    changeless laws ;
Only in submissive patience, waiting access to the Cause.

" And, they say, Centurion Altus, when he to Emania came
And to Rome's subjection called us, urging Cæsar's tribute
    claim,
Told that half the world barbarian thrills already with the
    faith
Taught them by the godlike Syrian Cæsar lately put to death.

" And the sun, through starry stages measuring from the Ram
    and Bull,
Tells us of renewing ages, and that Nature's time is full :
So, perchance, these silly breezes even now may swell the
    sail
Brings the leavening word of Jesus westward also to the
    Gael." *

 Conall died in exile. He had received a hospitable welcome at the court of Cruachan, but had slain Ailill by a cast of his spear, at the instigation of Maev, who was jealous of her husband. Conall fled, but was pursued and killed by the " Three Red-Heads," who were in the service of the king. Fergus MacRoy had previously fallen a victim to the not unmerited suspicions of Ailill, as tradition tells that Maev had borne to the aged hero three sons at a birth, from one of whom (Ciar) the

* S. FERGUSON.

county of Kerry derives its name. The occasion on which this access of jealous hate occurred was when Fergus was swimming in Loch Ein, in Roscommon, a lake not far from the royal residence at Rath Cruachan. Maev was seized with a fancy to contend with him in swimming, which so enraged Ailill that he commanded one of his kinsmen to cast his javelin at Fergus. Maev also met her death in the water, though not on this occasion. She had removed during her widowhood to the island of Inis-Clothran, in Loch Ree. Here she continued her natatory habits. Forbaid, son of Conor, learned that it was her custom to bathe daily at a spring on the coast of the island. He had the distance measured between this spot and the opposite shore of Loch Ree. Returning to Ulster, he set up as a mark at the ascertained distance, an apple on a stake, and practised daily, till he could truly and certainly hit it from a sling. Thus, habituated to cast unerringly at that exact distance, he repaired to the eastern shore of Loch Ree, watched his opportunity, and aimed a stone from his sling, which struck Maev on the forehead; and so died this Amazonian queen, having survived all her contemporaries, and reigned over Connaught for a period, it is said, of eighty years.

CHAPTER III.

THE ATACOTTIC PERIOD.

WE pass from the age of the heroes who surrounded the thrones of Conor MacNessa and of Ailill and Maev of Cruachan, to a period less prolific in chivalrous deeds. The great revolt of the "Un-free" tribes, or plebeians, — mainly descendants of the conquered Firbolgs, and sundry dissatisfied branches of the Milesian stock,— against the *Saer Gael*, or free tribes of the Gael, is known in our history as the Revolt of the Atacotti. But between the age of Conor and the civil war of which we are about to speak, two remarkable names, at which we would pause, occur on our list of kings. Conari Mór, ancestor of the Ernaian tribes of Munster, ruled Erin with impartiality and vigour. He banished from his court all those whose disorders impeded justice, not sparing his own foster-brothers, the four sons of Donn Desa, a great Leinster chief. The outlaws took to piracy on the seas between Britain and Ireland, and having landed at Malahide while Conari was in Munster, marched on Tara, devastating the surrounding country. On his return from the south, Conari found the plain of Meath wrapped in flames. He turned his chariot towards Dublin, and passing through

Lusk, crossed the Liffey, and repaired to Tallaght, where lay the mansion of the great *Brughaidh*, or Hospitaller, Da Derga.

The court of Da Derga, one of the six houses of universal hospitality which then existed in Ireland, was situated on the banks of the River Dodder. Here the monarch was welcomed and sheltered by his friend, Da Derga. But the hospitable house was attacked by the pirates, and, after an unavailing resistance, sacked and plundered. Conari Mór and his small retinue were put to the sword. The site where the court of Da Derga stood is indicated in the name yet retained, Bohernabreena—*Bothar-na-Bruigné*—or the Road of the Court, in the county of Dublin.

The second king on whose career we would pause was Criffan Niad-Nair. The "delightful adventures" which befell him while on a foreign expedition, are recounted in a poem ascribed to King Criffan himself. He was brought by a "fairy" lady into her palace. She bestowed on him a gilt chariot, a golden chessboard, inlaid with transparent gems, a cloak of divers colours embroidered in gold, a sword ornamented with serpents, a shield embossed with silver, and various other treasures which Criffan brought home with him to his fort of Dun Criffan, on the Hill of Howth. The dun was probably situated on that promontory of the peninsula where the Bailey lighthouse now stands. He also brought with him the fairy, Nair, whom he made his queen. He only lived for a few weeks after his return from his "fortunate" expedition, having been killed by a fall from his horse. In the eighth year of this monarch's reign, according to the Annals of the Four Masters, or the twelfth, according to Keating, was born, in Judea, Our Saviour, Jesus Christ.

About the middle of the first century of the Christian era, the Patrician tribes of the *Saer-Gael*, becoming more and more oppressive in their exactions, disgusted the poorer Milesians, as well as the plebeian remnants of the conquered races. The latter banded together, and planned in such profound secrecy an uprising against the dominant race, that no suspicion of their designs was entertained, though their plans were three years in preparation. These *Aitheach Tuatha*, or Atacotti, invited the monarch, the provincial kings, and great chiefs of the nation to a feast at a place in Connaught, since called *Magh Cru*, or the Bloody Plain. For three years they had stored up of their produce, the materials for this lavish entertainment. When the guests were enjoying the banquet and the delicious music of the harp, the plot was consummated by the entrance of armed men, who massacred them without remorse or pity. Tradition states that three ladies only escaped, wives of the provincial kings, Baini, daughter of the King of Alba (Scotland), Cruifi, daughter of the King of Wales, and Aini, daughter of the King of Britain. These queens sought refuge at their fathers' courts, and became the mothers of Feredach, Corb Olum, and Tibradi Tirech; and thus the Massacre of the Atacotti failed in its object, and representatives of the slaughtered kings were born to inherit the rights of their fathers. Meantime, the plebeians had elected Carbri Kin-Cait, or the Cat-headed, to be their monarch.

"Evil was the state of Ireland during his reign; fruitless her corn, for there used to be but one grain on the stalk: fruitless her rivers: milkless her cattle: plentiless her fruit, for there used to be but one acorn on the oak."

Carbri, who was an exiled son of the king of Lochlain (Scandinavia), reigned for five years. On his death the throne was offered to his son, Morann, who was noted for his wisdom and learning. Morann declined the crown, and advised that the three legitimate heirs should be recalled from exile. Then followed a Restoration: Feredach was installed Ard Righ, at Tara of the kings. His descendant in the fourth degree was the celebrated Con of the Hundred Battles. Corb Olum was the ancestor, also in the fourth degree, of Ollioll Olum, the great King of Munster, while Tibradi Tirech reigned over Ulster. Morann, who thus disinterestedly resigned all claim to the throne, acted as chief Brehon, or judge, and, by his wise decisions, won for Feredach the title of the "Just." He is feigned to have had a chain which, when placed round the neck of a guilty person, suffocated him, while it expanded when placed on an innocent man. The "Collar of Morann" is often alluded to in Irish song and fiction.

Civil contentions were not ended, for a second revolt of the Atacotti took place in this century. The reigning monarch was killed at the instigation of the plebeians, by the provincial kings at the slaughter of Magh Bolg, now Moybologue, in Cavan. Among the names of these provincial kings we recognize a son of Keth MacMagach, Sanb, King of Connaught. The slaughtered monarch, Fiacha, had a posthumous son, born in Scotland, who afterwards played an important part in our history as Tuathal Techtmar, or the " Acceptable."

Tuathal was twenty-five years old when he also was recalled from exile in Alba. He defeated the "Unfree tribes" in twenty-five battles, and convened the general assembly, or *Feis*, of Tara. The nobles of the Gael flocked to Tara, and there swore, according to the oath exacted in former days by Ugainé Mór, that the sovereignty of Ireland should belong to him and to his posterity for ever. To this king is ascribed the erection of Meath into a territory, to be the peculiar possession of the reigning monarch. Tlacta, Uisnech, Talti, and Temhair, or Tara, were the capital places of the kingdom of Meath. The first-named place was the seat of their worship; at the second a great annual fair was held; at Talti a fair was held, where marriage alliances were contracted; while at Tara, law, history, and genealogies were preserved. The "Psalter of Tara" is alleged to have been an historic register kept there even at this early period.

Eochy, King of Leinster, had married Darinni, daughter of Tuathal Techtmar; but on a subsequent visit to Tara he applied for the hand of her sister, Fithir, stating that Darinni, whom he kept concealed and imprisoned, was dead. His suit was granted. When he returned to Leinster with his bride, Fithir discovered that her sister was yet living, and died of shame, while the deserted first wife of the faithless Eochy died of grief. Tuathal marched on Leinster to avenge the wrongs of his daughters and the perfidy of Eochy. The Lagenians, unable to cope with the forces of the Ard Righ, submitted to a heavy fine, which was exacted every second year, and was called the Boromean Tribute, probably from Bo, a cow, as the tribute was paid by the Leinstermen in kine.

The Boromean Tribute became a fruitful source of conflict, the Lagenians resisting its levy whenever they found themselves strong enough to contend with any chance of success, and submitting only when they were powerless to resist.

The tribute was abandoned about the year 680, in the reign of Finnachta the Festive, at the instigation of St. Moling, but was reimposed in the eleventh century by the great Brian, as a punishment for the aid afforded to the Danes by the Leinstermen. Brian was probably thence called *Boru*, a name of glory and pre-eminence in the Irish annals.

Tuathal Techtmar fell in battle, after a prosperous reign of thirty years. He was slain and succeeded by Mal, a descendant of Conall Carnach. The sovereignty of Ireland remained in this prince of the Irian line for four years only, when the race of Eremon reasserted its supremacy in the person of Felemy Rectmar, son of Tuathal; and, in the person of his son, Con of the Hundred Battles, attained a permanent pre-eminence.

Before we enter on the important reigns of Con—of his son, Art—and his grandson, Cormac—we shall speak of the settlements effected by his brothers and their offspring :—

Felemy Rectmar left three sons. Con succeeded him as Ard Righ, or supreme monarch. Eochy Finn settled in Leinster, and received in fosterage Laeisech, a great-grandson of Conall Carnach, whom he educated. This young prince inherited the martial ardour of his great ancestor, and ably commanded the united armies of his foster-father and Cu Corb, the Leinster king, in a campaign against the Munstermen, who were expelled from the territory of Leinster. The grateful king bestowed on his allies some of the repossessed districts: Eochy Finn got a grant of the Seven Fotharts of Leinster, to him and his posterity for ever. The families of O'Nolan, and O'Lorcain, now Larkin, are his representatives. Laeisech received, as his guerdon, that part of the Queen's County which was named, from him, the territory of Leix. The chieftain sept thus established took at a later period the name of O'More, from Mordha "the Majestic," the twenty-eighth in descent from Conall Carnach. Many other privileges were bestowed by Cu Corb, in reward for the important services rendered him by Laeisech. He covenanted, for himself and his successors, that of every ox or swine slaughtered by the monarch of Leinster for his own use, the back and the ham should be given as "curadh-mir," or champion's portion, to the chieftain of Leix, who was also entitled to be one of the privy council of the king, and distributor of his gifts and presents. He had the privilege of leading the van of the Leinster army when entering an enemy's country, and to hold in battle the "bearna baeghail,"* or gap of danger. The chieftain of Leix paid no tribute, with the exception of seven oxen, to be sent to the hunting-booth of the sovereign; but he covenanted to maintain at his own cost forty warriors, always ready for the service of the King of Leinster, who on his part kept in his pay, and in constant attendance on his person, seven followers of the chieftain of Leix.

The third son of Felemy Rectmar, Fiachna Sraftiné, was settled in the Desi of Tara, now the Barony of Deece, in the county of Meath. His sons were exiled in consequence of one of them, Ængus, having killed his kinsman, Kellach, son of King Cormac, by a cast of a spear, in the presence of the monarch himself, whose eye was also transfixed by the weapon of the angry Ængus, hence called "Dreadspear." Ængus's safe-conduct had been violated by Kellach, on whom he thus avenged his wrongs. Cormac MacArt banished this family from Meath. The Desi settled in Waterford, where their name is perpetuated to our own day.

Having thus glanced at the settlement of the southern Desi, we return to the eldest son of Felemy Rectmar, Con of the Hundred Battles, who commenced his reign A.D. 123. This monarch found a formidable antagonist in Moh Nuad, or Owen Mor, an able prince of the line of Eber. The great Owen had passed much of his youth in exile. While in Spain he is said to have married Moméra, a princess of that nation, and to have received, in the wars he had to wage for his

* Pronounced *Barna Buyal*.

patrimony, valuable assistance from his continental allies. He defeated Con in several pitched battles, and forced him to yield the southern half of the island. The Esker Riada, a chain of low hills extending from Dublin to Galway, was the division between the northern Lea Con (Con's half) and the southern Lea Moha, or Moh Nuad's half. With the single exception of his successor, the posterity of Owen Mór ruled Munster uninterruptedly for a thousand years, while Con's descendants, the great families of O'Neill and O'Donnell, held sway in most parts of Ulster up to the "Plantation" of this province in the reign of James I. of England and VI. of Scotland. Owen Mór had other and more valuable qualities than those of military genius. His prudence saved his subjects from suffering during a famine, the account of which, however, seems to be framed on the Biblical model; and, like many other portions of these traditionary tales, may be referred to a comparatively modern origin. It is said to have lasted for seven years, and to have been foretold by a Druid. Owen, upon hearing of the prophesied scarcity, made use of his fish and flesh-meat, while he stored up his corn, and also bought up, to the extent of his revenue, grain, which he preserved in his granaries. Like Joseph also, he received the submission of those who, in the years of scarcity, repaired to him for food. His son, the celebrated Ollioll Olum, inherited much of his father's genius. Owen the Great perished in the battle of Moy Lena, or, according to some accounts, he was treacherously slain in his bed on the eve of that engagement, in which Con of the Hundred Battles was victorious.

Con's forces were inferior in numbers to those of his rival, Owen having a large Spanish contingent, under the command, as it is said, of an Iberian prince. The northern monarch determined on a night attack, to which all his chiefs agreed, with the exception of Goll MacMorna, the Firbolg chief of the militia of Connaught. "On the day that my arms were put into my hands," said the gallant Goll, "I swore never to attack an enemy at night, by surprise, or at any disadvantage. To this day I have adhered to my promise, and will not break it now." The attack was commenced without him, but, notwithstanding the advantage of the surprise, the troops of Moh Nuad fought so well that Con was well nigh discomfited. The morning dawned, and Goll, no longer bound by his vow to stand aloof, attacked the forces of Lea Moha, and Owen and his Spanish ally fell under his avenging sword. The soldiers of Goll raised the body of Owen on their shields, and exposed it in triumph to the armies. The noble Goll interposed:—"Lay down the body of the King of Munster," he said, "for he died the death of a hero."

The long and prosperous reign of Con was terminated at last by treachery. Tibradi Tirech assassinated him while the old king, who had entered his hundredth year, was preparing to hold the *Feis* of Tara.

Conari the Second, son-in-law to Con, whose daughter Sara he had married, succeeded him. This prince was father of the three Carbris;—Carbri Musc, from whom are descended the tribes of Muskerry; Carbri Baiscin, the progenitor of noble families in Clare; and Carbri Riada, giving name to the Dal

Riadic tribes of the north of Antrim, whose colonies in Scotland are mentioned by the Venerable Bede. The settlement first acquired by the Irish Gael or Scoti among the Picts of North Britain, received the name of *Airer-Gaedhil*, the district of the Gael, since corrupted into Argyle, for this western part of Scotland was the seat of the Dalriad colony. The blood of this grandson of Con of the Hundred Battles flows in the veins of her gracious Majesty, Queen Victoria.

Soive, another daughter of Con of the Hundred Battles, was twice married. By her first husband she had a son, MacCon, and by the renowned Ollioll Olum, her second husband, she was the mother of three sons, progenitors of great Munster families, who have contributed illustrious names to Irish history, and are not without distinguished representatives even at the present day. Owen was the ancestor of the Eugenian line, to which belong the MacCarthys, the O'Sullivans, O'Keeffes, and O'Callaghans, with their kindred branches. Cormac Cas, the second son of Ollioll Olum and Soive, had for his wife a daughter of the celebrated poet, Oisin or Ossian, son of Finn MacCumhal. From Cormac Cas is descended the great Dalcassian race represented by the O'Briens, MacNamaras, O'Gradys, O'Quinns, and other eminent native families of Clare and Munster.

The representatives of Cian, third son of Ollioll Olum, include, amongst others, the O'Carrolls, O'Meaghers, O'Haras, and O'Garas. Of the latter family sprang the illustrious patron of the O'Clerys, whose compilation, known as the " Annals of the Four Masters," is dedicated to Fearghal O'Gara, chief of Cuil O'Finn or Coolavin, in Sligo. "For every good that will result from this book," wrote Michael O'Clery, in his dedication, "in giving light to all in general, it is to you, O noble Fearghal O'Gara, that thanks should be given; and there should exist no wonder or surprise, jealousy or envy at [any] good that you do; for you are of the race of Eber MacMileadh, from whom descended thirty of the kings of Ireland and sixty-one saints: and to Tadgh, son of Kian, son of Ollioll Olum, from whom eighteen of these saints are sprung, you can be traced generation by generation."

CHAPTER IV.

THE OSSIANIC PERIOD.

ART THE SOLITARY succeeded his brother-in-law Conari as Ard Righ, A.D. 166. He obtained his name, *Aeinfer*, or the Solitary, being the only surviving son of Con of the Hundred Battles, his brothers having been assassinated by their kinsman, Eochy Finn. His wife was Maev, and from her is named Rath-Maev, near Tara. By a left-handed marriage with a beautiful girl named Eatach, the daughter of a smith, he became the father of Cormac MacArt, one of the most illustrious of our early kings. The future fortunes of Cormac were foreshadowed, according to the story, by a remarkable dream which his mother had previous to his birth. She dreamed that her head was severed from her body, and that from her neck grew a goodly tree, which overshadowed the land of Erin. This tree was prostrated by a sea which overwhelmed it, but again from its roots sprang another stately tree, which was in its turn laid prostrate by a whirlwind from the west.

This vision was supposed to be fulfilled by the loss of her *head*, her husband, King Art, who shortly after perished in the battle of Moy Mucrivé. The stately *tree* which overshadowed Erin symbolized her distinguished son, Cormac. The destroying *sea*, that fish-bone by which this king was choked. The *tree which sprang from its roots*, Cormac's illustrious son, Carbri Lificar, who again perished by the *whirlwind* which shadowed forth his fate when contending with the *Fianna Eirinn*, or revolted Militia, at the momentous battle of Gavra.

The battle of Moy Mucrivé, in which Art perished, was occasioned by the ambition of MacCon, son of Soive, daughter of Con of the Hundred Battles, by her first husband. He was consequently step-son to Ollioll Olum, then King of Munster. This southern kingdom was ruled alternately by representatives of the races of Eber and Ith. When the former gave a king to Munster—at that time in the person of Ollioll Olum—the tribe of Ith, from whom MacCon was descended, gave the Brehon and Tanist, or heir apparent. But this position did not satisfy the ambition of MacCon. He was obliged, however, to fly from home —the time being unpropitious for his schemes—and he was accompanied by Lugaid Laga, brother of Ollioll, who was displeased at the friendship which existed between that monarch and Art the Solitary; for Art's father, Con, had caused the death of their father, Moh Nuad, or Owen the Great. These exiles, aided by foreign allies, returned to Ireland, and in the pitched battle of Moy Mucrivé, gained a signal victory. Art Aeinfer himself fell by the hand of Lugaid Laga, and seven of the sons of Ollioll Olum fell beneath the swords of their half-brother's auxiliary troops.

MacCon, "son of the wolf-hound," for so his name

ignifies,—as he was reported to have been suckled by that animal,—now ascended the throne. He made himself beloved by poets and men of learning, to whom he distributed lavish gifts; and met his death at a place in Tipperary, whose name, Gort-an-oir—the field of gold—records his munificence. He was transfixed by the javelin of Ferchoas, as he was leaning against a pillar stone, engaged in his contributions to the poets and Ollaves. This treachery was instigated by Cormac MacArt, but he did not at the time reap any reward from the base act, as Fergus, a relative of the murdered prince, surnamed "of the black teeth," seized the crown, and, with his two brothers, also called Fergus, caused the disqualification of Cormac, for the time, by depriving him of his hair. The Ferguses applied a lighted torch to the long tresses of Cormac at a feast; and no one having a personal blemish could reign at Tara.

This injury was not irreparable. In due time the locks of Cormac grew, and he sought to revenge himself on the three Ferguses. There is something very characteristic in the story told of the way in which he accomplished his object. He desired to secure the services of the greatest champion of the day, Lugaid Laga. This was that son of Owen the Great who had embraced the cause of MacCon, and had slain the father of Cormac, King Art, with his own hand, in the battle of Moy Mucrivé. Cormac sought him out, and found Lugaid reposing in his hunting booth. He pricked him with his spear. "Who wounds me?" cried the warrior. "It is I, Cormac MacArt," replied the king. "Thou hast good cause for wounding me, for it was this hand that killed thy father, Art Aeinfor," rejoined Lugaid. "Award me an eric for that deed," said Cormac. According to Brehon law, if the family of a murdered man elected to accept a fine for the blood-shedding, in lieu of claiming the life of the murderer, they were at liberty to make the election; and, under some circumstances not explained, the law applied to Lugaid. "I claim a king's head on the battle field," said Cormac;—"the head of my enemy, Fergus of the Black Teeth, who opposes my accession to the throne of Ireland."

Lugaid Laga was compelled, by the custom of the times, to comply with this demand of his enemy, Cormac. A battle ensued, but Cormac took no part in the engagement. With a few attendants he watched the conflict from a hill overlooking the field of combat, and while there, exchanged his royal robes with an attendant, whose garments he assumed. His doughty champion, Lugaid, forced to pay his *eric*, sought out Fergus in the battle, conquered him, and returned to Cormac—or rather the disguised attendant who wore his robes—with the bloody trophy. "Is this the head of Fergus of the Black Teeth," he exclaimed, casting down the bleeding head. "Nay, this is but his brother," said the attendant, falsely. Lugaid again rushed into the battle, sought out and killed a second Fergus, and brought his head also on his spear to the king. "This is not the head of the King of Uladh," replied the disguised attendant. Lugaid again sought the field, and bearing away the head of the surviving

Fergus, dashed it with such force against the breast of the supposed Cormac, that his representative was killed by the blow. By this stratagem Cormac disposed of his formidable foes, and the Battle of Crinna—as this fight was called—paved the way to his accession to the sovereignty of all Ireland.

Notwithstanding these blemishes on the early career of Cormac MacArt, his reign is one of the most glorious recorded in the Irish annals. He maintained a princely retinue, and kept kingly state in Tara. He has the reputation also of having been a distinguished author. Many institutes ascribed to him are to be found in the books of the Brehon laws. He is there treated as the author of the *Tegasg Righ*, or book of precepts for kings, alleged to have been afterwards transcribed by his son, Carbri Lificar. In the great Hall of Tara, erected by him, and of which the foundations and fourteen doorways may still be traced, one hundred and fifty warriors stood in his presence when he sat down to the banquet. One hundred and fifty cup-bearers were in attendance with one hundred and fifty jewelled cups of silver and gold; and yet, with all this taste for magnificence, Cormac, in the choice of a wife, consulted only the dictates of his heart. His wooing of the fair damsel Ethni is highly romantic.

Cormac was ranging unattended through an oak wood in the vicinity of Cennanus, or Kells. To this spot had retired Buiked, a Leinster exile, with his wife and foster-child, Ethni. They lived in the closest retirement, for Buiked had impoverished himself, in his Leinster home, by his open-handed and unbounded generosity. The "cauldron of hospitality" was constantly on the fire, and all who entered his house were made welcome. At last he found all his flocks and herds exhausted; seven cows and a bull representing his remaining wealth. With this slender provision he retired to the oak wood at Kells, and here Ethni tended her foster-parents, performing for them all servile offices which were needed, with cheerful alacrity. She was engaged in milking the seven cows, when Cormac approached, unperceived, through the wood. The king paused to contemplate the maiden. She had brought with her two pails, into one of which she milked the first half-draught from the cows, and then, taking the second pail, she completed her task. With these she returned to the hut of her foster-parents, but speedily reappeared with two other pails and a horn. She then directed her steps to a stream which ran through the wood, and, with the horn, she filled both pails—one from the water which ran near the bank, the other from the middle of the streamlet. These she conveyed to the hut, and again appeared with a sickle in her hand. She next proceeded to cut green rushes, placing those that were long on one side. While thus employed, and—

"Duteous, in the lowly vale,
Unconscious of the monarch's gaze,
　She filled the fragrant pail;
And, duteous from the running brook,
　Drew water for the bath; nor deem'd
A king did on her labour look,
　And she a fairy seem'd—"

love and admiration and wonder filled the breast of Cormac. He approached her, and asked of her for whom she had made that selection of milk, and water, and rushes. "The person for whom I have made it," she replied, "has a right to still greater kindness from me, if it were in my power to render it."

"Of what name is he?" said Cormac.

"Buiked Brugh," she answered.

"Is not that the Leinsterman who was so famed throughout Ireland for his hospitality?"

"It is," replied the maid.

"Then art thou his foster-child Ethni, daughter of Dunlaing?" said the king.

"I am," replied Ethni.

"In a good hour," rejoined the king; "for you shall be my married wife."

"The disposal of me does not rest with myself, but with my foster-father," said the dutiful girl.

Cormac sought the hut of the impoverished Buiked, won his consent to his marriage with Ethni, and bestowed on his foster-father lands and gifts.

King Cormac had ten daughters. Two of them, Grania and Ailbe, played a memorable part in Irish story. Grania, "the golden-haired, the fleet and young," was affianced by her father to Finn, son of Cumhal, the great chief of the Fianna Eirinn, or Irish militia, the Finn MacCool of Irish, and Fingal of Scottish tradition. This military order, the Clanna Baisgne as they were sometimes called, was instituted for the defence of the kingdom against foreign foes. For the winter months this standing army was quartered upon the people of Ireland. During the summer, they lived by hunting and the chase, performing at all times the duties demanded of them by the sovereign, putting down public enemies, upholding justice, and preventing robberies. It was no slight honour to be admitted into this order of chivalry. Every candidate had to give proof, not only of his military skill and personal activity, but also of intellectual gifts. He should be a bard, and have mastered the twelve Books of Poesy; and four *Gesa*, or sacred injunctions, were laid upon each person admitted into the *Fianna*.

The first injunction was, never to receive a portion with a wife; but to choose her for good manners and virtue. The second, never to offer violence to a woman. The third, never to give a refusal to any mortal, for anything of which one was possessed. The fourth was, that no single warrior of the *Fianna* should flee before nine champions.

In addition to these vows of chivalry common to all the members of the order, each warrior might assume some particular *geis*, or obligation, by which he would be individually bound. Their great commander, Finn, in addition to his warlike accomplishments, is said to have possessed the gifts of Healing, Poetry, and Second-sight, which he won by his daring, from a fairy lady, into whose palace he had well nigh entered, one hand having passed her portals before she could close them against the intruder. Finn, a hero, but no longer a young man, when he was selected by King Cormac for his son-in-law, failed to find favour in the eyes of the beautiful Grania. His lieutenant, the "dark-haired

Dermid, of bright face and white teeth," reputedly the handsomest man of his age, and bound by his peculiar obligation to the service of distressed damsels, attracted the attention of Grania, who, at the marriage-feast at which she was to be united to Finn, cast herself on his protection, or, in the language of the romance, laid his "gesa" on Dermid, who was thus compelled, very reluctantly, to elope with her. Grania gained the opportunity for her interview with Dermid, by drugging the wine, with which, in compliance with the customs of the time, the lady filled her richest drinking-cup. This was sent by her to such guests as she desired to pledge. From this honour she excluded Dermid, and when her drugs had taken effect, she appealed to his gallantry and manliness, to save her from the hated bridal by making her his wife.

When Cormac and Finn awoke from their heavy sleep and found that Dermid and Grania had fled, they pursued them all over Erin. The lovers, aided by the sympathy of friends, and their own good fortune, avoided, by many hair-breadth escapes, a capture. Ignorant tradition has named from them, those ancient monuments which abound in our country, and are popularly called Cromlechs, or Druids' altars; and, as the supposed resting-places of the fugitive lovers are called *Leaba Diarmada agus Ghrainné*, the Beds of Dermid and Grania.

King Cormac, thus thwarted in his desire to honour Finn, consoled him by bestowing on him the hand of his daughter Ailbe. Dermid, after many varying fortunes and picturesque adventures, meets his death on the summit of the majestic mountain of Benbulben, in the county of Sligo, from the tusks of a wild boar. Finn arriving on the scene just before the death of his rival, gives occasion to a passage in the Irish romance of more than ordinary beauty and pathos, on which the following poem has been constructed. Dermid, notwithstanding the resemblance of his story to that of Adonis, is not altogether a fabulous character. The clan Campbell claim to be of "the race of Brown Dermid, who slew the wild boar," which still figures as the cognizance of the ducal house of Argyll.

The Death of Dermid.

Finn on the mountain found the mangled man,
The slain boar by him. "Dermid," said the king,
"It likes me well at last to see thee thus.
This only grieves me, that the womankind
Of Erin are not also looking on:
Such sight were wholesome for the wanton eyes
So oft enamour'd of that specious form:
Beauty to foulness, strength to weakness turned."

Dermid.

"Yet in thy power, if only in thy will,
Lies it, oh Finn, even yet to heal me."

Finn.

"How?"

Dermid.

"Feign not the show of ignorance, nor deem
I know not of the virtues which thy hand
Drew from that fairy's half-discover'd hall,
Who bore her silver tankard from the fount,
So closely follow'd, that ere yet the door
Could close upon her steps, one arm was in ;

Wherewith, though seeing nought, yet touching all,
Thou grasped'st half the spiritual world;
Withdrawing a heap'd handful of its gifts,—
Healing, and sight-prophetic, and the power
Divine of poesy: but healing most
Abides within its hollow:—virtue such
That but so much of water as might wet
These lips, in that hand brought, would make me whole.
Finn! from the fountain fetch me in thy palms
A draught of water, and I yet shall live."

    FINN.

" How at these hands canst thou demand thy life,
Who took'st my joy of life?"

    DERMID.

     "She loved thee not:
Me she did love and doth; and were she here
She would so plead with thee that, for her sake,
Thou wouldst forgive us both, and bid me live."

    FINN.

"I was a man had spent my prime of years
In war and council, little bless'd with love;
Though poesy was mine, and, in my hour,
The seer's burthen not desirable;
And now at last had thought to have man's share
Of marriage blessings; and the king supreme,
Cormac, had pledged his fairest daughter mine;
When thou, with those pernicious beauty-gifts,
The flashing white tusk there hath somewhat spoil'd,
Didst win her to desert her father's house,
And roam the wilds with thee."

    DERMID.

     "It was herself,
Grania, the princess, put me in the bonds

Of holy chivalry to share her flight.
'Behold,' she said, ' he is an aged man,
(And so thou art, for years will come to all;)
And I, so young; and at the Boltano games,
When Carbry Liffacher did play the men
Of Brea, I, unseen, saw thee snatch a hurl,
And thrice on Tara's champions win the goal ;
And gave thee love that day, and still will give.'
So she herself avow'd. Resolve me, Finn,
For thou art just, could youthful warrior, sworn
To maiden's service, have done else than I ?
No : hate me not—forgive me—give me drink."

FINN.

" I will not."

DERMID.

"Nay, but, Finn, thou hadst not said
' I will not,' though I'd ask'd a greater boon,
That night we supp'd in Breendacoga's lodge.
Remember : we were faint and hunger-starved
From three days' flight ; and even as on the board
They placed the viands, and my hand went forth
To raise the wine-cup, thou, more quick of ear,
O'erheard'st the stealthy leaguer set without,
And yet should'st eat or perish. Then 'twas I,
Fasting, that made the sally ; and 'twas I,
Fasting, that made the circuit of the court ;
Three times I cours'd it, darkling, round and round ;
From whence returning, when I brought thee in
The three lopp'd heads of them that lurk'd without—
Thou hadst not then, refresh'd and grateful, said
' I will not,' had I ask'd thee, ' give me drink.'"

FINN.

"There springs no water on this summit bald."

DERMID.

"Nine paces from the spot thou standest on,
The well-eye—well thou knowest it—bubbles clear."

Abash'd, reluctant, to the bubbling well
Went Finn, and scoop'd the water in his palms;
Wherewith returning, half-way, came the thought
Of Grania, and he let the water spill.

"Ah me," said Dermid, "hast thou then forgot
Thy warrior art, that oft, when helms were split
And buckler-bosses shatter'd by the spear,
Has satisfied the thirst of wounded men?
Ah, Finn, these hands of thine were not so slack
That night, when, captured by the King of Thule,
Thou layest in bonds within the temple-gate
Waiting for morning, till the observant king
Should to his sun-god make thee sacrifice.
Close-pack'd thy fingers then, thong-drawn and squeezed,
The blood-drops oozing under every nail,
When, like a shadow, through the sleeping priests
Came I, and loos'd thee; and the hierophant
At day-dawn coming, on the altar-step,
Instead of victim straighten'd to his knife,
Two warriors found, erect, for battle arm'd."

Again abash'd, reluctant to the well
Went Finn, and scoop'd the water in his palms,
Wherewith returning, half-way, came the thought
That wrench'd him; and the shaken water spill'd.

DERMID.

"False one, thou didst it purposely! I swear
I saw thee, though mine eyes do fast grow dim.
Ah me, how much imperfect still is man!
Yet such were not the act of Him, whom once
On this same mountain, as we sat at eve—
Thou yet mayst see the knoll that was our couch,

> A stone's throw from the spot where now I lie—
> Thou showed'st me, shuddering, when the seer's fit,
> Sudden and cold as hail, assail'd thy soul
> In vision of that just One crucified
> For all men's pardoning, which, once again,
> Thou sawest, with Cormac, struck in Rossnaree."
>
> Finn trembled; and a third time to the well
> Went straight, and scoop'd the water in his palms;
> Wherewith in haste half-way returned he saw
> A smile on Dermid's face relax'd in death.*

When Grania heard of the death of her husband, she uttered "a long, exceedingly piteous cry."—" And truly my very heart is grieved," said Grania, " that I am not myself able to fight with Finn, for were I so, I would not have suffered him to leave this place in safety." She summoned her sons, feasted them with mead, ale, and strong fermented drinks, and when thus excited, urged them to avenge her wrongs :—" Oh, dear children," said Grania, in a loud and bright clear voice, " your father hath been slain by Finn MacCumhal, against his bonds and covenants of peace with him; and avenge ye that upon him well." Thus speaking she bestowed on them their father's weapons, and dismissed them to learn feats of arms, till they should be old enough to measure swords with Finn.

When Finn heard of these projects for avenging the death of Dermid, he summoned his Fians to concert measures for repelling the meditated attack, but found his warriors unwilling to aid him in a cause in which they deemed him wholly in the wrong. In fact his

* S. Ferguson.

ungenerous treatment of Dermid had disgusted his friends, and among them even his own son Oisin. "According as thou hast planted the tree, so bend it thyself," replied Oisin, when refusing to bear out his father in the course into which his jealous rage had led him. Thus foiled, nothing was left to Finn but to appease the anger of Grania. This fickle lady was a prototype of Anne Neville, the widow of Edward Plantagenet, whose wooing, by the murderer of her husband, Richard, Duke of Gloucester, forms so fine a scene in Shakespeare's "King Richard the Third." In this ancient Irish romance of the *Pursuit of Dermid and Grania*, Finn is represented as endeavouring to overcome the enmity of the widowed Grania, with crafty cunning and sweet words. Grania, in reply, like the widow of young Plantagenet, assailed him with her keen, very sharp-pointed tongue. "Was ever woman in this humour wooed—was ever woman in this humour won?" is a query equally applicable to both. Grania yielded to the persuasions of Finn, the suitor whose love she had formerly rejected. She reconciled her sons to her new husband, and it is recorded by the romance-writer that from thenceforth Finn and Grania "stayed by one another till they died."

The heroic tales and legends connected with the Fians would fill a volume: much of this material is now accessible to English readers, through the translations of the Ossianic society. To Ossian, or Oisin, as his name appears in Irish story, are ascribed most of the poetic remains attaching themselves to this epoch. But this mighty bard's name shelters many compositions of much later date. Conversations with St. Patrick, to whose days he is fabled to have lived, form the subject of some of these poems. He appears as a very incorrigible convert, his Pagan sentiments strongly clinging to him. The fasts of the early saints, were specially repugnant to his nature, and he is represented as over looking back with regret, on the glorious days of his unregenerate youth.

> "Alas! were I in strength and vigor,
> As I was exultingly at the harbour of Finn-tragh,
> I should not be deafened in the church of the bells,
> And I would put a stop to their droning.
>
> "Alas! were I in lusty might,
> As I was against Fatha Chonain,
> With Finn and his hosts by my side
> I should not be listening to these howls."

It was in these disrespectful terms that Oisin is supposed to have designated the Psalmody of St. Patrick and his monks. But after all—such is the force of genius—we conceive of Oisin rather as the Ossian of MacPherson, or as in that still grander idealization of him, and of our ancient story, for which we are indebted to a living poet.*

> Long, long ago, beyond the misty space
>   Of twice a thousand years;
> In Erin old there dwelt a mighty race,
>   Taller than Roman spears;

---

* T. D. McGee.

Like oaks and towers they had a giant grace,
   Were fleet as deers,
With winds and waves they made their 'biding place,
   These western shepherd seers.

Their ocean-god was Mananán MacLir,
   Whose angry lips
In their white foam full often would inter
   Whole fleets of ships:
Crom was their Day-god, and their Thunderer,
   Made morning and eclipse;
Bride was their queen of song, and unto her
   They prayed with fire-touched lips.

Great were their deeds, their passions, and their sports:
   With clay and stone
They piled on strath and shore those mystic forts,
   Not yet o'erthrown;
On cairn-crown'd hills they held their council-courts,
   While youths alone
With giant dogs, explored the elk resorts,
   And brought them down.

Of these was Fin, the father of the Bard,
   Whose ancient song
Over the clamour of all change is heard,
   Sweet voic'd and strong.
Fin once o'ertook Griaun, the golden-haired,
   The fleet and young;
From her the lovely, and from him the fear'd,
   The primal poet sprung.

Ossian! two thousand years of mist and change
   Surround thy name—
Thy Finian heroes now no longer range
   The hills of fame.
The very name of Fin and Goll sound strange—
   Yet thine the same—
By miscalled lake and desecrated grange,
   Remains, and shall remain!

The Druid's altar and the Druid's creed
  We scarce can trace;
There is not left an undisputed deed
  Of all your race,
Save your majestic song, which hath their speed
  And strength, and grace;
In that sole song, they live and love, and bleed;
  It bears them on through space.

Oh, inspir'd giant! shall we e'er behold
  In our own time
One fit to speak your spirit on the wold,
  Or seize your rhyme?
One pupil of the past, as mighty soul'd
  As in the prime,
Were the fond, fair, and beautiful and bold,
  They of your song sublime!

To king Cormac we are said to owe the first erection of a water-mill in Ireland. Mithridates, king of Cappadocia, is reputed to have been the inventor of mills, about seventy years before the commencement of the Christian era. This memorable invention was celebrated by a Syrian poet, whose verses have been thus gracefully translated from the Greek:—

"Ye maids who toil'd so faithful at the mill,
Now cease from work, and from those toils be still;
Sleep now till dawn, and let the birds with glee
Sing to the ruddy morn on bush and tree;
For what your hands performed so long, so true,
Ceres has charged the water-nymphs to do:
They come, the limpid sisters, to her call,
And on the wheel with dashing fury fall,
Impel the axle with a whirling sound,
And make the massy mill-stone reel around,
And bring the floury heaps luxuriant to the ground."

Cormac is said to have brought over Pictish artisans from Alba to erect his mill at Tara. He had become enamoured of Carnait, a beautiful maiden of the Cruithni, who had been carried off from Alba on some plundering expedition. Ethni, the lawful wife of Cormac, treated Carnait with a severity inspired by jealousy, and compelled the fair captive to grind, with a quern, or hand-mill, nine pecks of corn each day. Carnait, about to become a mother, was unable to perform this domestic drudgery; she complained to Cormac, and probably informed him of the use of mills among her own people in Scotland. He sent thither for skilled workmen. To this day a mill—Lismullen—exists on the supposed site of the ancient erection of Cormac MacArt, and the present miller claims to be the representative of the Pictish millwright, brought to Tara by that monarch, to relieve the labours of the beautiful Carnait.

Cormac maintained unwonted state at Tara, and enacted that for the future the monarch of Erin should keep in constant attendance on his person, a prince of noble blood, a brehon, a druid, a physician, a bard, an historian, a musician, and three stewards. His banquets were on a scale of splendid hospitality. " Each king wore his kingly robe upon him, and his golden helmet on his head, for they never put their kingly diadems on but in the field of battle only. Magnificently did Cormac come to this great assembly. His hair was slightly curled, and of golden colour; a scarlet shield with engraved devices, and golden hooks, and clasps of silver; a wide-folding purple cloak on him, with a gem-set gold brooch over his breast; a gold torque around his neck, a white collared shirt, embroidered with gold, upon him; a girdle with golden buckles, and studded with precious stones, around him; two golden net-work sandals with golden buckles upon him; two spears with golden sockets and many red bronze rivets, in his hand, while he stood in the full glow of beauty, without defect or blemish. The world was full of all goodness in the time of Cormac, the grandson of Con of the Hundred Battles: there were fruit and fatness of the land, and abundant produce of the sea, with peace and ease and happiness in his time."

But Cormac was forced to abdicate, and leave his royal palace of Tara, for the comparative seclusion of his House of Cletty, near the Boyne; having lost his eye from the cast of that spear hurled by his kinsman, Ængus "Dread spear," as we have already mentioned: "and it was not deemed by the nobles of Ireland honourable or auspicious that any king disfigured by a personal blemish should reign at Tara." It was in the retirement of this House of Cletty that King Cormac is said to have composed his regal Institutes, the *Tegasg Righ*; and here, after ages have been willing to believe, abandoned the worship of idols, and refused to pay homage to any but the one great Creator of Heaven and Earth. "For I," said Cormac, "will offer no adoration to any stock or image, shaped by my own mechanic. It were more rational to offer adoration to the mechanic himself, for he is more worthy than the work of his hands." His death, occasioned by the bone of a salmon, which stuck in his throat, was ascribed by the Druids to the vengeance of their God, Crom Cruach. Cormac directed that he should not be buried at Brugh-na-Boinne, the resting-place of his Pagan ancestors, but at Rossnaree, on the southern bank of the Boyne, where he had first had his vision of the approaching light of a purer religion. The struggle between the powers of light and darkness for the possession of the dead king's body, is the subject of a characteristic legend on which is founded

THE BURIAL OF KING CORMAC.

"Crom Cruach and his sub-gods twelve,"
  Said Cormac, "are but carven treene:
The axe that made them, haft or helve,
  Had worthier of our worship been.

"But He who made the tree to grow,
  And hid in earth the iron-stone,
And made the man, with mind to know
  The axe's use, is God alone."

Anon to priests of Crom was brought,
  Where, girded in their service dread,
They ministered on red Moy Slaught—
  Word of the words King Cormac said.

They loos'd their curse against the king;
  They cursed him in his flesh and bones;
And daily in their mystic ring
  They turned the maledictive stones.

Till, where at meat the monarch sate,
  Amid the revel and the wine,
He choked upon the food he ate
  At Sletty, southward of the Boyne.

High vaunted then the priestly throng
    And far and wide they noised abroad
With trump and loud liturgic song
    The praise of their avenging God.

But ere the voice was wholly spent
    That priest and prince should still obey,
To awed attendants, o'er him bent,
    Great Cormac gathered breath to say—

"Spread not the beds of Brugh for me
    When restless death-bed's use is done;
But bury me in Rossnaree,
    And face me to the rising sun.

"For all the kings who lie in Brugh
    Put trust in gods of wood and stone;
And 'twas at Ross that first I knew
    One, unseen, who is God alone.

"His glory lightens from the east:
    His message soon shall reach our shore;
And idol-god, and cursing priest
    Shall plague us from Moy Slaught no more."

Dead Cormac on his bier they laid:—
    "He reigned a king for forty years,
And shame it were," his captains said,
    "He lay not with his royal peers.

"His grandsire, Hundred-Battle, sleeps
    Serene in Brugh; and, all around,
Dead kings in stone sepulchral keeps
    Protect the sacred burial-ground.

"What though a dying man should rave
    Of changes o'er the eastern sea?
In Brugh of Boyne shall be his grave
    And not in noteless Rossnaree."

Then northward forth they bore the bier,
    And down from Sletty side they drew,
With horseman and with charioteer
    To cross the fords of Boyne to Brugh.

There came a breath of finer air
    That touched the Boyne with ruffling wings;
It stirred him in his sedgy lair
    And in his mossy moorland springs:

And as the burial train came down
    With dirge and savage dolorous shows,
Across their pathway, broad and brown,
    The deep, full-hearted river rose.

From bank to bank through all his fords,
    'Neath blackening squalls he swelled and boiled;
And thrice the wondering gentile lords
    Essayed to cross, and thrice recoiled.

Then forth stepped four grim warriors hoar:
    They said, "Through angrier floods than these
Our link'd shields bore him once before
    From Dread-Spear and the hosts of Deece.

"And long as loyal will holds good,
    And limbs respond with helpful thews,
Nor flood, nor fiend within the flood,
    Shall bar him of his burial dues."

With slanted necks they stooped to lift;
    They heaved him up to neck and chin;
And, pair and pair, with footsteps swift,
    Locked arm and shoulder, bore him in.

'Twas brave to see them leave the shore;
    To mark the deep'ning surges rise,
And fall subdued, in foam, before
    The tension of their striding thighs.

'Twas brave, when, now a spear-cast out,
  Breast high the battling surges ran;
For weight was great, and limbs were stout,
  And loyal man put trust in man.

But ere they reached the middle deep,
  Nor steadying weight of clay they bore,
Nor strain of sinewy limbs could keep
  Their feet beneath the swerving four.

And now they slide, and now they swim,
  And now amid the blackening squall,
Grey locks afloat, with clutchings grim
  They plunge around the floating pall;

While, as a youth with practised spear,
  Through justling crowds bears off the ring,
Boyne from their shoulders caught the bier
  And proudly bore away the king.

At morning on the grassy marge
  Of Rossnaree the corpse was found,
And shepherds, at their early charge,
  Entombed it in the peaceful ground.

A tranquil spot: a hopeful sound
  Comes from the ever-youthful stream,
And still on daisied mead and mound
  The dawn delays with tenderer beam.

Round Cormac Spring renews her buds;
  In march perpetual by his side
Down come the earth-fresh April floods
  And up the sea-fresh salmon glide;

And Life and Time rejoicing run
  From age to age their wonted way;
But still he waits the risen Sun,
  For still 'tis only dawning Day.*

---

* From *Lays of the Western Gael.*

This tradition must be of great antiquity, for it is historically certain that Cormac's lineal descendant, St. Columba, in the sixth century, erected a Christian cell at Rossnaree on the spot where the king's body was then believed to have been deposited by this supernatural intervention of the elements.

Carbri Lificar, son of Cormac and Ethni, assumed the sovereignty of Ireland in the lifetime of his father, whose blemish unfitted him to sway the sceptre of Tara. He fell in the Battle of Gavra, A.D. 284. At this fatal engagement Oscar, the son of Oisin, and grandson of Finn MacCumhal, perished by the hand of King Carbri, who was himself so severely wounded by Oscar, that he did not survive the battle. The Clanna Baisgne had sided with Moh Corb, King of Munster, who was grandson to Finn, being the son of his daughter Samhair: she had married Cormac Cas, son of the great Ollioll Olum, and thus the blood of Finn yet flows in the veins of the O'Briens, and other families of the noble Dalcassian stock. Carbri Lificar had summoned to his aid, in his quarrel with Moh Corb, the Clanna Morna, or militia of Connaught, rivals of the Fians. Gavra is in the vicinity of the hill of Skreen near Tara in Meath. The battle was fiercely contested—long and bloody. Oscar was entombed in the rath which occupied part of the site of the battle-field. "The great green rath's ten-acred tomb lies heavy on his urn."

Carbri Lificar left two sons, Fiachaid and Eochy Domlen. The former succeeded him, and was again succeeded by his son Muredach. Eochy Domlen was the parent of three remarkable sons—the three Collas as they are called in our annals—Colla Uais, Colla Menn, and Colla Da Croc.

King Fiachaid had made his son Muredach commander of his armies, and presumptive heir to the throne. This aroused the animosity of his nephews, the three Collas. While Muredach was absent with his army in Munster, these princes resolved to give battle to the king, thus deprived of his most efficient troops. On the eve of one engagement Fiachaid was told by his Druid, that if any of his nephews should fall by him or his kinsmen, the posterity of that nephew should rule in Erin; but if he himself were slain, his descendants should triumph. The aged king determined to die, and preserve the throne of Ireland to his children.

Muredach ascended the throne vacated by the voluntary death of his father. He banished his cousins to Alba, where the Collas, with three hundred warriors who followed them into exile, were well received by the Scottish monarch. After three years passed in Alba, being warned in a dream that the time of fulfilling the prophecy had arrived, they returned to Tara, each bringing with him nine warriors only, in the hope that Muredach would avenge on them his father's death, and thus secure for their children, not his, the sway over Ireland. They presented themselves before the king. "Have you brought me any news, my cousins?" asked Muredach. "We have no sadder news to relate," said they, "than the deed which we have ourselves done, namely, the killing of thy father by our hands." Muredach, however, knew the prophecy as well as they did, and was resolved not to forfeit the sovereignty for his offspring, by any deed of violence. "The news you tell us is already known," replied the king; "but it is of no consequence to you now, for no vengeance shall be wreaked upon you therefor, save that the misfortune which has already pursued you shall not leave you." "This is the reply of a coward," said the Collas. "Be not sorry for it," replied the king, "you are welcome."

It was an object with Muredach to find employment for these daring and warlike kinsmen. He suggested to them an attack on Ulster, and gave them as an excuse for aggressive hostilities, the insult which their common ancestor, King Cormac MacArt, had received at the hands of the Ultonians, referring to that burning of his hair and beard, of which we have already spoken. "That deed," said Muredach, "is still unavenged."

Thus provided with a *casus belli*, the Collas marched on Emania. Fergus Fogha, King of Uladh, was slain, his capital plundered and burned, and the glories of Emania and Creeve Roe were extinguished for ever. Thus ended the Ultonian dynasty, overthrown by the three Collas, after it had lasted for more than 600 years, A.D. 332. Orgiall, giving name to the present territory of Oriel, was the name given to the "Sword Land" so won by the Collas: it comprised the greater part of the modern Ulster, Antrim and Down excepted, which remained the patrimony of the Rudrician race of kings, down to the conquest of Ulster, in the beginning of the thirteenth century, by John de Courcy. The descendants of Coll da Cree,—the O'Kellys, afterwards of Hy Many, in Connaught, — Maguires, MacMahons, and others, occupied the district comprising the counties of Armagh, Monaghan, and Fermanagh, down to the confiscation and settlement of Ulster in the reign of James I.

From Colla Uais are derived the Lords of the Isles, the Macdonalds of Scotland, and MacDonnells of Antrim, and their kindred clans; while the ancient inhabitants of Cremorne, in the County of Monaghan, claim Colla Menn as their progenitor.

Eochy, son of Muredach, reigned over Erin for seven years. He left children by two wives. Mongfinn, or the fair-haired, had four sons. Of these Brian, from whom are descended the O'Conors of Connaught, was her favourite. To pave the way for his elevation to the throne she poisoned her brother, Criffan, who had succeeded her husband Eochy. She sacrificed her own life to effect her ambitious schemes for her son, for she drank herself of the poisoned cup that she might induce Criffan to taste it. Her crime was unavailing. No descendant of hers ruled Erin till after a lapse of about eight hundred years. Then, Turlogh More O'Conor, of whom Mongfinn was ancestress, and his son Roderick, the last king of Ireland, filled the throne up to the time of the English Conquest. Criffan was succeeded by Nial of the Nine Hostages, son of Eochy, by a daughter of the king of Britain—a stepson, only, of the guilty Mongfinn.

Nial had to fight for the throne thus made vacant. He found a formidable competitor in Core, King of Munster. This prince, from whom are descended the

O'Donoghue of the Glens, the O'Mahonys, O'Moriartys, and also the Lennoxes and Marrs of Scotland, at length recognized Nial as sovereign, and received from that monarch, in accordance with the custom which enjoined such gifts to a former rival, one thousand steeds, five hundred suits of armour, gold rings and cups. This peace was granted to the entreaties of Torna, the bard of Nial. He filled the endearing position of foster-father to both these princes, and used his influence with Core and Nial to secure peace for his country.

The first military expedition undertaken by Nial, as soon as he found himself firmly seated on the throne of Erin, was directed to Alba. He desired to aid his kindred, the Dalriad colony, who had settled in the western district of Scotland, against the Picts or Cruithni. The Irish colonists, aided by Nial, were successful. These Scoti imposed their name on the country, and Alba became from thenceforth known as Scotland. To understand aright the relations of these Dalriads and Picts we must revert to the earlier traditions, and recount the settlement of the Cruithni, whose invasion of Alba is fixed at the period when Eremon, son of Miled, was king of Ireland.

The Cruithni, according to their own tradition, were a kindred race, and came from Thrace to Gaul. They had fled from the oppression of a monarch who sought to insult the beautiful daughter of their chieftain Gud. They were well received by the Gallic king, for whom, say their senachies, they built the city now called Poictiers. The beauty of Gud's daughter reached the ears of this sovereign also, and the Cruithnian exiles had again to fly from further insult. In a few long galleys they reached the Irish shore. Criffan Sciathbel, the Firbolg chief of Leinster, under Eremon, was at that time waging war with savage tribes, whose use of poisoned weapons was fatal to his soldiers. He accepted these new auxiliaries, making an alliance with the Picts, and availing himself of the skill of their Druid, Trosdan, who cured the wounds of Criffan's army by the simple application of a milk bath.

Eremon did not encourage the Cruithni to settle in Erin, but suggested to them the conquest of Alba; and as they were unprovided with wives, he supplied this want on condition that the throne should always be held by right of the female. This remarkable custom prevailed among the Picts to a late period. They became eventually amalgamated with the Scoti, or Irish colonists. The combined inroads of the Picts and Scots on the defenceless Britons, when the Roman legions evacuated their country, are familiar to all readers of English history. "The barbarians drive us into the sea—the sea throws us back upon the barbarians," was the mournful wail of the Britons to the Consul Ætius. The Romans returned for brief periods to Britain to repel these warlike Caledonians, and aided the Britons by the erection of those mighty ramparts, whose vast remains yet attest the power and mechanical skill of that great people.

When the Cruithni or Picts settled in Scotland there already existed there a people of the Firbolgic family. These early inhabitants of Scotland found themselves,

K

like their kindred in Ireland after the Milesian conquest, pressed by the superior race into the extremities of Alba and its outlying isles. From thence, still pressed by the Picts, a number of them sought refuge in Erin, and, shortly before the commencement of the Christian era, rented lands in Meath, where they settled under the protection of Carbri Niafer. This Firbolg colony, called from their leader Ængus, son of Umor, "the sons of Umor," finding the rents they were forced to pay exorbitant, migrated from Meath to Connaught, and were welcomed by Ailill and Maev, then ruling at Cruachan. The clan Umor were located along the coasts of Mayo, Galway, Clare, and the Aran, and other islands of the western shores of Ireland. Their *locale* may yet be determined by the names—still extant—of places called after their leaders. *Ængus*, son of Umor, was the founder of Dun Ængus, that great dry-stone fort, which we have before described, yet standing on Aran More, off Galway Bay; *Cutra* has left his name at Lough Cooter, near Gort; *Adhar* at Moy Adhair, in Thomond; *Measca*, at Loch Mask; and several other similar examples might be added. On their settlement in Meath Carbri Niafer had required and obtained for them the guarantees of four great heroes, with whose names we have made our readers already familiar—Keth MacMagach, Ross, Conall Carnach, and Cuchullin. When the sons of Umor abandoned his territories for those of Ailill and Maev, Carbri called on their sureties either to compel their return or to fight the fugitives; and accordingly the four heroes demanded of Clan Umor either of these alternatives.

The oppressed and impoverished Firbolgs chose the latter, and selected four of their mightiest champions to contend with the knights of the Red Branch and the Connacian and Munster heroes. Conall the Mild, son of Ængus, son of Umor, was opposed to Cuchullin; Kimi Kethir-Kenn to Conall Carnach; King to Ross; and Irgas-of-many-battles to Keth. The Firbolg champions were defeated. Conall the Mild and his father were buried under the cairn, called from him *Carn-Conaill.* The others were interred in the "delightful plain adjoining the *Rath Umaill,*" which has given name to the barony Burrisoole (*Burris-Umail*), in the county of Mayo.

We shall return, in our next Chapter, to Nial of the Nine Hostages, whose military expedition to Alba to assist his Scotic kindred of the Dalriads in their wars with the Picts has led us into this long digression.

CHAPTER V.

THE PATRICIAN PERIOD.

A STILL more important expedition, if we consider its after effects on the civilization of Ireland, and through Ireland, of Western Europe, than any we have hitherto recorded, was that undertaken by Nial against Armorica, as the north-western districts of France were called, in the fourth century.

Many captives, including children of noble birth, were brought back to Erin by King Nial from this plundering excursion. Among them was a boy of sixteen, Succoth, the son of the deacon Calphurnius, and Conchessa, a near relative of St. Martin of Tours, with his sisters Darerca and Lupida. His name, which is said to signify "brave in battle," was afterwards exchanged for that of Patricius, in allusion to his noble birth. But the boy, destined to become the patron-saint of Ireland, the great apostle and missionary St. Patrick, notwithstanding his gentle blood, was sold as a slave, and employed by his master, Milcho, in feeding cattle on the mountain of Slieve Mis, in the present County of Antrim. For many years the youthful Patrick tended, amidst hardship, suffering, and isolation, the flocks of the pagan Milcho. Amidst the solitudes of his mountain dwelling light broke in upon his soul. The teachings of his childhood, the meditations of his lonely youth, the very desolation of his lot, prepared his mind for the reception of those divine impulses, those spiritual intuitions which elevate the being who receives them above the vicissitudes of existence, and unite the soul to its Creator.

"When I had come to Ireland," says St. Patrick in his 'Confessions,' "I was employed every day in feeding cattle; and frequently in the day I used to have recourse to prayer, and the love of God was thus growing stronger and stronger, and His fear and faith were increasing in me, so that in a single day I would give utterance to as many as an hundred prayers, and in the night almost as many. And I used to remain in the woods, too, and on the mountains, and would rise for prayer before daylight, in the midst of snow and ice, and rain, and felt no injury from it, nor was there any sloth in me, as I now see, because the Spirit was fervent within me." And again he writes: "I was not from my childhood a believer in the only God, but continued in death and unbelief until I was severely chastened: and in truth I have been humbled by hunger and nakedness, and it was my lot to traverse Ireland every day sore against my will, until I was almost exhausted. But this proved rather a benefit to me, because by means of it I have been corrected by the Lord, and he has fitted me for being at this day what was once far from me, so that I should interest or concern myself about the salvation of others, when I used to have no such thoughts even for myself."

To a mind in such intimate communion with heaven, so elevated above earth, so filled with a desire to labour in the conversion of others, all things are possible. There is nothing miraculous when such men are deemed to have worked miracles, and are themselves convinced that they have seen visions and dreamed dreams. Patrick—escaped from his long captivity—restored to his parents—happy in their love—longs to return as a missionary to the people among whom he had lived a slave. "I saw in the visions of the night," he said,—and this passage, from a very authentic piece of antiquity, strongly supports the claim of the Irish to an early knowledge of the art of writing—"a person coming from Ireland with innumerable letters, and he gave me one of them, and I read in the beginning of the letter, 'The voice of the people of Ireland,' and I thought at that very moment that I heard the voice of those who were near the wood of Focluth, which is adjoining to the western sea, and they cried out thus, as it were with one voice, 'We entreat thee, holy youth, to come and walk still among us,' and I was very much pricked to the heart, and could read no further, and so I awoke. Thanks be to God, the Lord who, after very many years, hath granted to them according to their cry."

While the boy Patrick fed the swine of Milcho on the mountain of Slemish, King Nial of the Nine Hostages continued his depredations in Gaul. Hither he summoned to his aid his friends and allies from Alba; and an auxiliary army from the Dalriads of Scotland joined him on the Loire. Gabran, their leader, was accompanied by Eochy, King of Leinster, who had been banished from Erin by Nial. The exiled prince seized this opportunity of avenging himself. He transfixed the king with an arrow on the banks of the Loire. Thus perished the great monarch in the midst of his victorious career.

Nial of the Nine Hostages left eight sons. From Conall Gulban are descended the Kinel Conall, or race of Conall, the great family O'Donnells of Tyr-Conaill. From his twin brother, Owen, the Kinel-Owen, of Tyr-Owen, or Tyrone, the illustrious O'Neills. To all the descendants of Nial belongs the tribe name of Hy-Niall; but the families of O'Neill and O'Donnell, representatives of his twin sons, Owen and Conall Gulban, are distinguished as the Northern Hy-Niall from the progeny of another son, Conall Criffan, who are called the Southern Hy-Niall, and who, though giving some kings to Ireland, never attained the eminent place in her history which the O'Neills and O'Donnells filled. Conall Gulban obtained his name from the mountain already referred to as the scene of the death of Dermid. In this locality, and on this singularly formed and romantic mountain, he had been fostered. He was slain by the "old tribes" of Moy Slaught, that plain in Cavan where the idol Crom Cruach and "his sub-gods twelve" were formerly worshipped. His brother Owen died of grief. He was buried at Eskaheen, in Inishowen.

It will be remembered that Mongfinn, wife of Eochy, the father of Nial, had poisoned her brother, Criffan, to pave the way to the election of *her* son, Brian, to the throne, but that her perfidy, which cost her her own life, had failed in its object, and her step-son, Nial, had become King of Ireland, to the exclusion of her offspring. Brian, however, in the lifetime of his half-brother, Nial, had succeeded to the provincial throne of Connaught, and his brother, Fiachra, another son of Mongfinn, had become chief of a district in the west of Ireland. Dissensions arose between the brothers. Fiachra was defeated in battle by Brian, and delivered into the hands of Nial as a hostage. Feredach, afterwards better known by his acquired name of Dathi, son of the captive Fiachra, avenged his father's wrongs on his uncle Brian, and restored Fiachra to liberty and rule. Fiachra left two sons:—Dathi, who became Ard Righ on the death of his uncle Nial, and Awley, whose rule in Connaught has left its impress in the name of Tyrawley, in the north-west of Mayo. It was in the persons of the seven sons of Awley, converted by Patrick, and baptized with thousands of their followers by him in the land of Tyrawley, that the vision of the saint was realized; for these numerous converts to the faith were made in the vicinity of that wood of Focluth from whence in his dream Patrick had heard the voices entreating him to "come and walk among them."

Dathi is ancestor of the great Connaught families of O'Shaughnessy, O'Dowda, and O'Heyne. This king inherited the military ambition of his uncle Nial, and, like him, made war in Gaul. He had previously undertaken an expedition into Alba, stimulated by the praises of his Druids. In the seventeenth year of his reign he found himself at *Assaroe*, near Ballyshannon, whither he had gone from Tara to adjust some contentions between his kindred in the west. He arrived at the estuary of the Erne at the eve of the great Gaelic festival of *Samhain*, which was held on the last day of October. He commanded the presence of his Arch Druid, and demanded to know what would happen to himself and to his country in the year about to commence. "Then," said Doghra, the Druid, "if you will send nine of your noblest chiefs with me from this to the banks of the Moy, I will reveal something to them."—"It shall be so," said the king, "and I shall be one of the number myself."

Dathi and his chiefs departed secretly from the camp and arrived at Rath Archaill, near the Moy, where the Druids' altars and idols were. Dathi took up his abode at Mulloch Roe, near Screene, in the barony of Tireragh, County Sligo, where his queen, Rua, had a palace. At sunrise the Druid repaired to the chamber of Dathi. "Art thou asleep, O King of Erin and of Alba?" asked Doghra. "I am not asleep," said the monarch; "but have you made an addition to my titles?"—"I have consulted the clouds of the men of Erin," replied the Druid, "and found that thou wilt soon return to Tara, and wilt invite all the provincial kings and chiefs of Erin to the great feast of Tara, and then thou shalt decide with them upon making an expedition into Alba, Britain, and France, following the conquering footsteps of thy great-uncle Nial, and thy grand-uncle Criffan Mor."

The king was delighted with the prediction. He

returned to the camp and imparted it to his chieftains, and in due time retraced his steps to Tara, and invited, as the Druid had suggested, the chiefs of Erin to meet him there, at the approaching festival of *Beltainé*, which was held on May Day.

The feast was celebrated on this occasion with unusual splendour. The fires of *Tailti* were lighted, and the games, sports, and ceremonies, usually held there, passed off with great magnificence. War was resolved on, and Dathi made a successful foray into Alba, and from thence invaded Gaul, where he died; but his body was borne homewards by his soldiers, and now reposes among the mortal remains of his ancestors, the ancient kings of Connaught, at the *Relig na Ree*, near Rath Cruachan. Tradition ascribes his death at the foot of the Alps to a stroke of lightning. He fell, it is said, as he was storming the tower of Parmenius, a royal recluse, who had lived there secluded from the light of day. The Pagan monarch of Erin was not deterred by the sanctity of the royal hermit, and regarded not the recluse's vow of living in perpetual darkness. He proceeded to demolish the tower. When it was unroofed, and Parmenius "felt the wind coming to him, God raised him up in a blaze of fire, and he prayed for King Dathi that his reign might continue no longer; and he also prayed that his monument or tomb might not be conspicuous." Thereupon a flash of lightning struck Dathi dead upon the spot, while Parmenius formed for himself another dwelling lower down on the mountain side. Such is the wild and scarce intelligible form in which the story of Dathi has been transmitted from primitive times. The adventure, whatever may have been its real nature, took place in the same year in which Pharamond, king of the Franks, disappears from the page of history, and it might be suggested that he may have been the hermit king whom Dathi encountered at *Slieve Alpa*, probably some part of the Jura range, in the eastern districts of Gaul. The incident has had a great charm for the Irish imagination, and has been made the subject of many lyrical compositions, one of which is subjoined—

THE EXPEDITION AND DEATH OF KING DATHY.*

King Dathy assembled his Druids and Sages,
And thus he spake them—" Druids and Sages!
  What of King Dathy?
What is revealed in Destiny's pages
  Of him or his? Hath he
Aught for the future to dread or to dree?
Good to rejoice in, or evil to flee?
Is he a foe of the Gall—
Fitted to conquer or fated to fall?"

And Beirdra, the Druid, made answer as thus—
  A priest of a hundred years was he—
"Dathy, thy fate is not hidden from us!
  Hear it through me!
Thou shalt work thine own will!
Thou shalt slay—thou shalt prey—
  And be conqueror still!
Thee the earth shall not harm!
Thee we charter and charm
From all evil and ill!
Thee the laurel shall crown!
Thee the wave shall not drown!

---

* J. C. MANGAN.

Thee the chain shall not bind!
Thee the spear shall not find!
Thee the sword shall not slay!
Thee the shaft shall not pierce!
Thou therefore be fearless and fierce,
And sail with thy warriors away
   To the lands of the Gall,
There to slaughter and sway,
   And be victor o'er all!"

So Dathy he sailed away—away,
   Over the deep resounding sea;
Sailed with his hosts in armour grey
   Over the deep resounding sea,
Many a night and many a day,
   And many an islet conquered he—
He and his hosts in armour grey:
And the billow drowned him not,
And a fetter bound him not,
And the blue spear found him not,
And the red sword slew him not,
And the swift shaft knew him not,
And the foe o'erthrew him not:
Till, one bright morn, at the base
   Of the Alps, in rich Ausonia's regions,
His men stood marshalled face to face
   With the mighty Roman legions.
      Noble foes!
Christian and heathen stood there among those,
Resolute all to overcome,
Or die for the eagles of ancient Rome!

When, behold! from a temple anear
   Came forth an aged priest-like man,
Of a countenance meek and clear,
   Who, turning to Eire's Ceann,*

---

* Ceann:—Head; king.

Spake him as thus—" King Dathy, hear!
  Thee would I warn!
Retreat! retire! Repent in time
The invader's crime,
  Or better for thee thou hadst never been born!"
  But Dathy replied, " False Nazarine!
Dost thou, then, menace Dathy, thou?
And dreamest thou that he will bow
  To one unknown, to one so mean,
So powerless as a priest must be?
He scorns alike thy threats and thee!
On! on, my men, to victory!"

And, with loud shouts for Eire's king,
  The Irish rush to meet the foe,
And falchions clash and bucklers ring,—
  When, lo!
Lo! a mighty earthquake's shock!
And the cleft plains reel and rock;
  Clouds of darkness pall the skies;
    Thunder crashes,
    Lightning flashes,
  And in an instant Dathy lies
    On the earth a mass of blackened ashes!
Then, mournfully and dolefully,
The Irish warriors sailed away
  Over the deep resounding sea,
Till, wearily and mournfully,
They anchored in Eblana's Bay.
  Thus the Seanachies and Sages
  Tell this tale of long-gone ages.

And so, by the elements, not by the hand of man, perished the "fair king of Erin, Dathi, son of Fiachra, a generous king by sea and land," A.D. 426. His son Awley took command of the forces. They commenced their retreat, carrying with them the dead body of the king, whose very presence, though in death, served to discomfit their foes. Ten battles are recorded, won by the retreating host, whose victories are ascribed to the terror of Dathi's countenance, still kept turned towards the pursuers. When the army had reached Ireland, the body, borne by four servants of trust, crossed the island to Cruachan "with dirge and savage dolorous shows," and here, adjoining the *Relig na Ree*, where his ancestors repose, was erected the mound, and its red pillar-stone, over the grave of the last of Ireland's Pagan kings. According to the imprecation of Parmenius, it was "not conspicuous;" yet the pillar-stone, a block of red-grit sand-stone, about nine feet in height, is still standing on the grassy mound, amidst the earthworks, raths, and entrenchments, which, to this day, mark the site of the ancient capital of Connaught. Cattle feed around on the rich pasture land of Roscommon, but with the exception of an occasional cottier's house, the place is lonely, unmarked, and little known, save by the archæologist, or the survivors of the peasantry, who still cling fondly to these traditions of the olden time. More than fourteen hundred years ago, this red pillar-stone was raised. The years have rolled on to centuries, and yet it stands unchanged. How many works of succeeding generations has it not already outlived, how many yet destined to rise and fall, and crumble into ruin, may not this simple pillar survive, erected by his clansmen and soldiers to King Dathi.

Of his descendants we shall have much to speak. His son Ollioll Molt, became Ard Righ some years later, and his grandson Owen Bel, king of Connaught, is the hero of a very picturesque tradition. Owen Bel was the father of St. Kellach, whose story we shall return to, but may not now anticipate.

We resume the thread of the Christian story, laid aside for a space while recounting the fortunes of the sons of Nial. Patrick's captor was succeeded by his son Laery, or Laeghaire. It was in the fourth year of his reign that St. Patrick commenced his apostolic labours. A.D. 432 is the date generally agreed on for this event, which had been preceded by the mission of St. Palladius in the previous year. A few scattered Christians, principally in the south, were to be found in Erin before the time of Patrick. It has been asserted that Saints Ailbe, Declan, Kieran, and Ibar, afterwards consecrated by St. Patrick to the episcopal office, had been preaching in Munster before his coming.

St. Patrick was no longer a young man when he returned to Ireland, the scene of his former captivity as a Christian missionary. But the interval between his early manhood and mature life had not been idly spent. Bishops Germanus and Lupus, we are told, nurtured him in sacred literature, and ordained him, and made him the chief bishop of their school among the British and Irish. Thirty-three years has been assigned as the period of his pastoral labours. He first landed on the Leinster coast, but re-embarked, and directed his course to that northern district where he had passed his captivity. Here he laboured to convert to the faith of Christ his former master Milcho, but without success. Dichu, a prince of a territory in the present county of Down, was one of his earliest converts. He erected for the saint a church, Sabhall Padruic, Patrick's Barn, still called Saul, which afterwards became the seat of a considerable monastery. Here the saint, long after, died, and in the same neighbourhood was buried, though the Irish foundation of Glastonbury in England also claims the honour of possessing his remains. Many discrepancies and irreconcilable conflicts of testimony may be explained by the supposition that there were two Saint Patricks; one generally distinguished as *Sen* Patrick, or Patrick the Elder, not identical with Patrick the Apostle, and to whose labours may be ascribed the partial acceptance which Christianity had already obtained previous to the coming of Nial's captive. The first missionary tour of the great Apostle followed the course of the Boyne, and conducted him to Tara, and to the presence of King Laery, at the commencement of the Easter festival, A.D. 433. On his journey he visited, converted, and baptized a family, one of whose members attached himself from thenceforth to the Apostle, and was named by him Benignus, on account of the gentleness of his bearing. Benignus, it is said, became his successor in the see of Armagh.

Patrick, continuing his journey, reached Slane on the Boyne, on Easter eve. He commenced his preparations for the festival of the next day, and lighted the paschal fire at nightfall. The king was holding a high festival at Tara at the same time, and the law enjoined that no other fire should be lighted until the great fire should be kindled on the heights of Tara.

> The king is wrath with a greater wrath
>   Than the wrath of Nial or the wrath of Con!
> From his heart to his brow the blood makes path,
>   And hangs there, a red cloud, beneath his crown.
>
> Is there any who knows not, from south to north,
>   That Laegháire-to morrow his birthday keeps?
> No fire may be lit upon hill or hearth,
> Till the king's strong fire in its kingly mirth
>   Leaps upward from Tara's palace steeps.
>
> Yet Patrick has lighted his paschal fire
>   At Slane—it is Holy Saturday—
> And bless'd his font 'mid the chanting choir!
>   From hill to hill the flame makes way;
> While the king looks on it, his eyes with ire
>   Flash red, like Mars, under tresses gray.*

When King Laery inquired who had dared thus to infringe the law, his Druids told him that unless that fire were extinguished immediately, it would get the better of their fires, and occasion the downfall of his kingdom. Laery set out with a considerable force for Slane, and summoned St. Patrick to appear before him. He desired that no one should show the saint the respect of rising to receive him. Erc disobeyed the injunction, saluted Patrick, received his blessing, and became a believer. When St. Patrick preached before the king and nobles at Tara on the following day, Dubtach the bard in like manner rose, saluted him, and became a zealous convert. Dubtach was an eminent poet, both as a Pagan and a Christian. He was the instructor of Fiech, son of Erc, who afterwards became bishop of Sletty.

* AUBREY DE VERE.

This Easter Sunday of the year 433 was an eventful one.

>When the waters of Boyne began to bask,
>   And the fields to flash in the rising sun,
>The Apostle Evangelist kept his Pasch,
>   And Erin her grace baptismal won;
>Her birthday it was; his font the rock;
>He bless'd the land, and he bless'd his flock.
>
>Then forth to Tara he fared full lowly;
>   The staff of Jesus was in his hand;
>Eight priests paced after him chanting slowly,
>   Printing their steps on the dewy land.
>It was the Resurrection morn;
>The lark sang loud o'er the springing corn,
>The dove was heard, and the hunter's horn.
>
>* * * * *
>
>Like some still vision men see by night,
>   Mitred, with eyes of serene command,
>St. Patrick moved onward in ghostly white;
>   The staff of Jesus was in his hand.
>His priests paced after him unafraid,
>And the boy, Benignus, more like a maid,
>Like a maid just wedded he walked and smiled,
>To Christ new plighted that priestly child.
>
>They entered the circle, their hymn they ceased;
>   The Druids their eyes bent earthward still;
>On Patrick's brow the glory increased,
>   As a sunrise brightening some breathless hill.
>The warriors sat silent; strange awe they felt;
>The chief bard Dubtach rose up, and knelt!
>Then Patrick discoursed of the things to be,
>When time gives way to eternity;
>Of kingdoms that cease, which are dreams not things,
>And the kingdom built by the King of kings.

Of Him he spake who reigns from the Cross;
Of the death which is life, and the life which is loss
And how all things were made by the Infant Lord,
And the small hand the Magian Kings adored.
His voice sounded on like a throbbing flood
That swells all night from some far-off wood;
And when it was ended—that wondrous strain—
Invisible myriads breathed low, "Amen!"

While he spake, men say that the refluent tide
　On the shore beside Colpa ceased to sink;
And they say the white deer by Mulla's side,
　O'er the green marge bending forbore to drink;
That the Brandon eagle forgat to soar,
　That no leaf stirred in the wood by Lee,
Such stupor hung the island o'er,
　For none might guess what the end would be.

Then whispered the king to a chief close by,
" It were better for me to believe than die."*

Yet King Laery remained incredulous, although granting liberty to the saint to preach and to make converts. Among the most eminent who embraced Christianity at this time were the wife and daughters of the king, and his brother Conall Criffan, the progenitor of the southern Hy-Nials. Conall wished to become a cleric, but Patrick refused, telling the prince that the secular, and not the ecclesiastical, state was his vocation. He marked with his crozier the figure of a cross in the shield of Conall, which was ever after called *Sciath Bachlach*, or the shield of the crozier. This is the earliest notice that has been found in Ireland of armorial bearings.

* AUBREY DE VERE.

The conversion by Patrick of Ethna and Felimia, the daughters of King Lacry, has been detailed at length in the Book of Armagh. These princesses were residing in Connaught, near Cruachan, when St. Patrick and his attendants assembled at sunrise at the fountain of Clebach, at the east side of the rath.

Thither came the damsels to wash, and found at the well the holy men. "And they knew not whence they were, or in what form, or from what people, or from what country, but they supposed them to be *Duine Sidhe* (fairies), or gods of the earth, or a phantasm.

"And the virgins said unto them, 'Who are ye, and whence come ye?'

"And Patrick said unto them, 'It were better for you to confess to our true God, than to inquire concerning our race.'

"The first virgin said, 'Who is God?

"And where is God?

"And of what (nation) is God?

"And where is His dwelling-place?

"Has your God sons and daughters, gold and silver?

"Is he ever-living?

"Is He beautiful?

"Did many foster His Son?

"Are his daughters dear and beauteous to men of the world?

"Is He in heaven or in earth?

"In the sea?

"In rivers?

"In mountainous places?

" In valleys?

" Declare unto us the knowledge of Him.

" How shall He be seen?

" How is He to be loved?

" How is He to be found?

" Is it in youth—is it in old age that He is to be found?' "

" But St. Patrick, full of the Holy Ghost, answered and said:—

" ' Our God is the God of all men.

" The God of heaven and earth, of the sea and rivers.

" The God of the sun, the moon, and all stars.

" The God of the high mountains, and of the lowly valleys.

" The God who is above heaven, and in heaven, and under heaven. He hath a habitation in the heaven, and the earth, and the sea, and all that are therein.

" He inspireth all things.

" He quickeneth all things.

" He is over all things.

" He sustaineth all things.

" He giveth light to the light of the sun.

" And he hath made springs in a dry ground;

" And dry islands in the sea.

" And hath appointed the stars to serve the greater lights.

" He hath a Son co-eternal, and co-equal with Himself.

" The Son is not younger than the Father.

" Nor is the Father older than the Son.

"And the Holy Ghost breatheth in them.

"The Father, and the Son, and the Holy Ghost, are not divided.

"But I desire to unite you to the Heavenly King, inasmuch as you are the daughters of an earthly king —to believe.'

"And the virgins said, as with one mouth and one heart—

"'Teach us most diligently how we may believe in the Heavenly King. Show us how we may see him face to face, and whatsoever thou shalt say unto us, we will do.'

"And Patrick said :—

"'Believe ye, that by baptism ye put off the sin of your father and your mother?' They answered, 'We believe.'

"'Believe ye in repentance after sin?'—'We believe.'

"'Believe ye in life after death?—Believe ye the Resurrection at the day of Judgment?'—'We believe.'

"'Believe ye the unity of the Church?'—'We believe.'

"And they were baptized; and a white garment put upon their heads. And they asked to see the face of Christ. And the Saint said unto them, 'Ye cannot see the face of Christ, except ye taste of death, and except ye receive the sacrifice.'

"And they answered, 'Give us the sacrifice, that we may behold the Son, our spouse.'

"And they received the Eucharist of God, and they slept in death.

"And they were laid out on one bed, covered with garments; and (their friends) made great lamentation and weeping for them."

Before leaving the subject of St. Patrick's visit to Tara, we shall give at length his hymn composed on this occasion, " to protect himself with his monks against the enemies unto death, who were in ambush against the clergy. And this is a religious armour to protect the body and soul against demons, and men, and vices. Every person who sings it every day with all his attention on God shall not have demons appearing to his face. It will be a protection to him against every poison and envy. It will be a safeguard to him against sudden death. It will be an armour to his soul after his death. Patrick sang this at the time that the snares were set for him by Laegaire, that he might not come to propagate the faith to Temur; so that it appeared to those lying in ambush, that they were wild deer, and a fawn after them, that is Benen; and *Feth Fiadha* is its name."

This poem is interesting as illustrating the faith, not unmixed with credulity, of this great Evangelist of the fifth century, as well as for its antiquity. It is composed in that ancient dialect of the Irish in which the oldest tracts, and the Brehon Laws are written, and commences as follows:—

"At Temur, to-day, I invoke the mighty power of the Trinity. I believe in the Trinity under the unity of the God of the elements.

"At Temur, to-day (I place) the virtue of the birth of Christ with his baptism, the virtue of his Crucifixion, with his burial, the virtue of his Resurrection with His Ascension, the virtue of the coming to the eternal judgment ;—

"At Temur, to-day (I place) the virtue of the love of seraphim ; (the virtue which exists) in the obedience of angels, in the hope of the Resurrection to eternal reward, in the prayers of the noble fathers, in the predictions of the prophets, in the preaching of the apostles, in the faith of the confessors, in the purity of the holy virgins, in the deeds of just men ;—

" At Temur, to-day (I place) the strength of heaven, the light of the sun, the whiteness of snow, the force of fire, the rapidity of lightning, the swiftness of the wind, the depth of the sea, the stability of the earth, the hardness of rocks (between me and the powers of paganism and demons).

"At Temur, to-day, may the strength of God pilot me, may the power of God preserve me, may the wisdom of God instruct me, may the eye of God view me, may the ear of God hear me, may the word of God render me eloquent, may the hand of God protect me, may the way of God direct me, may the shield of God defend me, may the host of God guard me against the snares of demons, the temptations of vices, the inclinations of the mind, against every man who méditates evil to me, far or near, alone or in company.

" I place all these powers between me and every evil unmerciful power directed against my soul and my body (as a protection) against the incantations of false prophets, against the black laws of Gentilism, against the false laws of heresy, against the treachery of idolatry, against the spells of women, smiths, and Druids, against every knowledge which blinds the soul of man. May Christ to-day protect me against poison, against burning, against drowning, against wounding, until I deserve much reward.

"Christ (be) with me, Christ before me, Christ after me, Christ in me, Christ under me, Christ over me, Christ at my right, Christ at my left, Christ at this side, Christ at that side, Christ at my back.

"Christ (be) in the heart of each person whom I speak to, Christ in the mouth of each person who speaks to me, Christ in each eye which sees me, Christ in each ear which hears me.

"At Temur, to-day, I invoke the mighty power of the Trinity. I believe in the Trinity under the unity of the God of the elements.

"Salvation is the Lord's; Salvation is the Lord's; Salvation is Christ's. May thy salvation, O Lord, be always with us!"

St. Patrick is said to have borne part in that revision and purification of the laws of Erin, embodied in the great Brehon Law tract called the *Senchus Mor*. The Irish of the age of Alfred universally believed that these laws were reduced to their present form under the immediate inspection of the Apostle, and that the work of codification was carried on at Tara in summer on account of the amenity and freshness of the place; and at a neighbouring residence in the winter on account of facilities of shelter and firewood. One portion of this interesting tract has been published by the Brehon Law Commissioners, and exhibits an unexpected analogy to the rudiments of the Common Law of England, hitherto supposed to have been derived exclusively from non-Celtic sources.

Laery was constantly engaged in warfare with the Leinstermen, the "hated Lagenian race." The exaction of the Boromean tribute was the occasion of these contentions. In one of these campaigns he was defeated at *Ath-Dara*, on the Barrow, and compelled to swear by the Elements—that dreaded pagan oath—that he would not again seek to enforce the *Boru;* but afterwards, violating his oath, he was slain "by the Sun and Wind."

" So Laegháire by the dread God elements swore,
By the moon divine, and the earth and air.
He swore by the wind and the broad sunshine
That circle for ever both land and sea,
By the long-back'd rivers, and mighty wine,
By the cloud far-seeing, by herb and tree,
By the boon spring shower, and by autumn's fan,
By woman's breast, and the head of man,
By night and the noonday Demon he swore,
He would claim the Boarian Tribute no more.

But with years, wrath wax'd; and he brake his faith;—
Then the dread God-elements wrought his death:
For the Wind and Sunshine by Cassi's side
Came down and smote on his head that he died,
Death-sick three days on his throne he sate:
Then he died, as his father died, great in hate.

They buried the king upon Tara's hill,
In his grave upright:—there stands he still.
Upright there stands he as men that wade
By night through a castle moat, undismay'd;
On his head is the gold crown, the spear in his hand,
And he looks to the hated Lagenian land." *

---

* AUBREY DE VERE.

Laery was indeed buried, as described in the poem. He was killed by lightning, and interred in the external rampart of his rath at Tara, with his weapons in his hand, and his face turned towards the Leinstermen. This was in accordance with his own directions; and he assigned this predetermined hate which was to outlive him, as a cause why, though convinced by the teaching of St. Patrick, he could not himself embrace Christianity.

> "But my father, Nial, who is dead long since
> Permits not me to believe thy word;
> For the servants of Jesus, thy heavenly prince,
> Once dead, lie flat as in sleep, interr'd;
> But we are as men through dark floods that wade :—
> We stand in our black graves undismay'd;
> Our faces are turn'd to the race abhorr'd,
> And ready beside us stand spear and sword,
> Ready to strike at the last great day,
> Ready to trample them back into clay." *

To St. Patrick is ascribed the destruction of Crom Cruach, and the smaller idols by which it was surrounded, on the plain of Moy Slaught, in his progress towards Rath Croghan, where we have already noticed his conversion of Ethna and Felimia, daughters of this obstinate Pagan monarch. Passing thence, he spent the season of Lent on the mountain of Croagh Patrick, which was named from this visit of the Saint. In Tyrawley he baptized, as we have already mentioned, the sons and followers of Awley, brother of Dathi, in the vicinity of the wood of Focluth. Thence,

* From *Inisfail*, by AUBREY DE VERE.

the Apostle passed through the central district of Ireland, preaching, baptizing, and founding churches, and entered Munster. At the royal city of Cashel, he was met by Ængus, king of this southern province, who embraced the faith, and was baptized by Patrick. It is narrated that during the ceremony the pastoral staff of the saint, which terminated in a spike, entered the monarch's sandalled foot; but conceiving this to be part of the rite, king Ængus remained unmoved, submitting patiently to the pain which St. Patrick unconsciously inflicted.

Multitudes of people from Corca Baiscin, in Clare, crossed the Shannon in their curraghs, a simple hide-covered boat, of a kind still used on the western coast of Ireland, and were baptized by Patrick in the waters of this grandest of Irish rivers. In compliance with their entreaty, St. Patrick ascended a hill near Foynes, since called Knoc Patrick, and blessed the territory of Thomond, the land of the Dalcassians. A more liberal benediction bestowed by the Apostle upon Ireland and its inhabitants at large, has been preserved in the Book of Rights, and is thus translated:—

> " The blessing of God upon you all,
> Men of Eri, sons, women,
> And daughters; prince-blessing,
> Weal-blessing, blessing of long life,
> Health-blessing, blessing of excellence,
> Eternal blessing, heaven-blessing,
> Cloud-blessing, sea-blessing,
> Fruit-blessing, land-blessing,
> Crop-blessing, dew-blessing,
> Blessing of elements, blessing of valour,
> Blessing of dexterity, blessing of glory,

> Blessing of deeds, blessing of honour,
> Blessing of happiness, be upon you all
> Laics, clerics, while I command
> The blessing of the men of Heaven;
> It is my bequest, as it is a PERPETUAL BLESSING."

The year 453 is the date assigned to the founding of the metropolitan see of Armagh. Dairé, a chieftain of the Orgialla, gave the site for his church to St. Patrick. In the crypt of that venerable cathedral, the simple wattle outline of the roofs and doors of this portion of the very old, if not the original building, can yet be traced. Thither, when he felt his end approaching, the apostle of Ireland wished to turn, to die. He set out from Saul on his journey towards Armagh, when he was commanded by an angel—so the tradition goes—to return to Saul. He was buried at Downpatrick, and the legend, which, however, is shared with many other Lives of Saints, affirms that the place where his mortal remains should rest was also decided by heavenly interposition. A contest arose between the people of Armagh and those of Uladh, as to where he should be interred. It was agreed that two untamed oxen should be harnessed to the bier of the saint, sent forth, unguided, and that in the place where they halted the saint should be committed to the earth. The oxen rested at Dun-da-leth-glaisse, a fortified residence of the chieftains of Uladh, since the site of the present cathedral of Down. To allay the jealous feuds of the rival clans, each party followed, as they conceived, a bier, borne by two oxen, but as the Orgallian tribes neared Armagh, on the banks of a river, the bier and oxen, which they had followed, mysteriously vanished. The exact time of the death of the great apostle of Ireland is a disputed point. Wednesday, the 17th of March, 493, is the most probable date.

The marked success of St. Patrick's missionary labours may be in part ascribed to his wise policy in addressing himself, in the first instance, to the kings and chieftains of Erin. The clan readily followed the example of a baptized leader, and toleration, at least, was secured for Christian institutions. On his side, St. Patrick had little of the iconoclastic spirit. He respected, and even adopted, the pagan festivals, converting them into Christian holydays. The *Beltine* and *Samhain* of the Irish are celebrated to this day, not unmixed with some superstitious relics of paganism, in the corresponding festivals of May-day and All-hallow E'en.

The clan system, found and left by him in full operation, extended itself even to the monasteries. The abbot's sway was not dissimilar to that of the chieftain: every monastery was a centre of family influence, and always a refuge for houseless kin. In all respects, the church founded by St. Patrick conformed to the political institutions of the Irish tribes, as he had adopted himself, though a foreigner, their Gaelic speech. This church—endowed by the chieftains, recruited from the ranks of the people—in no way dependent on foreign aid for its prolonged existence—flourished at home and became a missionary church abroad, sending forth, during the sixth and seventh centuries, indefatigable labourers in the spiritual vineyard; to whose exertions we owe the evangelization of the greater part of Western Europe.

We have traced the useful, noble life of the great Irish saint, till it was closed in peace. "I protest in truth," says St. Patrick, in his *Confession*, "and can rejoice in the thought before God and his holy angels, that I never had any motive, save the Gospel and its promises, for ever returning to that people from among whom I had escaped. And I beg of all that believe in God and seek and fear Him, whoever of them may be pleased to examine or read this letter, which I, Patrick—poor sinful and ignorant creature as I am—have written in Ireland, that no one will ever say that my ignorance is to have the credit of it, if I have effected or performed any little matter according to the purpose of God; but believe and be assured for certain that it was God who has done it. And this is my confession before I shall die."

The mighty revolution which St. Patrick accomplished was inaugurated without bloodshed. No single martyr suffered for the faith in Erin; unless that servant of Patrick's, Oran, who exchanged places with the saint in his chariot, and received a death-wound designed for his master, be considered one. Her kings, though remaining pagan for two generations, permitted the preaching of the new doctrines, and were tolerant even to converts made among the members of their own families. It speaks well for the state of morals and manners among the pagan Irish that so mighty a change was effected with little bitterness, and no sacrifice of human life. While kings ruled at Tara, surrounded by their Druids, and worshipping idols, Christian communities were planted in every corner of the land. The zeal and fervour of St. Patrick and his disciples gathered to the infant church a peaceful and rich harvest of souls. Ireland became the land of saints: nor were these simple and pious men who belonged to the first and most perfect of the three orders of saints of the Irish Church, indifferent to secular knowledge. They did not, as the second and inferior order of saints of a succeeding age, shun the society of women, for they were "not afraid of the blast of temptation." The monasteries they established were schools of learning, whose reputation was deservedly so high, that students came from Britain and from the Continent, and received in Ireland gratuitous hospitality, and careful instruction. The Irish monks were the transcribers of those manuscript copies of Holy Writ, and of ancient learning, many of which are so exquisitely illuminated that they have been the wonder and delight of succeeding ages. These are true art-treasures, evincing the most refined perception of grace and beauty, with a delicacy of execution which has never been surpassed, and place Ireland, between the fifth and ninth centuries—a period when western Europe was sunk in barbarism—among the foremost seats of piety and learning, and in a position, as regards the arts of decoration, as applied to manuscripts and ecclesiastical objects, unapproached by any of the nations of Christendom.

King Leary was succeeded by Ollioll Molt, son of

Dathi, who had ruled Connaught for some years previously as provincial king. Ollioll was grandfather to Owen Bel, afterwards king of Connaught, whose hatred of the Clanna Neill of Ulster was as intense as that of Laery for the Leinstermen. Owen Bel was constantly engaged in conflicts against the northern clans, with varying success. At the Battle of Sligo, however, the Connacian army was defeated, and Owen Bel mortally wounded. He lingered for a week; and during that time gave directions about his burial. "Place me in my grave, on the north side of the hill by which the northerns pass when flying before the army of Connaught. Place me standing: my face towards the north, and my red javelin in my hand." The effect of this interment of Owen Bel was, that the Clanna Neill were always defeated, and compelled to fly before the Connacian hosts, until they came by stealth, disinterred the body of the hero, carried the corpse northward of the Sligo river, and there buried him, near the shores of Lough Gill, with his face downwards. A stone circle, still existing, on the southern bank of the Sligo river, close by the town, probably marks the site of the sepulchral cairn from which the men of Ulster stole the body of the dreaded monarch.

When Owen Bel found himself dying, he advised his clan, the Hi-Fiachrach, to elect his son Kellach king of Connaught, notwithstanding that he had become an ecclesiastical student, and was residing at Clonmacnoise under the tuition of St. Kieran, the founder of that monastic establishment. The youth, at the time, of

Owen Bel's second son, Cucongelt, unfitted him to be leader of his tribe. Kellach yielded to the persuasions of the messengers sent to him for this object, impelled by a not unnatural ambition; but accompanied them without the permission of St. Kieran, who pronounced a curse upon Kellach. To this the credulity of that age has ascribed all his after-misfortunes.

Kellach afterwards made his peace with St. Kieran, and became bishop at Kilmore-Moy, in Tirawley. His kinsman, Guary Aidhné, who was then king of Connaught, feared him as a rival; and bribed four students, who were under St. Kellach's instruction in a hermitage to which he had retired on Loch Con, to murder the ex-king and bishop. This wicked deed was accomplished in a wood, and the body of the murdered man was secreted in the hollow trunk of an oak-tree. What added to the enormity of the outrage was, that the four Maols, as they were called, were foster-brothers to St. Kellach. They were rewarded by Guary for their treachery by a grant of land in Tirawley, on which they erected a fort at Dun Finn.

Cucongelt, younger son of Owen Bel, and brother to St. Kellach, went to visit the recluse at Loch Con, and finding his brother had disappeared, and his four pupils become possessed of lands at the hands of King Guary, suspected that Kellach had been murdered. He sought for and found the body, sadly mangled by ravens and wolves. He brought the remains in succession to three churches; but the clergy, basely afraid of the vengeance of Guary, refused it interment. At last the remains of the hapless prince and bishop found a resting-place. Cucongelt chanted his funeral dirge, and vowed to avenge his death. He assembled in the neighbourhood of Dun Finn his friends and adherents; obtained entrance in the guise of a swineherd into the fort, while the murderers were feasting. He waited till they had become inebriated, and then, summoning his followers, captured the fort, and dragged the murderers in chains to a hill overlooking the River Moy, and since distinguished as Ard-na-ree, the "hill of executions," where they were mercilessly put to death.

The monument raised over the Maols is still in existence, and is called by the people the table of the giants, and *Cloch an togbhala*, "the raised stone," in Irish. It is a cromlech, formed by a level stone supported by three pillar-stones, and is interesting as being considered the only cromlech in Ireland which can undoubtedly be connected with history. It is spoken of in the *Dinnseanchus*, an Irish MS. of high antiquity, as the stone of the Maols, *Leacht na Maol*.

Ollioll Molt was slain in the Battle of Ocha, and Lugaid, son of Laery, son of Nial of the Nine Hostages ascended the throne of Ireland. While this king—who, like his predecessor, rejected Christianity and remained pagan—was on the throne, the final settlement of the Dalriads in Scotland took place. 503 is the date assigned for the emigration to Scotland of the six sons of Erc, the two Anguses, the two Loarns, and the two Ferguses. Fergus MacErc seized on the sovereignty of Scotland. This is the king who is said to have obtained from his cousin, Murkertach, the reigning monarch of Erin, who succeeded Lugaid, the Lia Fail, or stone of destiny, and to have brought this magical talisman which should secure the throne for ever to a prince of Scotic blood, from Ireland to the land named from these Scotic immigrants, Scotland. Its removal to Scone, and from thence to Westminster Abbey, has been already alluded to; but the Irish, in the 12th century, believed that the Lia Fail still existed at Tara: though the stone had ceased to "roar" under the rightful king, since the birth of Christ.

Lugaid was succeeded by Murkertach Mor MacErca, the first king of the Hy-Niall race of Owen son of Niall. This great family, in its various branches, furnished kings to Erin, with rare interruptions, for many centuries.

During his reign St. Brigid, or Bride, died. This celebrated foundress of the monastic establishment at Kildare is, in common with St. Patrick and St. Columba, a patron saint of Ireland. She was of noble birth, and claimed descent from Con of the Hundred Battles. She was remarkable from her early youth for her piety and charity to the poor. Vowed to perpetual virginity, she traversed Ireland, founding convents in various places; but her name and repute are chiefly connected with that "Church of the Oak," Kildare, where she was the foundress of the most famous convent that ever existed in Ireland. Her humility was such that she is said to have tended the cattle in her fields: she shared all she possessed with the poor, and scattered among those who surrounded her "the most wholesome seed of the word of God." She died at the advanced age of seventy, and was buried at the side of the altar in the cathedral church of Kildare. The 1st of February, 525, is the date assigned to this event. She was reverenced, not only in Ireland, but in Scotland also. The Western Isles, Hy Brides, are said to have their name from her. An annual festival in her house was there held in commemoration of the day of her death, and her name was invoked by the islanders to confirm their most solemn oaths.

St. Kieran of Saighir is called, by his biographer, "the first-born of the saints of Ireland." His church on Cape Clear Island is said to have been the earliest Christian church erected in Ireland. Its ruins, together with a cross sculptured on an ancient pillar-stone, yet exist on this remote island. He afterwards established the monastery of Seir-Kieran, on the brink of the well of Saighir, in the King's County, a spot dedicated to him, according to tradition, by St. Patrick. Round this a great village, in those days deemed a city, speedily clustered. He is supposed to have died in Cornwall, and to have been identical with St. Piran, an Irish saint, whose little church of Piranzabuloe, or Piran-in-the-Sands, has been covered and so preserved for centuries by the sands which have gained on that part of the English coast.

St. Finnian of Clonard, and St. Finnian of Moville, were saints of the second order, and, unlike the saints of the first order, dispensed with the society of women, separating them from the monasteries. St. Finnian of Clonard founded his celebrated school about the year 530. It was a place of great resort, and numbered among its students many eminent men, attracted to Clonard by the learning and sanctity of its founder. St. Columba, afterwards the evangelist of the Picts, was among the number.

The passion for a life of monastic seclusion characterised, to a remarkable degree, the religious Irish at this period. That ascetic temper of mind which is so much to be condemned, as separating men from the healthful duties of ordinary life, has some excuses in an age filled with strife and contention and endless turmoil. Nor can selfishness or indolence be justly charged on our Irish recluses, as they were teachers of learning, secular as well as ecclesiastical, zealous missionaries among heathen populations, and tillers of the soil around their monastic establishments. As might naturally be expected, the people became proud of their pastors, and sometimes contended for their possession. It is recorded of St. Ailbe of Emly, that, having converted the people of Munster, and established the Christian Church in that part of Ireland, he was about to seek the solitudes of Iceland, when he was coerced by King Ængus, the convert of St. Patrick, with all becoming respect, to abandon his intention.

Between the fifth and seventh centuries were founded those monastic establishments on the western isles of Aran, off Galway bay, whose remains yet abound on that sacred soil. " Aran of the Saints" contains, at this day, abundant impress of the anchorites of that period.

St. Enda obtained a grant of the largest of the three islands which constitute the group, and founded his monastic establishment at the southern extremity of Arnmore. Enda was son of the petty king of Orgiall, and was an accomplished warrior before his conversion. He had successfully avenged his father's death, and chanted a song of triumph as he happened to pass the cell of Fanchea, a female saint of the period. She came to the door of her cell, and asked why he disturbed her meditations. "I have been avenging the death of my father as becomes a son," he replied, "and I now sing my song of victory as becomes a warrior." "Knowest thou where thy father now is?" rejoined Fanchea. "I know not," said Enda. "Thy father," said Fanchea, "is now in hell." She proceeded to contrast the tortures of the damned with the bliss of the saved, the mournful gloom of hell with the celestial light of heaven. Her words made a profound impression on the mind of Enda. He frequently visited her cell, and listened to her instructions; but during these visits became strongly attached to one of Fanchea's sisterhood, and the novice returned the affection of the young prince. Fanchea interposed. "Whether wouldst thou have for spouse," she asked of the novice, "this young King of Orgiall, whom thou lovest, or that heavenly King whom I love?"—"Whom thou lovest Him also will I love," replied the girl. She sought her bed, and expired. Enda was brought by Fanchea to look on the dead face of his beloved. He renounced the world, travelled to Rome, returned, accompanied by one hundred and fifty monks, and founded, in 580, his church at Aran. His name yet survives in Kilany, but his church has disappeared, and the pure shining sands cover the adjoining cemetery, with its one hundred and twenty inscribed tombs of holy men. The foundations of the round tower only remain; but not far from the site of Enda's erections stands, to this day, the smallest church in Ireland, that of St. Benignus. Among the ruins of the seven churches in the north part of Aran, at Kilbrecan, still exists the tomb of their founder, St. Brecan. On a spherical black stone found in his grave, we read the inscription in Irish, " Pray for Brecan the Pilgrim." Another tomb at this place is inscribed to the memory of the "seven Romans," strangers from distant lands, seeking in this Irish Thebäid opportunity for indulgence in the contemplative life.

But the glories of the Irish church at this period culminate in the noble foundation of Clonmacnoise on the Shannon. It was established 548 by St. Kieran, generally called " the Son of the Artificer," to distinguish him from another saint of the same name. Dermid MacKervil, afterwards King of Ireland, passed his youth in exile, and was sheltered at Conmacnoise by St. Kieran, on whose foundation he subsequently bestowed a grant of lands. On the banks of the Shannon, a few miles below Athlone, amidst verdant meadows, gently rolling hillocks,—and beyond these a vast expanse of level bog, not black and dreary, but covered with a russet garment of heaths of the richest hues, and washed by the eddies of the broad placid river, with its sedgy margin of reeds and bulrushes—rise the graceful round towers, picturesque and exquisitely sculptured crosses, and other monastic ruins of Clonmacnoise.

St. Kieran, the original founder, was a descendant of Corc, one of the sons whom Maev of Cruachan bore to the hero, Fergus MacRoy, and was thus of the Irian stock. He had been one of the most distinguished pupils of St. Finnian of Clonard. He had also resided at Aran of the Saints, acquiring, under the austere rule of St. Enda, those lessons to be learned in seclusion from the affairs of secular life, in the comparative isolation of these rocky islets washed by the mighty waves of the Atlantic. But before entering into the particulars connected with this great ecclesiastical establishment, which was endowed by King Dermid MacKervil, we must complete our history of King Murkertach MacErca and his successor, Tuathal Mael-garv, who preceded King Dermid on the throne of Erin. Murkertach is said, in our annals, to have died a double death. He was both burned and drowned. He had abandoned the society of his queen for that of a beautiful girl named Sin. Her kindred had been slain by the king in battle, and Sin devoted her life to revenge them. With this object she threw herself in the way of the monarch, captivated him by her charms, and availed herself of opportunities thus obtained to burn his house of Cletty. Murkertach, maddened by his sufferings from fire, plunged into a butt of wine, in which he was suffocated. Tuathal Mael-garv succeeded him on the throne. This king banished out of Meath a rival claimant, Dermid MacKervil, who is said to have passed the nine years of his exile in a boat on the Shannon, befriended by sympathisers on both sides of the river. Among these was St. Kieran, then engaged in founding his church at Clonmacnoise.

On one occasion, Dermid was assisting St. Kieran in thrusting down in the earth one of the pillars or wattles of the house. He took the saint's hand, as they grasped the pole, and put it above his own hand, in sign of reverence. Kieran, touched by this mark of humility, fervently besought God of his great goodness that the hands of Dermid might have superiority over all Ireland. The prayer brought a bloody accomplishment. It was heard by the foster-brother of Dermid, who instantly devised a plan for realizing, by the murder of the reigning monarch, the saint's petition. Tuathal, in his hostility to the rival whom he dreaded, had offered a reward to any one who would bring him the heart of Dermid. Maelmora, the foster-brother, sacrificed a dog, placed its heart on a spear, and, mounted on a swift horse, rode into the presence of the king. When the attendants of Tuathal saw the man approaching with the bloody trophy, they made way, supposing it to be the heart of Dermid about to be laid at the sovereign's feet. Maelmora, in the act of presenting it, transfixed Tuathal with his spear. His own life paid the penalty of his deed, but his object was won. Dermid was at once proclaimed king at Tara.

Dermid became a liberal benefactor to Clonmacnoise. Round the little church, in whose foundation he had assisted—a fact corroborated by the figures of St. Kieran and his friend grasping the pole, carved on one of the stone crosses which yet remained to adorn the spot—

sprung up in after-ages those foundations which still stand to evince the piety and skill of their builders. There are few spots in our land so rich in interest. The larger of its two round towers was finished for King Turlogh O'Connor, A.D. 1127. Its crosses are beautiful specimens of the art of Sculpture, as it existed among the Irish before the eleventh century. On the great cross are sculptured inscriptions which read "A prayer for Flann, son of Maelsechlain," and "A prayer for Colman, who made this cross for the King Flann." Our annals record that King Flann erected the cathedral at Clonmacnoise, 909; and this cross will therefore belong to about the same date. The second cross is decorated with the peculiar interlaced pattern work so familiar in Irish art.

The tombs of kings, saints, and scholars, reposing for upwards of one thousand years, can yet be identified at this favourite burial-ground, which most of the princes of the southern Hy-Nial selected to be their last resting-place. Among them, we may enumerate the stone of Siubhne MacMaelbumai, one of the three "most learned doctors of the Irish," who visited Alfred in the year 891, and assisted at the foundation of Oxford. His death is recorded, not only in the Irish annals, but in the Saxon Chronicle, and also by Florence of Worcester, and Caradoc of Llancarvan.

The remains of the monastic establishment founded by St. Kevin at Glendalough, in the county of Wicklow, are familiar to multitudes who visit that mountain valley with its two lonely lakes: it lies within easy distance of Dublin. St. Kevin died 618: he had a brother of the same name, from whom the southern island of Aran took its designation, that

> Rocky eastern isle that bears
> The name of blessed Coemhan, who doth show
> Pity unto the storm-tossed seaman's prayers.

Another distinguished saint of this period was Brendan, who became in his advanced years Abbot of Clonfert. He voyaged, according to a highly poetic tradition, across the Atlantic with a few chosen companions in search of the mysterious island of Hy-Brasail. This enchanted land is supposed to be visible from the western coast of Ireland every seventh year. If once touched with fire, even by the flight of a kindled arrow, it would become subject to the ordinary laws of existence, and remain a delightful paradise for man, instead of disappearing with all its glories from the ken of the baffled discoverer. Missionary zeal, and love of discovery, stimulated St. Brendan to venture on the trackless ocean, in his small coracle of hides, with his few companions. He had been nurtured by the shores of the Atlantic, in his native Kerry, where his name yet lingers in Brandon mountain near Dingle.

> I grew to manhood by the western wave,
>   Among the mighty mountains on the shore:
> My bed the rock within some natural cave;
>   My food, whate'er the seas or seasons bore;
> My occupation, morn and noon and night,
>   The only dream my hasty slumbers gave,
> Was Time's unheeding, unreturning flight,
>   And the great world that lies beyond the grave.

* * * *

And then I saw the mighty sea expand,
    Like Time's unmeasured and unfathomed waves;
One with its tide-marks on the ridgy sand,
    The other with its line of weedy graves;
And as beyond the outstretched wave of Time,
    The eye of Faith a brighter land may meet,
So did I dream of some more sunny clime,
    Beyond the waste of waters at my feet.

Some clime where man, unknowing and unknown,
    For God's refreshing word still gasps and faints;
Or happier rather some Elysian zone,
    Made for the habitation of His saints;
Where Nature's love the sweat of labour spares,
    Nor turns to usury the wealth it lends,
Where the rich soil spontaneous harvest bears,
    And the tall tree with milk-filled clusters bends.

The thought grew stronger with my growing days,
    Even like to manhood's strengthening mind and limb;
And often now amid the purple haze,
    That evening breathed upon the horizon's rim,
Methought, as there I sought my wished-for home,
    I could descry amid the waters green,
Full many a diamond shrine and golden dome,
    And crystal palaces of dazzling sheen.

And then I longed with impotent desire,
    Even for the bow whereby the Pythian bled,
That I might send one dart of living fire
    Into that land, before the vision fled.
And thus at length fix thy enchanted shore,
    Hy-Brasail—Eden of the western wave,
That thou again wouldst fade away no more,
    Buried and lost within thy azure grave.

> But angels came and whispered as I dreamt,
>   "This is no phantom of a frenzied brain,
> God shows this land from time to time to tempt
>   Some daring mariner across the main;
> By thee the mighty venture must be made,
>   By thee shall myriad souls to Christ be won!
> Arise, depart, and trust to God for aid!"
>   I woke, and kneeling cried, "His will be done!"*

St. Brendan, after preliminary visits to Aran of the saints, and to the coasts of Connaught, launched his frail bark boldly on the Atlantic wave. Caught, probably, in the current of the Gulf Stream, he reached the distant land, it may be the New England shore. In the quaint language of the *Golden Legend*, "Soon after, as God would, they saw a fair island full of flowers, herbs, and trees, whereof they thanked God of his good grace; and anon they went on land, and when they had gone long in this, they found a full fayre well, and thereby stood a fair tree full of boughs, and on every bough sat a fayre bird. The number of them was so great, and they sang so merrily, that it was an heavenly noise to hear. Whereupon St. Brendan kneeled down on his knees and wept for joy, and made his praises devoutly to our Lord God, to know what these birds meant." The notes of these feathered songsters, from the mocking-bird, sweetest of singers, to the tiny and brilliantly-coloured humming birds of America, are charmingly described in the poem from which we have quoted. In the antique legend the birds are made to tell St. Brendan, that

---

* From *The Voyage of St. Brendan*, by D. FLORENCE MACCARTHY.

they are among those fallen angels who lost Paradise with Lucifer, "millions of spirits for his fault amerced of heaven, and from eternal splendours flung, for his revolt;" but yet, as they were not among the most guilty, "our Lord hath sent us here, out of all pain in full great joy and mirth, after his pleasing, here to serve him on this tree in the best manner we can." St. Brendan spent seven weeks among them, and continued his journey inland till he came to a great river flowing east and west, perhaps the River Ohio. Here he had a vision, and was desired by a man of commanding countenance to return home, as it was reserved to other times and other teachers to Christianize that pleasant land. Seven years after the wanderer had left the shores of Ireland, he returned to his native land, and founded his monastery at Clonfort. Here he is said to have presided over three thousand monks, who supported themselves by the labour of their own hands.

CHAPTER VI.

THE COLUMBAN PERIOD.

We turn from the legendary voyage of St. Brendan to the very real, very energetic, and active life of the greatest of our Irish saints after Patrick.

Colombkille (Columba of the Churches) was nobly born. His father, Felimy, and his mother, Ethna, were both of high rank. He was descended from King Nial of the Nine Hostages through his son, Conall Gulban, head of the Kinel Conaill, or branch of the northern Hy-Niall, who gave their name to the north-western part of Ulster, Tyrconnell. Gartan, near Letterkenny, in the County Donegal, is said to have been his birthplace. Columba studied in his youth at the school of St. Finnian of Maghbile (Moville), and is also claimed as a pupil of St. Finnian of Clonard and of Gemman, who was probably a Christian bard. It is certain that St. Columba became a scholar of no mean reputation, well versed in the Sacred Writings, and himself a poet. Of his personal appearance we can infer that he was of florid complexion, and his hair red or auburn. His temperament was hasty and passionate, yet generous and devoted. He had many and great faults. The impetuosity of his temper led him into much that was inconsistent with Christian duty. But he was a noble man, and did noble work. He was great and influential in his own time, and his memory is blessed and revered by succeeding generations. He founded in 546 the monastery of Doire-Calgaich, near Lough Foyle, on land bestowed on him by his kindred, the princes of Tyrconnel. To this establishment the town of Derry owes its name and origin. Durrow, in the King's County, a monastery which soon became very celebrated, was established by Columba a few years later. At Kells, a small stone-roofed building still exists which tradition connects with him. St. Columb's house probably served as a residence while part of the building was used as an oratory. The round church-towers of Swords, Raphoe, Tory Island, and Drumcliff, and the beautiful sculptured crosses at the latter place, though perhaps of later date, mark other foundations ascribed to him. He was indeed an indefatigable labourer in the cause of Christ in Ireland before those events occurred which drove him from his native land an exile to Iona. On this remote island of the Hebrides, he founded the celebrated monastic establishment from whence he evangelized the Picts, and where he trained his monks for the arduous missionary work which afterwards distinguished the community of Hy, as Iona in those days was called.

Among his early companions in study was Kieran, "son of the Artificer," afterwards illustrious as the founder of Clonmacnoise. The favour with which Columba was regarded by their common instructor awakened some feeling of jealousy in the breast of the young Kieran. This was allayed by a vision or dream, or, let us rather suppose, by the conviction of his own mind in moments of calm reflection. An angel appeared to him—so runs the legend—and showed him the carpenter's plane and saw, and other tools of his father's handicraft. With these were contrasted the insignia of royalty, symbols of the rank to which the high-born Columba might have aspired, had he not preferred the vocation of the monk to the earthly glories of the prince. "Look on these," said the angel to Kieran, holding before him the carpenter's tools:—"These are what thou hast given up for Christ; but Columba has made a higher sacrifice: let this reflection moderate thy unworthy thoughts." Kieran never forgot the lesson, and discarded from his breast all lingering remains of jealous feeling.

St. Finnian of Moville, in whose school Columba and Kieran had studied, was possessed of a remarkable copy of the Gospels, which he had brought with him from Rome, and valued most highly. It has been suggested that the MS. was a copy of St. Jerome's translation of this part of Holy Writ. The saint—who afterwards returned to Italy, and has been identified with Frigidian, patron saint and Bishop of Lucca—had been requested to lend this book to St. Fintan of Dunflesk, a pupil at the time of St. Comgall of Bangor. Finnian refused to part with his manuscript. Fintan complained of this churlishness to his master, Comgall, who exhorted the student to patience, and consoled him, predicting that the book should yet come into his possession. The very next day, the story goes, Moville was attacked by pirates, who carried off, among other spoils, the precious volume which St. Finnian had declined to lend. The plunderers meditated a further attack on Bangor. Their project was not carried into execution; for a storm dispersed their ships, and St. Fintan found on the shore the longed-for book, among other spoil, quite uninjured. Whether he retained it, or returned it, when read, to its owner, we cannot tell. The surreptitious copying of another manuscript of St. Finnian's, supposed to have been a copy of the Psalms, led to more serious results.

St. Columba is reported, during a visit he paid to Moville, to have remained daily in the church when the congregation had retired, for the study of St. Finnian's book. He ardently desired to possess a copy of it, and fearing to be refused should he ask the owner, made a hurried transcript of this highly-prized volume of the Psalms. He was observed, and his occupation reported to St. Finnian, who was highly indignant, and demanded the copy as his by right, as well as the original. Columba refused to surrender his transcript, and the matter was referred to King Dermid. The sovereign, who had been so great a benefactor to Clonmacnoise, pronounced for sentence, "To every cow belongeth her calf; so to every book belongeth its copy," and adjudged both to Finnian.

"This is an unjust decision, O'Dermid," said Columba, "and I will avenge it on you."

The breach was widened between the king and the saint by the following circumstance:—

The young son of the King of Connaught, at that

time a hostage at Tara, killed, at a game of hurling, the son of King Dermid's steward, and fled for sanctuary to Columba. Dermid had him dragged from the arms of the saint and put to death for having desecrated the precincts of his royal palace. The fiery temper of Columba was roused by these insults. King Dermid had placed a guard on his person to prevent his leaving Tara; but "the justice of God having thrown a veil of unrecognition around him," Columba made his escape, and traversed, alone, the mountains which interposed between Tara and his native wilds of Tyrconnell. Here, in solitude, alone with God, he expresses his confidence and trust in the protection of the Holy Trinity, and refers to pagan superstitions still blending with the religion of Dermid.

> "Alone am I upon the mountain.
> O King of Heaven, prosper my way,
> And then nothing need I fear,
> More than if guarded by six thousand men.
> Our fate depends not on sneezing,
> Nor on a bird perched on a twig;
> Nor on the root of a knotted tree,
> Nor on the noise of clapping hands.
> Better is He in whom we trust,
> The Father, the One, and the Son."

The powerful tribes of the Hy-Niall, the Kinel Conaill and Kinel Owen, near connections of Columba, with Aedh, King of Connaught, whose son had been put to death by Dermid, challenged that king to battle. The hostile armies encountered at Cuildrevné, near Sligo. Columba offered up petitions for the success of his friends.

"He will not refuse me—
My Druid—may he be on my side!—
Is the son of God: with us will He be aiding."

St. Finnian is stated to have offered up prayers for King Dermid. This entire story is doubted, as neither Bede nor Adamnan, the biographer of St. Columba, makes any mention of this quarrel between the saints. The battle of Cuildrevné, A. D. 561, is, however, an historical fact, the king having been defeated and the friends of St. Columba victorious. One man only is recorded to have fallen on their side. St. Columba, calmed and penitent for the blood shed in battle, sought the counsel of St. Molaise, of Devenish Island, in Loch Erne. His confessor enjoined on him, as penance for his fault, that he should leave Ireland, and never again look on his native land. Columba obeyed. He set forth with twelve companions for Scotland, where his kindred, the Dalriad kings, readily received him. It will be remembered that his grandfather had married Erc, daughter of Loarn Mór, and thus he was nearly connected with the sovereigns of Scotland as well as with successive kings of Ireland; for his cousins, Domnall and Fergus, became joint kings of Erin on the death of Dermid a few years after the Battle of Cuildrevné.

The copy of the Psalms, which was the original cause of all this trouble, yet exists, and is preserved as an heir-loom in the family of the O'Donnells of Newport, representatives of St. Columba's race. The Ca'ah or *Cathach* (The "Battler") "consists of fifty-eight leaves of fine vellum, written in a small, uniform but rather hurried hand, with some slight attempts at illumination." Of its inner cases nothing is recorded, but the magnificent external silver-gilt case, set with precious stones, in which it now reposes, was made at the expense of Cathbar O'Donnell, Chief of Tyrconnell, and Donnell O'Rafferty, Abbot of Kells, some time before the year 1098, at which time this Abbot of Kells died. The inscription on the shrine or case itself is as follows :—

"A prayer for Cathbharr O'Donnell, by whom this shrine was made; and for Sitric, the son of MacAedha, who made it; and for Domhnall Ua Robhartaigh, the Comharba of Cenannus, by whom it was made." The virtues of the Ca'ah are thus recounted in the life of St. Columkille by Manus O'Donnell:—

"The Cathach, indeed, is the name of the book on account of which the battle was fought; and it is it that is Colum Cille's high relic in Tir Conaill; and it is ornamented with silver, and it is not lawful to open it; and if it is carried three times to the right around the army of the Cinel Conaill when going to battle, it is certain that they would come out of it with victory; and it is upon the breast of a Comharba, or a priest without mortal sin upon him (as well as he can), that it is proper for the Cathach to be, at going round that army."

The after-fate of this manuscript, written by the pen of St. Columba, is not without interest. This precious heir-loom of the O'Donnells received some further decoration at the hand of Daniel O'Donnell in the year 1723. This O'Donnell, who had retired to the Continent, is believed to have fought in the battle of the Boyne. He placed the Cathach in a monastery in Belgium, with a written injunction that it should be kept till claimed by the head of the O'Donnell family. It was noticed by an Irish lady early in the present century, who spoke of it to Sir Neal O'Donnell, grandfather of the present baronet, and he obtained it on satisfying its keepers of his claim to the chieftainship of the race.

As this warlike sept used to go to battle under their book-standard, so the Kinel-Owen marched on their wars under the bell of St. Patrick; and another great family of Ulster origin, the O'Kellys of Hy-Many, bore the crozier of their patron Saint, Grellan, in like manner, as a battle-standard.

The story of their coming under the patronage of Grellan is too characteristic to be omitted. We have spoken before of the three Collas who destroyed Emania in the three hundred and thirty-first year of the Christian era. Mainé Mor, a descendant of Coll da Croe, resolved to migrate from the central districts of Orgiall to Connaught. "Numerous are our heroes, and great is our population," reasoned the chiefs of the clan, at a great family reunion held by them at Clogher about the end of the fifth century; "our tribe having multiplied, and we cannot all find room in any one province without quarrelling among ourselves, for nobles cannot well bear to be confined." And they also said: "Let us see which province of Banba is thinnest in population, and in which most Firbolgs remain; and let us narrow it on them. The province of Connaught is in the possession of these Atacots, excepting that they pay tribute to our relative, and let us attack it."

"These fine hosts suddenly and heroically proceeded in well-arranged battalions, with their flocks and herds" westwards across the Shannon. This formidable inroad on the territories of the Firbolg chief, Cian, was encountered by him with promptly raised levies of three thousand men. Grellan, a bishop in these semi-pagan parts—a strong favourer of the clan Colla, who had held out to him the inducement of increased tribute and duteous submission to his authority—at first endeavoured to mediate. A truce was agreed on, and hostages given to Cian, by Mainé Mor. The noblest of these was a son of Mainé's, who was given for safe keeping into the hands of Cian's lawgiver. But his wife becoming enamoured of the young captive, the Brehon, inflamed with jealousy, counselled Cian to put the hostages to death.

It is alleged that this treachery was intended to be carried into effect at a feast which Cian prepared for them, but that St. Grellan, having information of it, and apprehensive that his guarantee would be violated, called down from heaven a curse on the Firbolgs. "He obtained his request from God," says the Irish-written Life of the Saint," for the great plain was softened and made a quagmire under the feet of Cian and his people, so that they were swallowed into the earth; and the place received the name of Magh Liach, *i.e.*, the plain of sorrow, from the sorrow of the heroes who were thus cut off by the holy cleric. Then Mainé and his people came to where St. Grellan was, and bowed down their heads to him, and he told them how treachery had been designed for them, and how God and himself had saved them from those treacherous people. St. Grellan then said to them, 'Take possession of this territory, abominate treachery, and you shall have my blessing; observe brotherly love, and ordain my tribute and my own land for me from this day forth for ever.'—'Pass thy own award,' said Mainé, 'in whatever is pleasing to thee,' &c. —'I shall,' said St. Grellan, and he repeated these brief verses following:"—

The saint having enumerated the dues and tributes which he claimed, thus concludes his chant:—

" While they remain obedient to my will, they shall be victorious in every battle:
Let the warlike chiefs observe the advice of my successor,
And among the Gaels north and south, theirs shall be the unerring director.
Frequent my sacred church which has protected each refugee:
Refuse not to pay your tribute to me, and you shall receive as I have promised.
My blessing on the agile race, the sons of Mainé of chessboards;
That race shall not be subdued, so as they carry my crozier:
Let the battle standard of the race be my crozier of true valour,
And battles will not overwhelm them; their successes shall be very great."

The chiefs of Hy-Many—as the territory of about two hundred square miles in Galway and Roscommon, thus acquired by Mainé Mor, was called—bore from thenceforth the crozier of St. Grellan as their battle standard. This interesting relic was preserved for centuries in the family of Cronelly, hereditary coärbs of Grellan. In the year 1836 it still was in the possession of a poor man of the name. Nor is Mainé Mor without direct descendants yet possessed of estates on the soil thus conquered nearly thirteen hundred years ago. How bravely this branch of the Clan Colla contended with the foreign foe, in the great national conflict between Irish and Dane at Clontarf, we have yet to chronicle. Queen Elizabeth treated with the chiefs of Hy-Many of her day, and in 1585 made "agreement between the Irish chieftains and inhabitants of Imany, called the O'Kellie's country, on both sides of the river of Suek, in Connaught, and the queen's majesty. . . . that they and their heirs shall henceforth behave themselves like good subjects; shall put no ymposition or chardge upon the inhabyters of the lands, and shall bring uppe their children after the English fashions, and in the use of the Englishe tounge."

We now return from the long digression into which these singular ensigns of battle have led us, to the ardent young scribe of the *Cathach*. Columba was an accomplished poet.

There is much beauty and interest in these lines on Ben Edar, the hill of Howth, and the saint's favourite dwelling at Derry, thus rendered from the Irish—

> "Delightful to be on Benn-Edar,
> Before going o'er the white sea;
> The dashing of the waves against its face,
> The bareness of its shore and its border.
>
> Delightful to be on Benn-Edar,
> After coming o'er the white-bosomed sea,
> To row one's little coracle
> Ochone! on the swift-waved shore.

How rapid the speed of my coracle;
And its stern turned upon Derry;
I grieve at my errand o'er the noble sea,
Travelling to Alba of the ravens.

My foot in my sweet little coracle,
My sad heart still bleeding:
Weak is the man that cannot lead;
Totally blind are all the ignorant.

There is a grey eye
That looks back upon Erin;
It shall not see, during life,
The men of Erin, nor their wives.

My vision o'er the brine I stretch,
From the ample oaken planks;
Large is the tear in my soft grey eye
When I look back upon Erin.

Upon Erin my attention is fixed;
Upon Loch Levin; upon Liné,
Upon the lands the Ultonians own;
Upon smooth Munster; upon Meath.

Numerous in the East are tall champions;
Many the diseases and distempers there;
Many they with scanty clothes;
Many the hard and jealous hearts.

Plentiful in the West the apple-fruit;
Many the kings and princes;
Plentiful its luxuriant sloes;
Plentiful its noble, acorn-bearing oaks.

Melodious her clerics, melodious her birds,
Gentle her youths, wise her seniors,
Illustrious her men, noble to behold,
Illustrious her women for fond espousal.

It is in the West sweet Brendan is,
And Colum, son of Crimthann,
And in the West fair Baithin shall be,
And in the West shall Adamnan be.

Carry my inquiries after that
Unto Comgall of eternal life;
Carry my inquiries after that
To the bold King of fair Emania.

Carry with thee, thou noble youth,
My blessing and my benediction,
One half upon Erin, seven fold;
And half on Alba at the same time.

Carry my benediction over the sea
To the nobles of the Island of the Gaedhil;
Let them not credit Molaisi's words,
Nor his threatened persecution.

Were it not for Molaisi's words
At the cross of Ath-Molaisi,
I should not now permit
Disease or distemper in Ireland.

Take my blessing with thee to the West;
Broken is my heart in my breast:
Should sudden death overtake me
It is for my great love of the Gaedhil.

Gaedhil, Gaedhil, beloved name!
My only desire is to invoke it:
Beloved is Cuimin of fair hair;
Beloved are Cainnech and Comgall.

Were the tribute of all Alba mine,
From its centre to its border,
I would prefer the site of one house
In the middle of fair Derry.

> The reason I love Derry is,
> For its quietness, for its purity,
> And for its crowds of white angels
> From the one end to the other.
>
> The reason why I love Derry is,
> For its quietness, for its purity;
> Crowded full of heaven's angels
> Is every leaf of the oaks of Derry.
>
> My Derry, my little oak grove,
> My dwelling, and my little cell;
> O eternal God, in heaven above,
> Woe be to him who violates it!
>
> Beloved are Durrow and Derry;
> Beloved is Raphoe in purity;
> Beloved Drumhone of rich fruits;
> Beloved are Swords and Kells.
>
> Beloved to my heart, also in the West,
> Drumcliff, at Culcinne's strand.
> To behold the fair Loch Feval,
> The form of its shores, is delightful.
>
> Delightful is that, and delightful
> The salt main on which the sea-gulls cry,
> On my coming from Derry afar;
> It is quiet, and it is delightful.
>   Delightful."

Although, from internal evidences, this charming poem, in the complete form in which it has come down to us, may be later than St. Columba's age, yet as it is indeed "delightful," from its sweetness and tenderness, its love of nature, and love of country, and we doubt not truly expresses the yearnings of that noble exile's heart; so we shall not err in accepting its sentiments as those of the poet-saint, even if it be not all penned by his own hand.

St. Columba was in his forty-second year when he left his native land for the small island of Hy, or Iona, off the coast of Argyll. This retired spot, afterwards called from him I-Colm-Kill, was bestowed on the saint by his relative Conall, one of the Dalriad kings of Alba.

St. Columba belonged, as we have already noticed, to the second order of Irish saints. They had one head—one Lord, but used different liturgies and rules. They celebrated Easter on the fourteenth of the moon after the equinox. They had the eastern tonsure from ear to ear, instead of the Roman tonsure of the crown. They dispensed with the society of women, and were mainly presbyters in rank, having few bishops among them—only such as were required for the laying on of hands—and their monasteries were ruled by abbots, whose jurisdiction extended over the entire community, even when including bishops among them. This order, more national though more ascetical than the first order of Irish saints, may be regarded as "the development of a native ministry."

The question as to the time of celebrating Easter was that on which the Irish and British Christians dissented, not without much bitterness on both sides, from the other Christian churches of Europe. The general rule for fixing the time on which this festival should be held was, that it should be the Sunday following that fourteenth day of the moon which fell next after the vernal equinox. The Eastern Church acquired the opprobrious name of Quarta-decimans, because they celebrated Our Lord's resurrection on the fourteenth, or Passover Day itself—on whatever day of the week that might chance to fall, whether it were Sunday or not. The Irish observed their Easter on the Sunday between the fourteenth and twentieth day of the moon, not always on the Sunday *after* the Passover, as celebrated by the Roman Church; but sometimes on the day of the Passover itself, when that happened to fall on Sunday. The Irish also used for their calculations, as to the moon's age, the cycle of Sulpicius Severus, which consisted of eighty-four years, while Rome adopted the more accurate cycle of nineteen years, known as the cycle of Anatolius. On this point endless disputes were waged for centuries; the Irish ecclesiastics being unwilling, even for the sake of conformity, to abandon the habits practised by their venerated saints.

Worship, labour, study, such were the domestic occupations of the monks of Hy. Columba himself was a noted scribe. That most beautiful manuscript of western Europe, the Book of Kells, now preserved in the Library of Trinity College, Dublin, is ascribed to Columba. Its illuminated letters are glorious specimens of calligraphic art. The rich shrine in which it was enclosed had, a few centuries later, almost proved fatal to this valuable manuscript. It was stolen by night from the sacristy of the church of Kells. It was found "after two months and twenty days, its gold having been stolen off it, and a sod over it."

The Book of Durrow, another Irish MS. of great antiquity, is also ascribed to Columba. The silver-mounted case has been lost, but the book and its beautiful illuminations may be seen in Trinity College, Dublin.

Durrow—the field of the oak—sometimes called Ros-Grencha, was a spot dearly loved by St. Columba. Looking back from the land of his exile to the monastery he had founded there, and left in care of his friend Cormac, he exclaims—

" How happy the son of Dimma,—Of the devout church,
When he hears in Durrow,—The desire of his mind,
The sound of the wind against the elms,—When 'tis played,
The blackbird's joyous note,—When he claps his wings,
And listens at early dawn in Ros-Grencha,—To the cattle,
And the cooing of the cuckoo from the tree,—On the brink of summer.
Three objects I have left, the dearest to me,—On this peopled world,
Durrow, Derry, the noble angelic land, And Tir Luighdech."

In another poem, ascribed to Columba, and, if not from his pen, at least of great antiquity, a dialogue between the saint and his friend Cormac is given. The scene is Hy; and Cormac has escaped the perils of *Coire-Brecain*, the whirlpool of Corryvreckan, on the west coast of Scotland, and other dangers of the ocean. Columba is the first speaker :—

" Thou art welcome, O comely Cormac,
From over the all-teeming sea ;
What sent thee forth ; where hast thou been
Since the time we were on the same path ?
Two years and a month to this night
Is the time thou hast been wandering from port to port,

From wave to wave: resolute the energy
To traverse the wide ocean!
Since the sea hath sent thee hither,
Thou shalt have friendship and counsel:
Were it not for Christ's sake, Lord of the fair world,
Thou hadst merited satire and reproach."

CORMAC.

"Let there be no reproach now,
O descendant of Niall, for we are a noble race;
The sun shines in the west as in the east:
A righteous guest is entitled to reception."

Columba bids him welcome, but expresses surprise at his leaving Ireland; and to the regret of Cormac, predicts to him that his resurrection should be in Durrow. Cormac does not sympathise in the yearning love which the exile felt for the soil of Erin. "Death is better," exclaims Columba, "in reproachless Erin, than perpetual life in Alba!" Cormac, moved doubtless by the earnestness of his master, expresses his willingness to return to Durrow:—

"O Columcille of a hundred graces,
For thou art a prophet, thou art a true poet,
Thou art learned, a scribe, happy, perfect,
And a devout accomplished priest;
Thou art a king's son of reddened valour,
Thou art a virgin, thou art a pilgrim;
We shall abide in the west if thou desire it;
Christ will unfold his mysterious intentions."

COLUMBA.

"O Cormac, beautiful is thy church,
With its books and learning;
A devout city with a hundred crosses,
Without blemish, without transgression;

> A holy dwelling confirmed by my verse,
> The green of Aedh, son of Brenann,
> The oak-plain of far-famed Ros-Grencha;
> The night upon which her pilgrims collect,
> The number of her wise—a fact wide spread—
> Is unknown to any but the only God."

Conall, the ruler of the Dalriad colony, in the west of Scotland, who had sanctioned the settlement of his saintly kinsman on the outlying Isle of Iona, which the missionary exile and his companions probably found unclaimed and unoccupied, died soon after, and was succeeded by his relative Aidan, who came to Iona to be inaugurated at the hands of Columba. By this prince, who was a man of much vigour and ability, the real foundations of the Scottish monarchy were laid. He repaired to Ireland, and took part in the convention of Drumceat, near Newtown-Limavady, in the county of Derry, A.D. 575, and there obtained the recognition of his independence. For this success he was indebted to the good offices of Columba, who also returned for the purpose of bearing a part in affairs in which, from his near relationship to the princes of the Hy-Niall dynasties, he also was deeply interested.

Aedh, son of Ainmiré, was monarch of Ireland at the time of the convention of Drumceat. During the reign of Dermid MacKervil, A.D. 554, Tara had been cursed by St. Ruadhan of Lorrah, and ceased from that time to be the residence of the supreme monarch. The kings of the northern Hy-Niall, who succeeded Dermid, made Aileach, near Derry, between Loughs Foyle and Swilly, their residence; while the princes of the southern Hy-Niall ruled from Dun-na-Sgaith, on Lough Ennell, near Mullingar. Donall and Fergus, sons of Murkertach MacErca, were the successors of Dermid; and the throne was successively filled by Eochy and Baedan, Ainmire, and Baedan II., till Aedh, son of Ainmire, assumed the sovereignty of Ireland, 568.

King Aedh endeavoured to banish the bards from Ireland. Their numbers had become excessive, and their exactions most oppressive. The provincial king of Connaught at this period, Guary Aidhné, had been well nigh impoverished by his gifts to them.

A romantic story is told of this king and the poet Sancan, which casts some light on the probable age of that remarkable composition, the *Tain Bo Cuailgné*, referred to in an earlier chapter. The *Tain* was, says the legend, originally composed by Fergus MacRoy himself, one of the chief actors in the foray, who rode beside Maev's chariot and recounted what had passed before his own eyes. But in process of time the memory of the piece had been lost, so that though it was in the list of recitations which might lawfully be demanded of every bard, even Sancan himself was unable to repeat it; and this blot on the chief bard's pretensions was well known; but from a feeling of reverence, his entertainers were careful not to expose his deficiency, and the *Tain* had long ceased to be called for. At last, on a visit of Sancan with a great retinue of other bards to Guary, the stores of the king were well-nigh exhausted by the rapacity of his guests, and Guary, to be relieved of their company, called on Sancan to recite the *Tain*. The bard and his com-

poers retired in extreme indignation; and his son
Murgen undertook a pilgrimage into "the East"—that
is, to the continent of Europe—in search of the lost lay.
He was accompanied by Eimené, who joined himself as
the companion of his pious wanderings. On reaching
the shores of Loch Ein, in Roscommon, Murgen, faint-
ing from fatigue, stopped to rest, while Eimené went in
search of a house of entertainment. It will be remembered, it was in Loch Ein that Fergus himself had
perished; and the story goes that the spot where
Murgen lay down to rest happened to be the grave of
the poet-warrior. Murgen, comprehending that he was
now close to the very author of the piece he was in
quest of, extemporized an invocation to the shade of
Fergus, so earnest, that presently the grave gave up its
dead.

Fergus rose; a mist ascended with him, and a flash was seen
As of brazen sandals blended with a mantle's wafture green:
But so close the cloud closed o'er him, Eimené, returned at
    last,
Found not on the field before him but a mist-heap grey and
    vast.

* * * * *

Thrice to pierce the hoar recesses faithful Eimené essayed;
Thrice through foggy wildernesses back to open air he
    strayed:
Till a deep voice through the vapours filled the twilight far
    and near,
And the night, her starry tapers kindling, stooped from
    heaven to hear.

Concealed within the mist-cloud, Murgen learns
from the shade of Fergus the perfect version of the

Tain, and restores his father to the unquestioned supremacy of the bards of Erin. Such was the order of men in whose favour Columba interposed his authority at Drumceat. Guary's device has not prevented his name continuing to be renowned for liberality. He bestowed gifts with both hands: but the right hand was the larger, "for with it he gave to the poor."

St. Columba used his influence with the king to persuade him, instead of banishing the bards, to reduce their number only; and instead of demanding tribute from the kindred princes of the Dalriad colony in Scotland, which would have resulted in war, thus to limit his requirements:—" Their expeditions and hostings to be with the men of Erin always; for hostings always belong to the parent stock. Their tributes, and gains, and shipping to be with the men of Alba. And when one of the men of Erin or Alba should come from the east, the Dal Riada to entertain them, whether few or many; and the Dal Riada to convey them on, if they require it."

There is a tradition that when he arrived from Iona he brought with him a sod of grass on which to place his feet, and wore a bandage over his eyes, in fulfilment of the penance enjoined on him by St. Molaise never to set foot again, or even look, on the soil of Erin.

Columba, having visited the monasteries he had founded in Ireland, returned to Iona, where he died on the 9th of June, 597, in the 77th year of his age, having lived in exile from his native land for nearly thirty-five years.

Adamnan, a subsequent abbot of Iona, has been the

biographer of St. Columba. He has recorded that, on the last day of his life, the aged saint had visited the granary of his monastery, blessed it, and congratulated his brethren on the store of food which was there laid up. He then, with cautions of secrecy, told his attendant, Dermid, of his approaching end. "This day," said he, "is in the sacred volume called the Sabbath, which is interpreted, Rest: and to-day is verily a Sabbath for me, because it is the last with me of this present toilsome life, upon which, after all my toils and sorrows, I come to enjoy my Sabbath; and at the approaching hour of midnight, as the hallowed day of the Lord begins, I shall, as the Scripture saith, be going the way of my fathers. For now my Lord Jesus Christ vouchsafes to invite me to himself, and when this midnight, as I say, comes, I shall go at his own bidding to be with him."

He ascended the hill which overhung the monastery, and "stood at the top of it a little while; and as he stood there, with uplifted hands, pronounced a blessing on his community." On his return, he is recorded to have caressed—as with the consciousness that it was for the last time—an old white horse belonging to the community, which, being too feeble for work, had been permitted to graze in the abbey-close, and had approached the saint, as if to solicit his notice. Having returned to the monastery, he spent the afternoon of that Saturday in his chamber writing the *Psalter*. He paused, at evening, at the close of his page, at that verse where it is written, "They that seek the Lord shall not want any good thing."

The saint, whose hours on earth were numbered, attended the Vesper service, and leaving the church, sought a brief repose on the bare stone which served him for a bed. He was roused by the midnight bell summoning the community to their devotions. "Rising up hastily, he goes to the church, and running before the rest, and coming in alone, he sinks on bended knees in prayer." His faithful attendant, Dermid, was the first to follow. He discovered his master in a dying state, raised him, and supported his head on his breast. The monks had by this time arrived. Columba, speechless, yet filled with tender love, raised his feeble right hand to bless them, "so that he might appear, even with a motion of his hand, to convey to his brethren that benediction which he was unable to express orally, from his breath failing him. And after having thus imparted to them his solemn blessing, he immediately breathed forth his spirit."

And so died one who is represented by his friend and biographer as "angelic in aspect, pure in conversation, holy in his employments, of excellent abilities, so eminent for wisdom, that, although his dwelling was on earth, yet he showed himself by his disposition to be fit for the society of the inhabitants of heaven."

Nor did the influence of Columba cease with his life: the monasteries which he founded were nurseries of learning and piety. The Venerable Bede has borne testimony on this point:—"Whatever kind of person he himself was," writes the Anglo-Saxon historian, "this we know of him for certain, that he left successors distinguished for their great chastity, divine love, and strict attention to their rules of discipline; following, indeed, uncertain cycles in their computation of the time of the great festival (Easter); because, far away as they were out of the world, no one had supplied them with the synodal decrees relating to the Paschal observance; yet withal diligently observing such works of piety and chastity as they could find in the prophetic, evangelic, and apostolic writings."

Columba was interred at Iona; but after the lapse of years, probably in the eighth century, his bones were exhumed and enshrined. Saul, Downpatrick, Durham, and Dunkeld contend for having had possession of the relics of this saintly man. The shrine, which became "the title-deed of the Columban community," was from time to time taken over to Ireland as the warrant for levying religious contributions. Its rich decorations fatally excited the cupidity of the plundering Northmen; and when in the ninth century Iona was devastated by these pirates, the shrine was permanently deposited in Ireland for greater security. In the twelfth century it was carried off by the Danes of Dublin, but restored—probably despoiled of its gold and silver—at the end of a month. Its after-fate is unknown.

When Columba, with the cerecloth over his eyes, and a sod from the land of Alba under his feet, revisited his native land to take part in the convention of Drumceat, the queen, wife of Aodh, son of Ainmire, suggested to her sons to receive the saint with insult.

To this advice, our ecclesiastical writers tell us, her eldest son, Conall, hearkened, but Donall, the younger, courteously saluted the stranger, and was rewarded by his blessing, and a prediction that he should fill the throne of Ireland. Some years after the death of his father, who was succeeded by sovereigns of little note, this prince attained to the promised position.

CHAPTER VII.

THE SCHOLASTIC PERIOD.

The period extending from the convention of Drumceat to the first arrival of the Danes, was the least disturbed, and, in intellectual progress, the most flourishing epoch in the history of Ireland before the Conquest. Yet the native accounts we have of it are meagre in proportion to the paucity of those events which were alone thought worthy of being chronicled—battles, usurpations, and violent deaths. The local annals being thus barren, we have to look for the picture of Ireland during this, which we have called the Scholastic, period, by the reflected light of external literature, which certainly borrowed a great part of its lustre from the schools for which Ireland began to grow famous shortly after the regal and ecclesiastical power had cemented their alliance at Drumceat. But, before these comparatively halcyon days were attained to, there remained one grand contest in which all the old pagan and bardic influences, uniting with provincial jealousy of the central government, arrayed themselves for a decisive struggle against the newly consolidated strength of the church and crown.

This was the battle of Moy Rath, an event well marked as an historical fact, and which has been made the subject of a bardic poem-story, for the better appreciation of which it will be necessary to trace downward the influence impressed on his generation by St. Columba.

King Aedh's household had received him with insult, with one exception. This was Donall, a younger son, and who had then little prospect of the crown. Twenty years later, King Aedh (or Hugh, as the name is Anglicised) met his death at Dunbolg, in the county of Wicklow, while endeavouring to exact the Boromean tribute from the then king of Leinster. The stratagem by which the provincial king, with inferior numbers, defeated the Ard-Righ, is thus recorded:—He entered the camp disguised as a leper, and reported that the men of Leinster, unprepared for resistance, were coming to the king with overtures of peace, and stores of provisions for the royal army. As evening closed in, a drove of bullocks, laden with leathern bags, approached the camp, and entered unchallenged, when they announced that they were the bearers of stores and gifts for Aedh. Each sack contained a soldier, and, when night closed in, they attacked the camp and killed the king himself. Two princes of the same name, but not of his immediate family, succeeded. In 626, his son Maelcova reigned for a brief period, when he resigned his authority to Sweeny Menn, and became a cleric.

Sweeny banished from Erin the Donall of whom we have spoken; and his prospects of the throne, predicted for him by St. Columba, appeared more distant and hopeless than ever.

Donall sought refuge in Scotland, accompanied by his foster son, Congal Claen, provincial king of Uladh or Ulster. The Dalriad monarch was Congal's maternal grandfather, and he hospitably received the exiles. Here Donall incited his foster son to attempt the life of King Sweeny Menn, promising, if he thus became king of Erin, that he would reinstate Congal in all the lands of Ulster, once ruled by his ancestors, but of late circumscribed by the encroachments of the Clan Colla and the Hy-Niall to the present counties of Antrim and Down. Congal Claen made the attempt. He thus recounts the assassination of Sweeny, which, in those days, seems to have been regarded as a legitimate exploit:—

"I was nursed by thee," he says to Donall in after years, "until thou wast expelled by the king of Erin, Suibhne Menn. . . . and thou didst repair to the king of Alba, taking me along with thee in that exile; and thou didst receive great honour from him, and you formed a treaty, thou and the king of Alba, and he protested to thee that he would not oppose thee as long as the sea should surround Erin. Thou didst afterwards return to Erin, and I returned along with thee, for I was in exile along with thee. . . . And what thou didst say was, that whoever thou shouldst get to destroy the king of Erin, thou wouldst be bound to restore his territory to him whenever thou shouldst become king over Erin. I went on the enterprise, O king, for a promise that my patrimony should be wholly restored to me, whenever thou shouldst become monarch of Erin; and I delayed not until I reached Ailech Neid (the dwelling of the northern Hy-Niall princes, near Lough Swilly), where the king held his residence at that time. The king came out upon the green, surrounded by a great concourse of the men of Erin, and he was playing chess amidst the hosts; and I came into the assembly, passing, without the permission of any one, through the crowds, and made a thrust of my spear, Gearr-Congail, which I held in my hand, at the breast of the king; and the stone which was at his back responded to the thrust, and his heart's blood was on the head of the javelin, so that he fell dead."

Donall, son of Aedh, son of Ainmiré, whose accession to the throne was thus secured, found himself unable to fulfil his promise to the "son of Scannlan of the Broad Shield, the haughty, famous, intelligent, arch-king of Ulster," Congal Claen. The Clan Colla were in too firm possession of Orgiall (now Armagh and Monaghan), and the Hy-Niall, of the north-western districts of Ulster, to permit of Donall restoring Uladh to its ancient boundaries.

King Donall fixed his royal habitation at Dun-na-n'-geadh, on the banks of the Boyne; Tara, as we have before said, having been deserted, since it was cursed by St. Ruadhan of Lorrah. The attainment of his utmost desires could not secure for the monarch tranquil enjoyment. In his home, in the beautiful valley of the Boyne, his nights were haunted by ill-omened dreams. To his queen first, and afterwards to his hermit brother, the ex-king Maeleova, Donall revealed his visions.

Maelcova thus interpreted the dream: "A greyhound whelp, in a dream," said he, "is the same as a king's son; thou hast two foster-sons, O king, Conal Caev, and Congal Claen, the son of Scannlan of the Broad Shield. Either of these will rise up against thee, O king, and will bring the plunderers and the doers of evil of Alba, France, Saxon-land, and Britain with him to Erin, who will give seven battles to thee and the men of Erin, so that great slaughter shall be made between you both, and in the seventh battle which shall be fought between you, thy foster-son shall fall. Now it is proper for thee, O king, to prepare a banquet, and to invite to it the men of Erin, and to obtain the hostages of every province in Erin, and also to detain in fetters, to the end of a year, these two foster-sons of thine, because it is one of them who will rise up against thee, and because the venom goes out of every dream within the year. Then set them at liberty, and bestow many jewels and much wealth upon them."

"This shall not be done by me," said the king; "for sooner would I quit Erin than deal treacherously by my own foster-sons, for they will never rise up against me; and if all the men of the world should oppose me, Congal would not."

That part of his brother's advice which related to the banquet found more favour in the mind of Donall. He summoned his guests, and sent out purveyors to bring in store of provisions, for "Donall did not deem it honourable that there should be in Erin a kind of food that should not be found at that banquet." These men appropriated for their purpose a store of goose eggs, the property of Erc of Slane, an anchorite who passed his days immersed to his arm-pits in the Boyne, having his *Psalter* before him on the river bank, constantly engaged in prayer: and whose sole repast was daily made on cresses of the Boyne and these goose eggs. When Erc found his store so invaded, he "cursed the banquet as bitterly as he was able to curse it."

When the ill-omened feast was prepared, Congal, at the request of the king, went to inspect the arrangements. He saw the goose eggs, and marvelled at them, and ate a part of one of them, and took a drink after it. He then came out, and said to Donall, "I think," said he, "if the men of Erin were to remain for three months in the palace, that there is a sufficiency of food and drink for them there."

The bishops present at the feast bless the entertainment. Unfortunately, Congal Claen has eaten already of the eggs cursed by the hermit Erc. And now the hosts are seated. "First of all the king sat in the golden couch; and the custom and law at this time was, that when the monarch of Erin was of the southern Hy-Niall, the king of Connaught should sit at his right hand; but if of the northern Hy-Niall, the king of Ulster should be at his right hand, and the king of Connaught at his left hand." Unhappily this order was infringed, Malodar Macha, king of Orgiall, being placed at the king's right hand, the position which belonged to Congal Claen.

Nor did the mortifications of Congal end here. The goose egg, presented to each of the other kings in a silver dish, assumed, in his case, the contemptible form of a hen egg on a wooden platter. He starts

up, angrily recounts his wrongs, and, followed by
the men of Ulster, leaves the feast. The bishops
present, at the request of the king, follow to entreat
his return. Congal is deaf alike to persuasions
and curses. "I swear by my valour," said Congal,
"that not one cleric of you shall reach the king's
house alive, if I or any Ultonian be cursed by you."
Terror then seized the saints, " whereupon Congal went
far away from them, and they cursed him afterwards."
The poets are then sent by the king. Congal receives
them graciously, gives them presents, yet refuses to
return. He proceeds to the abode of his uncle, Cellach,
who, though now aged and a cripple, had been a hero
in his youth. His voice was strong for war. "I
pledge thee my word," he exclaimed, disclosing his
weapon, which, unknown to his attendants, he wore under
his gown, when Congal had told his story," that shouldest
thou receive any considerations from the king but a
battle, all the Ultonians could not save thee from me,
because I would thrust this sword through thy heart;
for it is not the custom of the Ultonians to accept of
considerations in place of battle until they take revenge
for insults. I have seven good sons, and they shall
go with thee into the battle, and if I were able myself
I would go also, and the Ultonians should not be
defeated while I had life."

Congal continued his journey, and sought for allies
and auxiliary forces in Scotland, Scandinavia, France,
and Britain. With these foreign mercenaries, and
aided by the dispersed remnant of the Bards and Druids,
Congal returned to Ulster, and encountered the forces

of King Donall at Moy Rath, now Moira, in the county of Down. A.D. 636 is the date of this eventful battle, which may be considered as the expiring struggle of paganism in Ireland.

The Druids who accompanied the host of Congal could not encourage hopes of ultimate success; but "whoever felt dejection for the battle, it was not the arch-king of Ulster that was sorrowful, dejected, or pusillanimous at the approach of this final defeat, and it was in vain for his Druids to make true magical predictions for him, and it was not profitable for his clergy to seek instructing him; for his friends might as well converse with a rock as advise him."

On the morning of the battle, Congal, lulled to sleep by the "soft sounds of the musical pipes, and by the warbling vibrations and melancholy notes" of the stringed instruments, was aroused by the chant of his Druid:—

> O Congal Claen, arise.
> Thy enemies approach thee;
> The characteristic of an imbecile is the desire of constantly lying asleep;
> Sleep of death is an awful omen;
> Little energy forebodes the destruction of the coward;
> The desire of the hero and the watchman is early rising;
> An inciter of valour is a proud and fearless fiery-champion;
> Fervour of blood—the characteristic of a hero—
> Be to thee, O Congal.

Congal, though hopeless of success, is unflinching in his determination to fight. "Which of the great descendants of Ir," he asks, "has got protection against final destruction, or will live without being killed?

P

And it is a good king like Donall, with the arch-chieftains of Erin about him, to whom it belongs by fate to have the killing and slaughtering of the Ultonians on this occasion," said Congal. "But though I should attempt to avoid this battle, and save myself from final destruction (for my Druids are making true predictions to me that I shall fall in this battle), yet flight has never saved a wretch: it is profitless to fly from death."

King Donall, on his side, although deeply lamenting the necessity of the appeal to arms, cheerfully addresses his army :—

" Arise, arise, O youths ! quickly and unanimously, firmly and prudently, vigorously and fearlessly, to meet this attack of the Ultonians and foreigners. . . . that so the battle-reparations which Congal so loudly demands may be the battle in which his own final destruction shall be wrought ; for a furious enraged bull is not entitled to protection, nor a man with the daring deeds of a demon to forgiveness, unless indeed he is purified by repentance (for even though the beloved nursling of my heart, Congal, should be slain, his sorrow and regret for his crimes would make me lighter, and his anguish for past offences would render my wounded heart calmer). . . . Let the conduct of your heroes be brave and headstrong to maintain the field of battle ; let the feet of your mighty men be firm, solid, cemented, and immovable on the earth, and let the hands of your champions be quick, expert, and wounding in using your swords, lances, and warlike shields, and let none of you go into the conflict except one who longs to approach it ; for it would be trusting to shadows in a prince to trust to the exertions of his heroes unless they were all equally desirous to rush to the scene of action to defend him."

King Donall further reminds them of the blessing invoked on his head of yore by St. Columba. His army, thus animated, performed great feats of valour. The doomed Congal fought with equal bravery.

That Congal's ambition might the more signally be mortified, he met his death at the hands of an idiot, a foster-son, as he himself also was, of King Donall. Cuanna had been sent back to his father's house when his infirmity had been discovered, because "the king did not think it becoming to have an idiot as a foster-son." On the day when the hosts were mustering at Moy Rath, the despised youth was sent by his stepmother to collect firewood, and was met by her reproaches for the selection he had made. "The firewood thou hast brought with thee is a bad present, O Cuanna," said the woman; "and it is becoming and like thyself; and alas! thou art not the kind of a son we stand in need of having here to-day, but (we need) a son who would assist his father and his fosterer on this day of battle; for Congal, with his Ultonians and foreigners, has been killing and overwhelming them these six days; and it was thy father's turn to fight yesterday, and we know not whether he has or has not survived."

The despised Cuanna, stung by these reproaches, follows on the track of the hosts till he reaches Newry, and from thence continues his route to Moy Rath.

"Cuanna came forward in rapid course, on the strong track of the hosts, till he arrived at Magh Rath, where he saw the great forces of both parties attacking each other. As the men of Erin were there, they saw one lone man in the plain approaching them from the south-west, and they ceased till they recognised him. 'He is Cuanna, the idiot,' said one of them; 'He is Cuanna, the fool,' said a second man; 'It was no small cause of waiting,' said a third man. In a short time Cuanna came on to where the king of Erin was. The king bade him welcome. 'Good, my dear Cuanna,' said he; 'wherefore hast thou come to us to-day?'—'To assist thee, O monarch,' said Cuanna, 'and to lay Congal prostrate, though he is my foster-brother.'—'It behoves thee,' said the monarch of Erin, 'though thou knowest it not, to press thy share of this battle against Congal, for he slew thy father in yesterday's battle.' Cuanna grew red as he heard this, and said, 'Give me weapons, O monarch, and I pledge my word that I will repel any fighter of a hundred men, who is against thee this day.' All gave a great shout of derision aloud on hearing Cuanna. Cuanna said to them, 'I swear by my word,' said he, 'that if I had arms, or edged weapons at hand, I would revenge on some of you your having mocked me.'—'Not so,' said Domhnall (Donall); 'take no heed or notice of them; and here is for thee the second missile javelin which I have to spare, and it is the third best spear in Erin, the other two being the spear which is along with it, and the javelin called Gearr Congail, for an erring cast cannot be given with either of them.' The idiot took the lance, and brandished it in the presence of the king, and said that he would achieve with it a deed which would be pleasing to the king."

Congal had vanquished all opponents, and was in the full flush of his conquering progress, when he encountered his imbecile foster-brother.

Congal, on seeing his companion and foster-brother, " bade him welcome, and said, 'Terrible is the enmity, and heroic is the muster, when fools and madmen are waging battle against me.'—'It is not the act of a prince or a true hero in thee, indeed,' said Cuanna, ' to cast reflections on the son of any good man or good hero who should come to give his day of battle to assist his relatives in the struggle of a great battle.' —'Be not enraged, O Cuanna,' said Congal, 'for I know that it was not for martial achievements, or to perform feats of arms or valour, thou hast come to Magh Rath on this expedition.'—'It is not the saying of an arch-king for thee to say so,' said Cuanna; 'why should I not lend my aid in battle to my tribe, and my monarch? But, however, I can more easily bear a reproach than forbear giving assistance to my friends on this day of battle.' Then Congal passed by the idiot. But Cuanna pressed his foot against the support and the solidity of the earth, and putting his finger on the cord of his broad-headed spear, he made a bold, terrible, destructive cast at Congal, and it passed beyond the angle of his great shield, so that the handspear pierced the armour of Congal and entered his abdomen, and pierced all the viscera, so that as much as would kill a man of its blade was to be seen at the other side of his body, and of the armour which defended it. Congal looked on one side, and observed that it was the idiot that wounded him; and it was in his power to slay him on the spot, but he did not like to see the blood of an idiot on his arms: he laid his heroic weapons on the ground, and made a drag and a mighty pull to draw back the spear, but he failed; he made a second effort, and failed; but in the third effort he dragged it out, and he extended his strong warlike hand and drew his belt to close the wound, and took up his arms off the ground, and proceeded to address the idiot, and said to him, 'Woe is me, O Cuanna,' said Congal, 'that it was not a mighty puissant lord, or a hundred-killing champion, that sent that shot to destroy me. It grieves me, moreover, that it was not the mighty, many-battled, populous champion, Cellach, the son of Maelcobha, that has to boast of having first wounded my body. I lament that it was not the pillar, numerously-attended-in-battle, Crummhael, the son of Suibhne, that chanced to wound me, for I slew his father at the instigation of the monarch of Erin, so that a debtor might not owe the debt of enmity.'—'Desist, O Congal,' said Cuanna; 'old is the proverb that his own danger hangs over the head of every rash man.'—'That is not the same, O Cuanna,' said Congal, 'as that I should fall by the deeds of an imbecile idiot without a firm mind, and without a cause for destroying me.' After this Congal recognized that he was neither king of Ulster nor Erin after this one wound."

Thus perished Congal Claen, the last of the Rudrician kings of Ulster. Well might the victorious Donall exclaim—

> Alas for him who destroyed all Erin
> For a dispute about one egg!

Donall was ever a friend to the church and submissive to ecclesiastics. Under the influence of St. Fechin of Fore, he became the founder of many monastic establishments. Among these we may pause to mention the Abbey of Cong, on the neck of land which divides Lough Corrib from Lough Mask. Cong became, in subsequent times, the residence and last resting-place of several kings of Connaught. Roderic O'Connor, monarch at the time of the Conquest, died in that retreat. The ruins which stand on this most interesting spot date probably from his time—the latter part of the twelfth century.

St. Fechin, himself of noble blood, was a builder of no mean merit. He erected the beautiful little church at Fore, which is yet standing; and to him also is ascribed an ancient mill which adjoins it, in the green secluded valley of Westmeath, where this anchorite and his community sought for solitude and holy meditation. The monks of old must have had an exquisite feeling for nature, at least we may so infer from the sites they selected for their monasteries and cells. The ecclesiastical establishment on High Island, off the coast of Connemara, one of this saint's foundations, though one of the most secluded of all the Irish *lauras*, commands a prospect of wondrous grandeur, the billows

of the Atlantic on one side, the varied outlines of
the Connemara coast and its grand mountains on the
other.

St. Fechin died of the *Buidhe Chonnaill*, or " yellow
plague," a fearful pestilence, which desolated Ireland
as well as Wales at this period. In both countries the
visitation was impersonated in the popular imagination.
The Welsh prince, who shut himself up to avoid the
pest, was struck by a glance of the yellow destroyer,
which looked in at him through a chink of the door.
The *Buidhe Chonnaill* of the Irish fell, like another
Python, before a shaft of prayer and the tinkling of
a bell of St. Patrick aimed at it by St. MacCreiché.
Three sovereigns died of the pestilence, which was
followed some years later by a cattle plague, in the
reign of Finnachta the Festive, or Hospitable. This
calamity lasted for four years, and was succeeded by
a season so severe that all the lakes and rivers were
frozen, and even the sea between Ireland and Scotland
blocked with ice. To the intercession of another ecclesiastic, St. Moling of Ferns, is ascribed the remission
of the Boromean tribute, which, after occasioning many
ages of strife, was abandoned about A.D. 690 by this
monarch Finnachta. During his reign Adamnan, the
great abbot of Iona, visited Ireland, and pitched his
tent at Tara. Already this deserted capital, no longer
the abode of " chiefs and ladies bright," was a grass-
covered hill, on which, as at the present day, the
ruins only of former royal residences could be traced.
St. Adamnan, like his illustrious predecessor Columba,
of whom he was the biographer, was of noble Irish

blood. His life of St. Columba is written in Latin, of remarkable purity for that age. This book, next to the history of the Venerable Bede, is the most valuable specimen we possess of the literature of that time.

One of the earliest and most authentic accounts of the holy places of Palestine has been preserved by the learned diligence of Adamnan, who took down, from the narration of Arculf, a Saxon bishop, shipwrecked on his return from Jerusalem, and cast ashore on one of the western Scottish islands, a very detailed and exact account of the holy city and its chief monuments, including the Chapel of the Holy Sepulchre, of which the pilgrim bishop gave the abbot of Iona a ground plan, transcribed into the manuscript of Adamnan.

At the time of which we speak, Iona had become widely celebrated for its sanctity. In its cemetery had been recently interred Egfrid, King of Northumbria, who had been slain in war with the Picts and Scots. This prince had sent in 683 an expedition to ravage the coasts of Leinster. This is memorable as the first instance on record of a Saxon raid into Ireland. During the reign of another Northumbrian prince, Aldfrid, St. Adamnan visited York, and obtained by his influence the release of many Irish captives, restored by these efforts of Christian philanthropy to their native land.

To return, however, to the text of our chapter, and to its starting-point at the battle of Moy Rath. Amid much that is grotesque and fantastic in this story, there occur incidental illustrations of life and manners, valuable as showing what the early Irish themselves considered to have been the state of civilization existing in the country at the period commemorated. Not the least interesting of these relate to the progress which had already begun to be made in the wider diffusion of scholastic education.

Amongst Donall's warriors in this engagement was one who afterwards became famous in the peaceful pursuits of letters, Kenfalla, son of Ollioll. Kenfalla was a professional scholar; but, hitherto, not noted for superior intellectual ability. It was his chance in the fight to encounter the terrible Congal himself, from whom he received a sword-cut in the hinder part of his head which penetrated to the brain. Being cured of the wound, it was found that his memory had acquired a wonderful strength and acuteness, and he afterwards became the Admirable Crichton of his age, and is still remembered traditionally as the Scholar, *par excellence*, of early times. Hence the battle of Moy Rath has been called a triple victory, that is, a victory of truth over untruth; a victory of tale-and-story-telling over dull moments, owing to the multitude of stories founded on the madness of Sweeny (one of Congal's chiefs, who lost his reason in the terrors of the conflict); and a victory of rough surgery, "by reason of the taking of the brain of forgetfulness out of the head of Cennfaeladh."

In the story of the cure of Kenfalla we get a glance at the nature of the schools in which the Irish youth of the seventh century conducted their studies. His *leech* was Bricin of Tomregan, who resided at the meeting of three roads, neighbouring the houses of three *säis* or professors; a *sai* (*sage*) of the Fenechus (or old Brehon) law, a *sai* of poetry, and a *sai* of letters (literally of "legends"); and from frequenting their classes during his convalescence, he acquired the first great accession to his stores of knowledge.

These scattered teachers at cross-roads were merely the outposts of the great hosts of men of learning who about this time began to congregate in the shelter of abbatial and episcopal seats: cities they have been termed, but great villages would probably be a more accurate designation of Armagh, Bangor, Clonard, Lismore, and other resorts of pious and studious persons. In these central places of learning, provision was made for the maintenance and instruction of strangers, and there was a Saxon quarter and an Albanian quarter in Armagh, just as there still remains a Latin quarter in Paris. Among other British and Brito-Saxon youths educated at Armagh during this period of its growth was Aldfrid, son of Oswy, who became King of Northumbria A.D. 685. He has recorded his experiences in a poem, which gives a picture of early Irish society—simple, pure, and joyous—as pleasing and instructive as it will be considered singular, having regard to the time it was composed. The translation is one of the most faithful that has proceeded from the pen of its author, J. C. Mangan:—

> "I found in Innisfail the fair,
> In Ireland, while in exile there,
> Women of worth, both grave and gay men,
> Many clerics and many laymen.

I travelled its fruitful provinces round,
And in every one of the five I found,
Alike in church and in palace hall,
Abundant apparel and food for all.

Gold and silver I found, and money,
Plenty of wheat, and plenty of honey;
I found God's people rich in pity,
Found many a feast, and many a city.

I also found in Armagh the splendid,
Meekness, wisdom, and prudence blended,
Fasting, as Christ hath recommended,
And noble councillors untranscended.

I found in each great church, moreo'er,
Whether on island or on shore,
Piety, learning, fond affection,
Holy welcome, and kind protection.

I found the good lay monks and brothers
Ever beseeching help for others,
And in their keeping the holy word
Pure as it came from Jesus the Lord.

I found in Munster, unfettered of any,
Kings and queens, and poets a-many;
Poets well skilled in music and measure,
Prosperous doings, mirth and pleasure.

I found in Connaught the just, redundance
Of riches, milk in lavish abundance;
Hospitality, vigour, fame,
In Cruachan's land of heroic name.

I found in the country of Connall the glorious
Bravest heroes, ever victorious;
Fair-complexioned men and warlike,
Ireland's lights, the high, the starlike.

I found in Ulster, from hill to glen,
Hardy warriors, resolute men;
Beauty that bloomed when youth was gone,
And strength transmitted from sire to son.

I found in the noble district of Boyle
 [*MS. here illegible.*]
Brehons, Erenachs, weapons bright,
And horsemen bold and sudden in fight.

I found in Leinster the smooth and sleek,
From Dublin to Slewmargy's peak,
Flourishing pastures, valour, health,
Long-living worthies, commerce, wealth.

I found besides, from Ara to Glea,
In the broad rich country of Ossorie,
Sweet fruits, good laws for all and each,
Great chess-players, men of truthful speech.

I found in Meath's fair principality
Virtue, vigour, and hospitality,
Candour, joyfulness, bravery, purity,
Ireland's bulwark and security.

I found strict morals in age and youth,
I found historians recording truth;
The things I sing of in verse unsmooth,
I found them all—I have written sooth."

In this there may be some interpolations of a later age; but the poem is a valuable proof of what at an early period was the popular belief in both islands regarding the condition of Ireland during the generation which succeeded the defeat of Congal, and forms at once a commentary on, and illustration of, the authentic statement of Bede:—"There were in that country

(Ireland), at the time we speak of, many of the nobility and also of the middle classes of the English people; some of whom devoted themselves to the monastic profession, while others chose rather to pay visits to the chambers of different masters, and so to carry on their studies; all of whom the Scots received most cordially, and provided with daily food free of charge, as likewise with books to read and gratuitous instruction."

Another voice from beyond sea, which testifies to the same enviable condition of the island during these days of comparative happiness, comes from a greater distance. Donatus (Donagh), bishop of Fiesole (A.D. 844), saw nothing in Tuscany fairer or more amiable than the aspect of the land and people from amongst whom he had come to fix his habitation beside the Arno. His verses have the tenderness of home-affection mingled with a pardonable pride in his country :—

> " Far in the confines of the west
> There lies a land of lands the best;
> An island, rich in all good store
> Of robe, and gem, and golden ore;
> An isle, in soil, and sun, and wind,
> Most healthful to the human kind.
> With honey all the land abounds,
> With lovely lawns and pasture-grounds;
> With weeds of peace and peaceful arts,
> With arms of war and manly hearts.
> * * * * * * *
> And worthy of that blessed spot,
> There dwell the nations of the Scot;
> A race of men renowned high
> For honour, arms, and courtesy."

The Scòts of that day, emigrating from Ireland, obtained a character for the energetic prosecution of their enterprises, not dissimilar to that since so honourably earned for themselves by the Scots of North Britain. Eric of Auxerre, writing of Elias, bishop of Angouleme, an Irishman, who died A.D. 875, exclaims: "What need to speak of Ireland, setting at nought as it does the difficulties of the sea, and coming almost in one body to our shores, with its crowd of philosophers, the most intelligent of whom are subjecting themselves to a voluntary exile?" The number, indeed, of travelling Irish was destined ere long, after the repeated Danish incursions had begun to drive them abroad for shelter as well as for missionary and scholastic adventure, to become burthensome to neighbouring countries. The Council of Chalons on Saone (A.D. 813), and the English Synod of Calcytho (A.D. 816), both made canons against these wandering Scots.

The reproach of ingratitude might with some justice be made against the authors of these canons. But, notwithstanding occasional opposition of this character, the Irish Scots continued, for at least another century, to maintain their place in the foremost British and European seminaries of learning. Sweeny of Clonmacnoise, whose bell bearing his name may still be seen in the Museum of the Royal Irish Academy, was one of the sages who assisted at the foundation of the University of Oxford; and the story of the "Wisdom-sellers" before Charlemagne, introduces us to Clement, another of the same race and origin, for whom the honour is claimed of having been one of the first teachers in the University of Paris. "When the illustrious Charles had begun to reign alone in the western parts of the world, and literature was almost forgotten, it came to pass that two Scots from Ireland, men incomparably learned both in human knowledge and in the Holy Scriptures, came over with some British merchants to the shores of France." These persons, says the writer of the History of the Reign of Charlemagne, soon attracted attention by standing in the public market-place, and crying out to the passers-by, "If any person wishes for wisdom, let him come to us and receive it, for we have it to sell." There seems no doubt that both the strangers were well received by the great monarch, and that both of them were placed over scholastic seminaries, one at Paris, and the other near Pavia.

The great associations connected with the name of Armagh have led us so far down the course of the centuries, that in adverting to the other eminent school of Lismore, we must return to the commencement of the period inaugurated at Moy Rath.

There is a beautiful little church at Rathin in Westmeath, where, about A.D. 650, Carthagh, a descendant of Fergus Mac Roy, who had adopted a religious life, took up his abode with other monks of Kerry. "They led so pious a life in this house, it was said an angel was wont to hold conversation with every third man of them." The ecclesiastics of the Hy-Niall race became jealous of the Munster monks' superior reputation for holiness, and they appealed to Blathmaic and Dermid, their joint kings, to expel the intruders. Blathmaic was in favour of their expulsion; but Dermid, at the sight of Carthagh, relented, whence his *sobriquet* of the "Ruthful." However, the "holy men of the Clanna Niall" insisted on the expulsion of the strangers, and Carthagh (in popular hagiology, Saint Mochuda), after a twelvemonth's negotiation, being finally driven out by the resolute Blathmaic, went forth and established himself among the tribes of the Desi in their new seats in the south, where he founded the long-celebrated school of Lismore.

Bangor is another name which raises a train of associations, carrying the mind across a wide tract of Europe, and through a series of most interesting, though turbulent, events. St. Columbanus, a pupil of this school, evinced that fervour of missionary zeal so characteristic of his age and country. Accompanied by twelve monks of Bangor, he set forth on his wanderings, and became the evangelizer of eastern France, and parts of Switzerland and Italy. He established himself at Luxeuil in Burgundy. Columbanus warred no less with nature, in the then well-nigh impenetrable forests of the Vosges and Jura, where his community toiled, and cleared and cultivated the soil, than with the stormy passions of those long-haired Merovingian kings of the Frankish dynasties, who were swayed, at that period, by the savage impulses of two remarkable and unscrupulous women. Brunehault, the wife of Sigebert, the grandson of Clovis, and Fredegonde, the beautiful fury who ruled his brother Chilperic, have filled a prominent part in French history. Their very names recall a period of giant crimes, unregulated passions, and unparalleled bloodthirstiness. Among these ferocious Franks Columbanus preached and laboured. Expelled from his monastery by the peremptory orders of Queen Brunchault, whose sins he had fearlessly denounced, he dared to return; and when again cast forth, turned his steps towards Northern Italy, leaving to the Helvetians, among whom he tarried for some months, his disciple, the Irish St. Gall, whose name and fame still survive throughout the northern cantons of Switzerland.

St. Columbanus died at Bobbio in Italy, where he had established his confraternity under the protection of Agilulf, king of the Lombards. He has left behind him a great reputation as a letter-writer. His famous epistles to Pope Gregory the Great, and Pope Boniface the Fourth, are yet extant. So also are his tender addresses to his loved brethren at Luxeuil; "his dearest sons, his dearest pupils, to his brethren in abstinence, to all the monks." In a letter to the bishops of Gaul he thus speaks:—

"Finally, fathers, pray for us, as we also do, unworthy though we be, for you: and do not regard us in the light of aliens; for we are fellow members of one body, whether we be French, or Britons, or Irish, or whatever be our nation. Let us then, all nations, rejoice in the acknowledging of the faith, and confession of the Son of God; and hasten forward all of us, to advance to the perfect man, to the measure of the stature of the fulness of Jesus Christ, in whom may we love one another, speak well of one another, correct one another, visit one another, pray for one another, that with one another we may reign, and have joy in His presence."

Even the Danish inroads, of which we shall speak in our next chapter, failed wholly to quench, although they greatly diminished, the flame of learning in these cultured spots. A remarkable evidence of the continued reputation of Ireland for superior intellectual culture, even so late as the middle of the eleventh century, is afforded by a poem written by John, son of Sulgen, who was bishop of St. David's about A.D. 1070. In this piece John tells us that his father went to Ireland to study the Scriptures, and spent upwards of ten years in that employment. The Latin verses have been well rendered :—

> " With ardent love for learning, Sulgen sought
> The school in which his fathers had been taught;
> To Ireland's sacred isle he bent his way,
> Where science beamed with bright and glorious ray:
> But lo! an unforeseen impediment
> His journey interrupted as he went ;
> For, sailing toward the country where abode
> The people famous in the word of God,
> His bark by adverse winds and tempests toss'd,
> Was forced to anchor on another coast ;
> And thus the Albanian shore the traveller gained,
> And there for five successive years remained.
> * * *
> At length, arriving on the Scottish soil,
> He soon applies himself to studious toil.
> * * * *
> Then, having gained a literary fame,
> In high repute for learning, home he came,
> His gathered store and golden fruit to share
> Among admiring friends and followers there."

We have placed under the eyes of our reader the contemporaneous evidence of Bede—let us add the testimony of another learned and candid Englishman, derived from the wider range of inquiry afforded by the subsequently accumulated learning of nearly nine hundred years. We refer to the illustrious William Camden, whose words will carry the weight of historic truth, as well as the solemnity of a pious philosophy, to whatever mind will receive them.

" Our Anglo-Saxons of that day," he says, speaking of this, which we have ventured to call our Scholastic Period, " used to flock together to Ireland, as a market of learning; whence it is that we continually find it said in our writers concerning holy men of old, *He was sent away to be educated in Ireland*. . . And it would appear that it was from that country the ancient English, our ancestors, received the first instructions in forming letters, as it is plain they used the same character which is still used in Ireland. Nor need we wonder that Ireland, which is now (*i.e.* in A.D. 1607) for the most part wild, half-savage, and destitute of education, should at that time have abounded in men of such holiness, piety, and splendid geniuses, while the cultivation of literature elsewhere in the Christian world lay neglected and half buried; since the providence of the Almighty Ruler of the universe is pleased to scatter the seeds of holiness and virtues in the different ages of the world, now among these nations, now among those, as it were in so many beds and flower knots; thus producing blossoms which, as they appear in one place and another with fresh vigour, may thrive and be preserved, for His own glory and the benefit of mankind."

CHAPTER VIII.

THE DANISH PERIOD.

THE eighth century affords little beyond the series of successions of kings, to be recorded, until we reach A.D. 795. From thence extends a period of gloom, in which depression and disaster characterize the Irish annals. For upwards of two centuries, learning, piety, almost Christianity itself, succumbed before pagan invaders. Danes, Northmen, Scandinavians, whom the Irish writers distinguish according to their complexions, into Dubh-Galls, or dark, and Finn-Galls, or fair-haired foreigners, hovered round our coasts, in ships manned by hardy, but sanguinary pirates. The leaders—Vikings, as they are called—were brave and daring adventurers, glad to exchange their barren mountains for the plunder, and afterwards the colonization, of more fertile lands. These ruthless invaders spared neither age, nor sex, nor station. The monasteries were ever their first objects of attack. Here were deposited articles of chiefest value in the land; precious manuscripts, which were only prized by the plunderers for the rich decorations in gold and gems that graced the cases in which they were enclosed; shrines of exquisite workmanship, on which all that was costly and precious had been lavished, to fit them for receptacles of the relics of some venerated saint; illuminated manuscripts, to produce which had been the life-long labour of pious and saintly men, lovers of literature, and decorative artists of no mean skill:—all these were scattered to the winds by the ignorant and ruthless hands of these sea-robbers. The Danes did not confine their ravages to the coasts—they boldly ascended the rivers, and, secure in the protection of their ships, descended on the defenceless population when and where they would, and that so unexpectedly, that they encountered little or no organized resistance.

The fatal defect of the Irish political system was its want of centralization. The Ard-Righ, or supreme monarch, was but nominal ruler of the entire island, and could only act vigorously in his own patrimony. The provincial kings were virtually independent, and frequently in open collision with the central authority. The power of combination has ever been deficient among the Gael. Unrestricted individual freedom has been so much a passion with the race, that combined action has been rarely achieved, or sustained for any considerable length of time. At the period of which we speak, this difficulty was greatly augmented; for the vigorous rule of a succession of princes of the northern Hy-Niall line was, at this time, exchanged for the ascendency of the southern branch of this great family; and the comparatively limited patrimony of the southern Hy-Nialls rendered them less efficient general rulers. The neighbourhood of Mullingar, in Westmeath, was their place of abode. Malachy of the

Shannon, the first Ard-Righ of this line, in 845 succeeded King Niall, surnamed of Callan, who met his death while attempting to save the life of one of his followers, swept away by the current when entering a ford of the river Callan, in advance of the king's army. Niall had called in vain for aid for the drowning man; and seeing those around him hesitate, had sprung himself to the rescue of the *gilly*. As he spurred his horse for the plunge, the bank beneath him gave way, and rider and steed were precipitated into the river. That is no ignoble death which is encountered in an act of self-sacrifice for others, and the name of Niall *Caillé* lives, though his other actions are forgotten.

A romantic but somewhat apocryphal story is told of Malachy and his Danish neighbour Turgesius. This chieftain had established himself in the very heart of Ireland, and possessed a fleet on the inland waters of Lough Ree. The youthful daughter of Malachy attracted his regards: he demanded her from her father, who dared not refuse. The king proposed to Turgesius to send her to his court, accompanied by fifteen maids of honour, attendants of her own age and sex, befitting her rank and birth. Instead of these, however, he selected fifteen beardless youths, who carried weapons concealed beneath their feminine garb. The disarmed and unsuspecting Turgesius was seized; his fortress-gates thrown open to the troops of Malachy, who were prepared, on a given signal, to rush in and possess themselves of the fort. Turgesius himself was drowned in Lough Owel, and the land for a time once more breathed freely.

The dire pressure of Danish tyranny, enforced by the "Nose-gelt," was felt by each individual, however humble, as well as by the kings and chiefs of Ireland. A soldier was quartered " over every homestead, and the man of the house was not allowed the disposal of as much as one egg of his own property; and though a family owned but one stripper, they were not allowed on any night to give its milk to either infant or child, but were obliged to keep it up for the use of the soldier; and though the man of the house owned but one in-calf cow, he was forced to kill the same for the use of his unwelcome guest; and if he could not satisfy the latter therewithal, he was compelled to place his inheritance in pledge for the maintenance of the said soldier. Besides this, the Lochlannaigh should either get an ounce of gold each year for every man in Ireland, or they would have the nose from off his face. Then no lord or lady of the Irish was allowed to wear any mantles or garments, except the cast-off clothes of the Lochlannaigh. It was not allowed to give instruction in letters, nor to live in religious communities, for the Lochlannaigh dwelt in the temples and in the duns: no scholars, no clerics, no books, no holy relics, were left in church or monastery, through dread of them: neither bard, nor philosopher, nor musician, pursued their wonted professions in the land."

But a time was approaching when these fierce invaders, themselves succumbing to Christian influences, should become here and there permanent dwellers in the land, intermarry with the Irish, and even join with them in repelling marauding assaults of their own countrymen. To the Northmen we may trace the foundation of most of our seaport towns, Dublin, Waterford, Cork, Limerick, and others. The Finn Galls—for the Norse element predominated among them—showed a great aptitude for trade and commerce. Their fearlessness at sea, and skill in navigation, fitted them to become foreign merchants. They had a coinage of their own. Their nomenclature may be traced in the names of places, especially on the east coast of Ireland, where their settlements were most permanent. The Norwegian *fiord*, or arm of the sea, reminds us of their presence in the bays of Strang*ford*, Carling*ford*, Wex*ford*, Water*ford*, &c. Lambey, Ireland's *ey*, show the Scandinavian affix of *Ey*, for island. The names of three out of the four provinces of Ireland announce the Norse influence, which has changed the Celtic Uladh into Ul*ster*, Laighin into Leins*ter*, and Mumhain into Mun*ster*. They gave much of what we may term municipal life; they took in return the Christian faith, and, in a degree, its humanizing lessons and virtues, in lieu of their stern yet heroic paganism.

We have alluded to the frequent intermarriage between Irish and Dane. A singular example, illustrating the connection between Irish and Norwegian history, may be found even in the case of the great Brian Boru, with whose history we shall be occupied hereafter. He had married, when a widower, Gormley, daughter of the king of Leinster, who became the mother of his sons Tiege and Donogh. By her former husband, Anlaf the Dane, Gormley was the mother of Sitric "Silk-Beard" (afterwards the husband of Brian's daughter Save) and of Olaf Cuaran, Danish king of Dublin. The Norwegian king and saint, Olaf, was the guest of this Olaf Cuaran, and received baptism, most probably, in Ireland. There was an inherent sternness and cruelty in the Norse character, which indisposed it to the acceptance of the mild religion of Christ, on the one hand, and to the gentle modes of inculcating it which had proved so successful among the Celtic populations, on the other. No contrast can be imagined more remarkable than that between the conduct in accepting and propagating the faith, of the Irish and the Norsemen. Receiving the message of peace from his Irish instructors, the canonized Scandinavian king carried it into the *fiords* and *fells* of Norway, with fire and sword for his apostles. A great poet has majestically versified one of the *sagas* of Olaf, which presents the difference of character in question so vividly that we will crave our reader's indulgence for a moment's departure from Irish ground, while making better acquaintance with the fierce but noble race of men whose extirpation at Clontarf is so important an event in the Irish story.

> Loud the angry wind was wailing,
> As King Olaf's ships came sailing
> Northward out of Drontheim haven,
>   To the mouth of Salten Fiord:
>
> Though the flying sea-spray drenches
> Fore and aft the rowers' benches,
> Not a single heart is craven
>   Of the champions there on board.

All without the Fiord was quiet,
But within it storm and riot,
Such as on his Viking cruises
   Raud the strong was wont to ride;

And the sea through all its tideways,
Swept the reeling vessels sideways,
As the leaves are swept through sluices,
   When the flood-gates open wide.

" 'Tis the warlock! 'tis the demon
Raud!" cried Sigurd to the seamen;
"But the Lord is not affrighted
   By the witchcraft of his foes;"

To the ship's bow he ascended,
By his choristers attended;
Round him were the tapers lighted,
   And the sacred incense rose.

On the bow stood Bishop Sigurd,
In his robes, as one transfigured,
And the Crucifix he planted
   High amid the rain and mist;

Then with holy water sprinkled
All the ship; the mass-bells tinkled;
Loud the monks around him chanted,
   Loud he read the Evangelist.

As into the Fiord they darted,
On each side the water parted:
Down a path like silver molten,
   Steadily rowed King Olaf's ships;

Steadily burned all night the tapers,
And the White Christ through the vapours
Gleamed across the Fiord of Salten,
   As through John's Apocalypse.

Till at last they reached Raud's dwelling
On the little isle of Gelling:
Not a guard was at the doorway,
    Not a glimmer of light was seen;

But at anchor, carved and gilded,
Lay the dragon-ship he builded;
'Twas the grandest ship in Norway
    With its crests and scales of green.

Up the stairway, softly creeping
To the loft where Raud was sleeping,
With their fists they burst asunder
    Bolt and bar that held the door:

Drunken with sleep and ale they found him,
Dragged him from his bed and bound him,
While he stared with stupid wonder
    At the look and garb they wore.

Then King Olaf said: "O Sea King,
Little time have we for speaking,
Choose between the good and evil,
    Be baptized, or thou shalt die."

But in scorn the heathen scoffer
Answered: "I disdain thine offer;
Neither fear I God nor devil,
    Thee and thy gospel I defy!"

Then, between his jaws distended,
When his frantic struggles ended,
Through King Olaf's horn an adder,
    Touched by fire they forced to glide:

Sharp his tooth was as an arrow,
As he gnawed through bone and marrow;
But without a groan or shudder
    Raud the Strong, blaspheming, died.

> Then baptized they all that region,
> Swarthy Lap and fair Norwegian,
> Far as swims the salmon leaping,
> > Up the streams of Salten Fiord:
>
> In their temples Thor and Odin,
> Lay in dust and ashes trodden,
> As King Olaf onward sweeping,
> > Preached the gospel with his sword.
>
> Then he took the carved and gilded
> Dragon-ship that Raud had builded,
> And the tiller single-handed
> > Grasping, steered into the main:
>
> Southward sailed the sea-gulls o'er him,
> Southward sailed the ship that bore him,
> Till at Drontheim haven landed
> > Olaf and his crew again.*

Among the proofs which still attest the influence on the popular mind, produced by these inroads, and the deep-seated terror of the Danish name which they excited, we may mention the habit of the Irish peasantry of ascribing to this race the cairns, cashels, forts, and duns of a more primitive period. So far from being builders of these monuments, we have on record, both in the Irish chronicles and the Norse *Sagas*, that in the year 861 the three earls, Olaf, Sitric, and Ivar, opened, for purposes of plunder, the sepulchral mounds of New Grange, Dowth, and Knowth on the Boyne, and the mound of the wife of the Gobaun Saor, the mythic builder, or Wayland Smith of the Irish Celts, still a conspicuous object at Drogheda. But it may be that the Danes referred to in popular tradition are

* From the *Saga of King Olaf*, by H. W. LONGFELLOW.

those older *Tuath De Danaan* of the archaic period. To return to the Christian period: we have in Waterford, in very good preservation, an interesting specimen of the Norwegian art of fortification. The Round Tower, popularly called Reginald's Tower, is said to have been built in 1003, by the Scandinavian ruler of Waterford, Ragnvald. At the time of the Norman invasion of Ireland, Earl Strongbow possessed himself of it, and kept there as his prisoner the last "Eastman" king of Waterford, Reginald the Dane.

We must return to King Malachy, and speak here of his desire to make a pilgrimage to Rome. He sent an embassy to Charles the Bald, then reigning in France, requesting a safe-conduct through his territories, and acquainting him with his successes against the Northmen. A friendly intercourse appears to have been maintained between France and Ireland up to the time of the English Conquest.

Malachy died without having accomplished his pilgrimage. He was much regretted:—

"Mournfully is spread the veil of grief over Ireland since the chieftain of our race has perished," writes the chronicler; "Red wine has been spilled into the valley; Erin's monarch has died."

Aedh Finnliath—better known as Hugh of Aileach, son of Nial, of the Callan—succeeded Malachy as Ard-Righ. He prosecuted the war with the Danes with vigour. He gained a victory at Lough Foyle, which, with its savage incidents, is thus recorded:—

"After Aedh, king of Ireland, had learned that this gathering of strangers was on the borders of his country, he was not negligent in attending to them, for he marched towards them with all his forces, and a battle was fought fiercely and spiritedly on both sides between them. The victory was gained over the foreigners, and a slaughter was made of them. Their heads were collected to one place in presence of the king; and twelve score heads were reckoned before him, which was the number slain by him in that battle, besides the numbers of them who were wounded and carried off by him in the agonies of death, and who died of their wounds some time afterwards."

This king "of the long flowing hair," was a generous, wise, and staid man, if we are to credit the bard who uttered his funeral lamentation :—

"Long is the wintry night, with rough gusts of wind;
Under pressing grief we encounter it, since the red-speared
    king of the noble house liveth not.
Fearful it is to watch how the waves heave from the bottom;
To them may be compared all those who with us lament him."

Aedh had to wife Maelmuri, daughter of Kenneth MacAlpin, the first king of all Scotland. His Irish kinsmen had aided the Scotic monarch in his final contests with the Picts. This lady afterwards married Aedh's successor, Flann of the Shannon, the son of Malachy—thus restoring the throne to the branch of the Southern Hy-Niall.

Flann had a daughter, Gormley, whose gifts, beauty, and tragical fate, have made her name celebrated in Irish story. Many poems of this lady have survived to our day. She was betrothed, while still very young, to the celebrated Cormac MacCulinan, King of Cashel;

but when the period had arrived when he should claim his bride, he failed to appear, having resolved to lead a life of celibacy. Gormley, who is said to have been tenderly attached to Cormac, was married to the King of Leinster against her own inclinations, and for political motives, by her father Flann. Her hated husband treated her with contumely. Gormley appealed for redress to her cousin Niall " Black-Knee," afterwards king of Ireland, who espoused her cause, and, on the death of the King of Leinster, married Gormley. The most touching of her poems which survive express her maternal tenderness for her child, sent by his father Niall, according to the custom in Ireland, to be fostered. Gormley has recorded her grief at this separation from her son, and also her agonizing sorrow when the young prince was afterwards drowned in Lough Corrib. She long survived her husband Niall, whose death she also lamented in verse—

> " Where is the chief of the western world?
> Where the sun of every clash of arms?
> Sorrowful this day is sacred Ireland,
> Without its valiant chief."

This daughter, sister, and wife of kings, is said to have died of absolute want; having long survived the greatness of her kindred, and seen other dynasties arise—no longer near to her in blood and family ties—indifferent to, and careless of her woes. Her first sorrow—the disclaiming of her hand by Cormac MacCulinan—was one of the causes which led to the battle of Belach Mughna (Moone, near Ballytore, in the county of Kildare), in which her father, King Flann was opposed to the celebrated Cormac MacCulinan, king-archbishop of Cashel. To this Cormac is ascribed the erection of the beautiful Romanesque church yet standing on the Rock of Cashel. He was author of the compilation (*Cormac's Glossary*), which has made his name a household word with modern scholars. The lost *Psalter* of Cashel was also a work of Cormac. To understand aright the further circumstances which brought this great and good man into collision with his suzerain, we must revert to times long anterior to his age (the latter part of the ninth century), and remind our readers of the old compact which divided Erin between Con of the Hundred Battles, of the race of Eremon, and Owen Mor, the descendant of Eber, A. D. 125. The Esker Riada was the boundary—a range of low limestone ridges extending from Dublin to Galway.

Hitherto we have been more concerned with the northern district, Lea Con, or Con's half; as the race of Eremon gave a greater number of kings to Ireland, and filled a more prominent place in the page of history; but now we shall find the foremost historic names belonging rather to the Munster clans.

We must also bear in mind the will of Ollioll Olum, which assigned the sovereignty of Munster alternately to the descendants of his sons Owen and Cormac Cas. . . . The Eugenians—as the families derived from Owen are called—MacCarthys and others, ruled in Desmond, or South Munster; while the Dalcassians

R

—descendants of Cormac Cas—O'Briens, and others—were lords of Thomond, or North Munster.

But in process of time it happened that the Dalcassian family—whose possessions in Clare and Limerick were removed from Cashel, the capital of Lea Moha—found themselves passed by in the succession, which had more and more fallen into the hands of the Eugenian tribes. To the latter belonged Cormac MacCulinan, who, in 896, was called to the throne of Cashel.

The state of Munster during the reign of this " king, bishop, anchorite, and scribe profoundly learned in the Scotic tongue," is thus described in the annals :—

" Great was the prosperity of Ireland during his reign ; for the land became filled with the divine grace, and with worldly prosperity, and with public peace in his days, so that the cattle needed no cowherd, and the flocks no shepherd, as long as he was king. The shrines of the saints were then protected, and many temples and monasteries were built; public schools were established for the purpose of giving instruction in letters, law, and history ; many were the tilled fields, numerous were the bees, and plenteous the beehives under his rule ; frequent was fasting and prayer, and every other work of piety ; many houses of public hospitality were built, and many books written at his command. And, moreover, whenever he exacted the performance of any good work from others, he was wont to set them the example himself, by being the first to practise it, whether it were a deed of alms, or benevolence, or prayer."

Cormac had applied to his own tribe for " food and

treasures" wherewith to celebrate Easter, but was refused. The Dalcassians, on hearing of his need, voluntarily supplied his wants. He then applied to the Eugenians for "jewels and valuables for the purpose of making presents to strangers." Here again he found his own kin less liberal than his Thomond subjects. "Thus did Cormac feel again most grateful to that tribe, as he tells us himself in the following verse :—

> "May our truest fidelity ever be given
> To the brave and generous clansmen of Tal;
> And for ever may royalty rest with their tribe,
> And virtue, and valour, and music, and song."

Impelled by gratitude, and still more by a sense of justice, Cormac desired that his successor should be a prince of Thomond. His efforts were not crowned with success, and lessened the regards of his own tribe. His unpopularity with the Eugenians became apparent, when he summoned them to his standard to wage war with Leinster, and enforce a demand for chief rents from that principality.

He had reigned peacefully and prosperously for seven years, when he most reluctantly undertook this war at the instigation of his nobles, and especially of Flaherty, a man of royal blood, abbot of Inis-Cathaigh or Scattery Island, near the mouth of the Shannon. Haunted by presentiments of disaster, Cormac made his will before commencing the campaign.

> "'Tis time my testament were made,
> For danger's hour approacheth fast;
> My days shall henceforth be but few;
> My life has almost reached the goal.

My golden cup of sacrifice
Wherewith I holy offerings make,
I will to Senan's brotherhood
At Inis-Cathaigh's sacred fane.

The bell that calleth me to prayer,
Whilst on the green-robed earth I stay,
Forget not with my friend to leave
At Conall's shrine where Forgus flows.

My silken robe of graceful flow,
O'erlaid with gems and golden braid,
To Roscrè, Paul and Peter's fane,
And Cronan's guardianship, I leave.

My silver chessboard of bright sheen,
I will to Uladh's royal chief;
My well-wrought chain of faultless gold,
To thee, Mochuda, I bequeath.

Take thou my amice and my stole,
And take my manuple likewise,
To Lenin's son who lies at Cluain,
To Colman, who has found his bliss.

My *Psalter* of illumined leaves,
Whose light no darkness e'er can hide—
To Caisel I for ever leave
This potent gift without recall.

And my wealth I bequeath to the poor,
And my sins to the children of curses;
And my dust to the earth whence it rose,
And my spirit to Him who has sent it."

We give the details of this disastrous campaign, which resulted in the death of Cormac MacCulinan, in the quaint language of the historian Keating:—

"After this, Cormac, having mustered a large host,

and armed himself, and armed Flathbertach (Flaherty), son of Inmanen, marched into the territory of the Leinstermen, and demanded of them to give him hostages, and to pay him tribute as king of Munster, upon the grounds that their country (Leinster) formed part of Lea Moha. Now when the host of Munster had come together, and was all collected into one camp, previous to marching upon the intended expedition, it happened that Flathbertach, son of Inmanen, the abbot of Inis-Cathaigh, having mounted upon horseback, rode through the street of the encampment, and that whilst he was thus engaged, his horse fell beneath him into a deep trench. This was esteemed an unlucky omen, and its consequence was that a large portion both of his own people and of the whole army retired from the expedition, having first proposed the adoption of peaceful measures—so unfavourable a prognostic did they deem the sudden fall of the holy abbot when he had mounted his steed.

"Then ambassadors arrived from the Leinstermen, and from Kerball, son of Murighen, charged with proposals of peace to King Cormac. These proposals were: first, to have one universal peace maintained throughout Ireland until the following month of May, for it was then the fortnight of the harvest; and for that end to place hostages in the hands of Macnach son of Siadal, abbot of Disert Diarmada, who was a holy, pious, learned, and wise man; and, next, to give a large quantity of jewels and valuables to Cormac himself, and also to Flathbertach, son of Inmanen, as a recompense for having assented to such a peace.

Cormac was most willing to grant their request; whereupon he immediately proceeded to acquaint Flathbertach that these ambassadors had come to him from the king of Leinster, demanding peace until the ensuing month of May, and offering jewels and valuables to them both, from the people of Leinster, provided they would return home in peace to their own country. But when Flathbertach had heard him out, he fell into a violent rage, and he exclaimed, 'How easily seen is the weakness of thy mind, and the littleness of thy intellect and thy spirit!' And after this fashion he then addressed much of abusive and contemptuous language to Cormac. The latter replied to him in the following words: 'I know full well what will be the result of all this, to wit, a battle will be fought with the men of Leinster, in which I shall be slain, and in which it is probable that thou shalt meet thy death likewise.'

"Having uttered these words, Cormac proceeded, sad and dejected, to his own tent. When he had taken his seat therein, a basket of apples was set before him, which he began to share amongst his attendants, saying, 'My dear friends, I shall never more share any apples amongst you, from this hour forth.'—'Dear lord,' said his people, 'thou hast cast us into sadness and grief. Why art thou thus wont to prophesy evil for thyself?'—'Believe what I now say, friends of my heart,' said Cormac, 'for though I am wont to distribute apples amongst you with my own hands, it will be little wonder if some one else in my stead should share them amongst you henceforward.'

"The war proceeded, and a battle was imminent.

The army of Munster was drawn up in three divisions, under the command of Flaherty, assisted by Kellach, son of the prince of Ossory; Cormac himself; and Cormac son of the prince of the Desi. The warriors were disheartened by reason of the multitude of their enemies, and of the fewness of their own host, for some authors assert that the army of Leinster was four times more numerous than that of Munster.

"Woful, indeed, was the tumult and clamour of that battle; for there rose the death-cry of the men of Munster as they fell, and the shouting of the Leinstermen exulting in the slaughter of their foes. There were two reasons why the fight went so suddenly against the Munstermen. The first was because Keilichar, a relative of Kennghegan, a former king of Munster, jumped hastily upon his steed, and as soon as he found himself mounted, cried out, 'Flee, O free clans of Munster, flee from this terrible conflict, and let the ecclesiastics fight it out themselves, since they would accept no other condition but that of battle from the people of Leinster!' Having thus spoken, he quitted the field of strife, followed by many of the combatants. The other reason why the men of Leinster were routed was because Kellach, son of Kerball, king of Ossory, when he perceived the carnage that was made amongst his people, jumped likewise with haste upon his steed, and thence addressed his host in these words :—'Mount your steeds,' said he, 'and banish these men who stand up against you.' But though he used this language he did not mean to encourage them to drive off their enemies by fighting, but he thus let them know that it was time for themselves to run away. The result of these two causes was that the ranks of the men of Munster were broken, and they were put to sudden and general rout. Alas! great indeed was the carnage that then spread over Magh-n-Ailbi. Neither layman nor ecclesiastic found quarter therein, both were slaughtered indiscriminately; and if any man of either class happened to be spared, he owed his life not to the mercy but to the cupidity of the vanquishers, covetous of his ransom.

"Hereupon Cormac proceeded toward the van of the first division, but his horse fell beneath into a ditch, and he was himself dashed upon the ground. Some of his people, who were running away from the battle, saw him in this position, and they came at once to his relief, and replaced him upon his steed. It was then that Cormac met one of his own pupils, a free-born man, named Aedh, who was distinguished for his proficiency in wisdom, laws, and history, and in the knowledge of the Latin tongue. To him the royal prelate addressed these words:—'Dear son, do not follow me; but betake thyself hence, as well thou mayest, and remember that I had said that I should myself be slain in this battle.'

"Cormac then rode forward, and full of the blood of horses and of men was the way before him; but the slipperiness of that field of carnage soon caused the feet of his horse to glide from under him, and he reared and fell backwards, crushing his rider beneath him. The neck and back of Cormac were broken in that fall, and he died, saying, 'Into thy hands, O Lord, I commit my spirit!'" Then some wicked persons came up and pierced his body with their javelins, and cut off his head."

It is creditable to Flann that, far from insulting his fallen enemy, he honoured the mortal remains of Cormac of Cashel. He took the severed head in his hands and kissed it, severely censuring those who had mutilated the corpse of the prince-bishop. "What heart would not feel saddened at that deed?" writes the old chronicler; "to wit, the death and mutilation of so sacred a personage, who was the wisest of the men of Ireland in his own day; a learned scholar in the Gaelic and Latin languages; an archbishop who was filled with devotion, and sincerity, and prayer, and chastity, and godliness; the head of doctrine and true philosophy, and good morals, and the chief king of the two pentarchates of Munster?"

Flaherty, the warlike ecclesiastic who had been the chief instigator of this campaign, retired to his cell on Scattery Island, and passed some time in penance and retirement; till summoned himself to fill the throne of Cashel, which he afterwards resigned to Lorcan.

King Flann, after a long and, on the whole, a prosperous reign, died A.D. 916. This "pleasant and hospitable" prince rebuilt the cathedral church at Clonmacnoise, one of the chief stone-built edifices of its kind in Ireland at that period.

Amongst the successors of Cormac on the throne of Munster was the provincial king Callaghan, whose chequered fortunes will now have our notice. It is said that he owed the sovereignty of Munster to the influence of his mother, who appealed to the justice of Kennedy, son of Lorcan, reminding him of the law of Ollioll Olum, which gave alternate rule to the tribes of Owen and Cormac Cas. Kennedy resigned his claims, which, at a later period, centered in his son, the great king of Munster, Brian Boru.

Callaghan waged successful war with the Danes. Their chief, Sitric, sought to repair his losses by stratagem. Tradition tells us that for this purpose he made overtures of peace to Callaghan, offering him the hand of his sister in marriage. The king of Cashel acceded to the proposal, having heard much of the beauty of Bebinn, as the lady was called; and set forth for Dublin, escorted only by a small body of horsemen, to celebrate the marriage.

The wife of Sitric inquired of her husband why he proposed this marriage between his sister and his enemy. The treacherous Sitric told her that his design was to secure the person of the king of Cashel. The lady had cherished in secret an attachment for Callaghan, and, alarmed for his safety, she privately set out to meet him, and warn him of the snare laid by her husband. But the warning came too late. When Callaghan endeavoured to retrace his steps he found himself surrounded by foes, placed in ambush along the path he had to traverse, and was led into captivity.

Kennedy, son of Lorcan, mustered the clans of Munster, and marched to the rescue of the prince. The troops were supported by a fleet, under the command of Falvy Finn, a Kerry chieftain. Callaghan had been removed from Dublin to Armagh, and thence, when the Munster forces appeared before Armagh, was sent to Dundalk. The Danes placed their prisoner on board ship for security, not anticipating the arrival of an Irish fleet. Falvy Finn appeared in the Bay of Dundalk, boarded the Danish ship, freed Callaghan, who was tied to the mast, but sank himself covered with wounds. His brave followers, inspired by his example, and conscious that they should eventually be outnumbered by the Danes, closed with Sitric and his brothers Tor and Magnus. Each grappled with a foe, and sprang with his enemy into the sea. Such was the first liberation of Callaghan of Cashel.

Callaghan found himself a second time a prisoner, as hostage to Murkertagh, prince of Aileach, under circumstances which we must now narrate. King Flann, in the latter years of his life, had to contend with rebellion in his own family. His sons had been undutiful, but were compelled to submission by Niall "Black-knee," the husband of his daughter Gormley. Niall succeeded Flann as Ard-Righ, and died, as we have already seen, in battle with the Danes, being himself succeeded, according to the usual course, by Donogh, son of Flann—while his own vigorous son, Murkertagh, filled the position of Roydamna, or heir-apparent.

Murkertagh, surnamed "Pell-Cloak," or of the Leathern Cloaks, in A.D. 941 assembled the northern clans, and, with a thousand selected troops, commenced a circuit of Ireland, from Aileach, accompanied by his bard, whose narrative of the expedition is yet extant. Commencing his journey in winter, he provided his troops with cloaks of leather—whence his name—as a protection from the inclemency of that season. He " kept his left hand to the sea " till he arrived at Dublin. Thence he led as a hostage Sitric, a Danish lord, and carried off Lorcan, king of Leinster, also. He next proceeded to Cashel, where Callaghan was surrendered to him, not without his own consent, if we interpret aright the lay of Cormacan Eigeas—

We were * * a night at Cashel of Munster ;
There the great injury was inflicted on the men of Munster :
There were arrayed against us three battalions brave,
    Impetuous, red, terrible,
So that each party confronted the other,
In the centre of the great plain.
    We cast our cloaks off us,
As became the subjects of a good king ;
The comely, the bright Muircheartach was at this time
Engaged in playing his chess.
The hardy Callaghan said,—
(And to us it was victory) :—
" O men of Munster ! men of renown !
    Oppose not the race of Eoghan.
Better that I go with them as an hostage
Than that we should all be driven to battle ;
    They will kill man for man,
The noble people of Muircheartach."
We took with us, therefore, Callaghan the just,
Who received his due honour,
Namely, a ring of fifteen ounces on his hand,
And a chain of iron on his stout leg.

This was harsh treatment for Callaghan, for he was the only hostage who was bound in fetters. Conor, son of the king of Connaught, was also taken to

Aileach, and here Murkertagh and his hostages feasted for five months. He then committed them to the custody of the Ard-Righ. Two years later he fell in battle against the Danes. His son, Donall O'Neill, became Ard-Righ in 954, and was among the first in Ireland to assume a surname. The prefix Mac implies "son of;" O, "descendant of." King Donall assumed the name of his grandfather Niall, father of Murkertagh, and from him, in direct descent, were the lords of Tir Owen, closing with Hugh, Earl of Tyrone, who died in Rome, A.D. 1616, and also the younger branch of O'Neills of Clanaboy.

The Danes, during this period of their domination, were almost universally Pagans, and delighted in exhibiting their contempt for the sacred things of the Christian religion. Thus, it is recorded of Auda, wife of Turgesius, that she made the high altar at Clonmacnoise her seat of state for receiving her courtiers. It is surmised, with some show of probability, that Turgesius is the Regner Lodbrog of Norse tradition; and the profaner of Clonmacnoise, that Aslauga to whom he addressed one of the stanzas of his Death-song, when about to be cast into the lake which, in the Scandinavian legend, is supposed to be full of serpents:—

> "We have fought with our swords—hurrah!
> How our sons would all be storming,
> Aslauga! how they'd roar to-day,
> Could they see their sire's deforming!
> For, through and through, the serpent blue
> Must gnaw me here, 'mong strangers;—
> But I've given my sons a mother, who
> Will rear me meet avengers."

The museums of Denmark are now full of objects of rich and characteristic Celtic workmanship, drawn from the sepulchral tumuli of Jutland and Holstein, many of which were, no doubt, carried off from the shores of Ireland during this period.

CHAPTER IX.

THE DALCASSIAN PERIOD.

MALACHY II., who ascended the throne in 980, in the commencement of his reign exhibited vigour and ability. He defeated the Danes at Tara, and again at Dublin. The attack on the city lasted for three days, and the siege of the castle for twenty days, "so that they (the Danes) drank no water during that time but the brine." He carried thence two thousand hostages, jewels, and other valuables, and freed the country from tribute and taxation from the Shannon to the sea. His proclamation was as follows:—"Every one of the Gaeidhil (Gael) who is in the territory of the foreigners, in servitude and bondage, let him go to his own territory in peace and happiness." It was in these contests that Malachy carried off "the collar of gold, which he won from the proud invader."

Unhappily all the wars of this king were not waged with the foreign foe. A powerful rival to Malachy had appeared in the person of Brian Boru, son of Kennedy, son of Lorcan, of the Dalcassian tribe, now rising to great power and importance in Munster. Malachy, alarmed and jealous of the Dal-

Gais,* ravaged Clare, and uprooted the "great tree of Magh Adair," under which the kings of Thomond had been inaugurated from time immemorial. This outrage did not pass unavenged.

A long succession of able and vigorous princes, descended from King Niall of the Nine Hostages, had secured for this northern clan the sovereignty of Ireland. They had eclipsed the fame of the Munster families descended from Ollioll Olum. The will of this great ruler of Lea Moha—as the southern half of the island was called—had vested the succession alternately in the descendants of his sons, Owen and Cormac Cas. At the period at which we have arrived the Dalcassian tribe, representatives of Cormac Cas, were emerging from comparative obscurity, under the leadership of the sons of Kennedy, Mahon and Brian, princes of vigour and genius.

"There were then governing and ruling that tribe," writes the contemporary chronicler, "two stout, able, valiant pillars—two fierce, lacerating, magnificent heroes—two gates of battle, two poles of combat, two spreading trees of shelter, two spears of victory and readiness of hospitality and munificence of heart, and strength of friendship and liveliness, the most eminent of the west of Europe, viz., Mathgamhain (Mahon), and Brian, the two sons of Cennidigh, son of Lorcan," &c., &c.

These chieftains, like Alfred of England—with whose story theirs has many points of resemblance—were trained in the school of adversity. The Danes

* Dal-g'Cais, that is, the Tribe of Cas.

had firmly riveted their chains on Munster. Limerick and Waterford were strongholds of the hated foreigner. As in England in the time of Alfred, it seemed hopeless to attempt to dislodge the Northmen, "because of the greatness of their achievements, and of their deeds, their bravery, and their valour, their strength, and their venom, and their ferocity; and because of the excess of their thirst and their hunger for the brave, fruitful, nobly-inhabited, cataract-abounding, rivery, bayey, pure, smooth-plained, sweet-grassy land of Erinn."

But it was not "honourable to the mind, or to the courage, or to the nature," of the tribe of the Dal Gais, "those animated, high-minded ones, who never brooked injustice or tyranny from any king of the kings of Erinn; and not only that, but who never gave them pledges or hostages in token of obedience;—to submit of their own accord to cruel slavery from Danars, and from fierce, hard-hearted pirates." Accordingly the Dalcassians, from the fastnesses and forests into which they were driven, ceased not to carry on a guerilla warfare. But the strength of the Northmen became so overpowering, that most of the Munster princes—Mahon among the number—submitted to the Danish domination.

It was not so with Brian. "He was not willing to make peace with the foreigners, because, however small the injury he might be able to do to the foreigners, he preferred it to peace. . . . It is not easy to enumerate or tell all that Brian killed of the foreigners of that garrison in twos, and in threes, and in fives, and in scores, and in hundreds; or the number of conflicts and combats that he frequently and constantly gave them. Great, on the other hand, were the hardship and the ruin, the bad food and bad bedding which they inflicted on him in the wild huts of the desert, on the hard knotty wet roots of his own native country; whilst they killed his people and his trusty officers and his comrades—sorrowful, dispirited, wretched, unpitied, weary. For historians say that the foreigners cut off his people, so that he had at last no more than fifteen followers."

His brother, Mahon, became alarmed for Brian's safety. He visited him secretly, and mourned with Brian over the loss of their brave clansmen. Brian, on his side, tenderly reproached Mahon for his submission to the Danes, a subjection which their father, Kennedy, or their grandfather, Lorcan, would never have brooked. The chronicler, who is supposed, with seeming probability, to have been MacLiag, the bard of Brian, thus describes the conference between the brothers, and the decision of the whole clan, on the momentous question submitted to them—of peace or war with the powerful foe.

Mahon said that " he had not the power to meet the foreigners, because of the greatness of their followers, and the number of their army, and the greatness of their champions, and the excellence of their corslets, and of their swords, and their other arms in general. And he said, also, that he would not like to leave the Dal Gais dead in following him, as he (Brian) had left the most of his people."

"Brian said that that was not a right thing for him (Mahon) to say, because it was hereditary for him to die, and hereditary for all the Dal Gais; for their fathers and grandfathers had died, and death was certain to come upon themselves; but it was not natural or hereditary to them to submit to insult or contempt, because their fathers or their grandfathers submitted not to it from any one on earth. He said, also, that it was no honour to their courage to abandon, without battle or conflict, to dark foreigners, and black grim Gentiles, the inheritance which their fathers and grandfathers had defended in battle and conflicts against the chiefs of the Gaedhil" (Gael).

"After this, all the Dal Gais were convened to one appointed place before Mathgamhain (Mahon); and he asked them what decision they wished to come to, namely, whether they would have peace or war with the foreigners, and with the Danars. Then they all answered, both old and young, that they preferred meeting violent death and destruction and annihilation, in defending the freedom of their patrimony, and of their race, rather than submit to the tyranny and oppression of the pirates, or abandon their country and their lands to them. And this was the voice of hundreds, as the voice of one man."

But before they resumed hostilities, their chief proposed to the Dal Gais to return from their then seats in Clare and Limerick, in which they appear to have been, themselves, invaders, to Cashel, the headquarters of their race. He said, "that it was better and more righteous to do battle and combat for their inheritance, and for their native right, than for land acquired by conquest and the sword."

The Danes of Limerick mustered their forces, with a contingent of the subject Irish of Munster. Their king, Ivar, "whose spite was little short of death to him," determined to extirpate the clansmen of Mahon and Brian, and so to ravage and depopulate the Dal Gais "that there should not be left of them a man to guide a horse's head over a channel, an abbot, or venerable person, who should not be murdered and put to death, or brought under tribute and subjection to the foreigners like all others."

The warriors of the Dal Gais and the troops of Ivar met at Sulcoit, near the present town of Tipperary, A.D. 968. It was a decisive battle; "bloody, crimsoned, violent, rough, unsparing, implacable." It lasted from sunrise till mid-day, and resulted in the utter defeat of the Danes. The foreigners "were at length routed, and they fled to the ditches, and to the valleys, and to the solitudes of that great sweet-flowery plain."

Limerick fell into the hands of the victors. Mahon divided the spoil among his clansmen, "according to persons and rights, according to accomplishments and fair performances, according to bravery and valour."

We obtain an insight into the wealth and trade of the Danes of Ireland from the enumeration of the spoils of Limerick. "They carried off their jewels and their best property, and their saddles beautiful and foreign; their gold and their silver; their beautifully-woven cloth of all colours and of all kinds; their satins and silken cloth, pleasing and variegated, both scarlet and green, and all sorts of cloth in like manner. They carried away their soft, youthful, bright, matchless girls, their blooming silk-clad young women, and their active, large, and well-formed boys."

A Gaelic song of triumph, a pæan for Mahon, thus concludes :—

> "Luimnech (Limerick) was totally ravaged by thee:
> Thou didst carry away their gold and their silver;
> Thou didst plunder their fort at that time;
> Thou didst surround it with a wall of fire.
>
> For Mumhain (Munster) hast thou well contended,
> O Mathgamhain! thou great chief!
> Thou hast given, O king, a stern defeat,
> To banish the foreigners from Erinn.
>
> King of Mumhain methinks thou art,
> High king of Caisel (Cashel) renowned :—
> Bestow gold on those who merit,
> They are many, O Mathgamhain!"

Mahon did not long survive the victory of Sulcoit. He was treacherously murdered by Donovan and Mulloy, sons of the rulers of South Munster, instigated by the Danish king of Limerick. Jealousy of the growing power of Thomond was the actuating motive with these scions of the Eugenian line. Their mode of carrying their treachery into effect was base in the extreme. Donovan invited Mahon to a banquet, and finding that the chieftain of the Dal Gais hesitated to comply, obtained for him a guarantee of safety from the bishop of Cork and others of the Munster clergy. Thus assured, Mahon accepted his invitation. His person was seized and delivered up to a body of troops who lay in wait.

"Mulloy had ordered his people, when they should get Mahon into their hands, to despatch him at once; and this order was obeyed. A bright and sharp sword was plunged into his heart, and his blood stained St. Barry's Gospel, which he held to his breast to protect himself by its sanctity. When, however, he perceived the naked sword extended to strike him, he cast the gospel in the direction of the clergy, who were on an adjacent hillock, and it struck the breast of one of the priests of Cork; and those who were looking on assert that he sent it the distance of a bow-shot from the one hillock to the other."

When Mulloy, who was within sight of this tragic scene, observed the flashing of the sword raised to strike the victim, he understood that the bloody deed was done, and mounted his horse to depart. One of the clergy who knew Mulloy, asked him what was to be done. Mulloy replied, with sardonic sneer, "cure that man if he come to thee," and then took his departure. The priest became wroth, and, cursing him bitterly, predicted that he would come to an evil end. "Mulloy MacBran was the chief instigator of this deed; but it were better for him he had not accomplished it, for it afterwards caused him bitter woe and affliction." When the news of it reached Brian and the Dal Gais they were overwhelmed with grief; and Brian vented his grief and rage in an extemporaneous effusion, which the chronicler gives in the form of a poem, lamenting that his brother had not fallen in battle behind the shelter of his shield before he had relied on the treacherous word of Donovan. He concludes thus:—

> "My heart will burst within my breast
> Unless I avenge this great king;
> They shall forfeit life for this foul deed,
> Or I shall perish by a violent death."

Brian accomplished his revenge. He attacked the Danes of Limerick, and slew their king, Ivar, who had plotted against his brother; and put Ivar's sons also to the sword. He then turned his victorious arms with like success against Donovan. Mulloy had previously fallen by the hand of Murrogh, eldest son of Brian, in conflict at the ford of Bealach-Leachta. The young prince desired to avenge with his own hand his uncle Mahon's murder. Brian Boru was now undisputed king of Munster, and fixed his royal seat at Kincora, not far from the falls of the Shannon at Killaloe.

Brian's personal rivalry with Malachy did not prevent his joining the Ard-Righ with his forces in a campaign against the Danes. The Northmen were defeated at Glen Mama, near Dunlavin, in the county of Wicklow. Afterwards, Malachy and Brian entered Dublin in triumph, spent a week in the Danish capital, burned the fortress, expelled Sitric, and carried off immense spoil, in gold, silver, and prisoners.

This cordial co-operation with Malachy was not of long continuance. The monarch was gallant, hospitable, and joyous in temperament; a fearless rider, delighting in a mettlesome, unbroken steed; open-handed in his generosity, but lacking the statesman-like qualities which distinguished Brian. This clear-sighted, resolute man had, by the glory of his achievements and the policy of his alliances, undermined the authority of King Malachy. Brian had married, in succession, daughters of the powerful Connaught clans of O'Heyne and O'Connor, and thirdly Gormley, sister of Maelmurra, king of Leinster, who had been previously the wife of Olaf Cuaran, Danish king of Dublin, and was afterwards wife of Malachy II. He had a numerous family, for whom he made alliances which extended his influence. The daughter of Earl Godwin of Kent became the wife of one of his sons. His own daughters were married, one to Sitric "Silk-Beard," son of Gormley by her former husband, Danish king of Dublin, and another to a Scottish prince. His oldest son, Murrogh, was a distinguished man, and father to a promising boy; and five younger scions gave stability to this branch of the Dalcassian line.

Brian, deeming himself now strong enough to aspire to the monarchy, soon after the battle of Glen Mama, marched on Tara, at the head of the Munster clans, and challenged Malachy to open battle, or to give hostages in acknowledgment of Brian's supremacy. Malachy, unprepared for resistance, asked a respite of a month, that he might summon the provincial chieftains to his aid, promising at the end of that time either to stake his sovereignty on the event of battle, or to resign it into the hands of Brian. He stipulated that in the interval Brian should not devastate Meath. The Munster king agreed to these terms.

Malachy, who was himself a prince of the South Hy-Niall line, sent envoys to the Northern Hy-Niall princes, and to the chieftains of Uladh and of Connaught, summoning them to his aid, to fight against Brian. From Aedh O'Neill he received a reply which indicated how little he had to expect at the hands of these princes. "Whenever," said he, "Tara happened to be possessed by the Kinel Owen, they were themselves wont to defend its rights, and sought no other aid: therefore let him who holds it now stand up himself and fight for its freedom as best he may."

Malachy tried, with no better result, the effect of a personal interview with the proud chief of Aileach. Having besought Aedh in vain, he tempted him by the offer of the sovereignty for himself.

"If thou wilt not fight in defence of Tara for my sake," said Malachy, "defend it for thine own, and I shall give thee hostages, as sureties for my leaving thee in the quiet possession thereof; for I prefer that thou shouldst hold it, rather than Brian." This was a much more attractive proposition to the selfish Aedh O'Neill. He summoned his clan, and consulted them on the offers made to him by Malachy. But they were not willing to encounter the veterans of Brian. "It was their opinion that it was likely that very many of them would never return from the war, in case they should now march against the Dal Gais. For which reason they declared that it was meet that they should first acquire an inheritance for their children after them. 'Because,' said they, ' it is idle to expect that any possessions or any wealth will ever come to them from our return to our homes, if we once march against that tribe, namely, the Dal Gais, whose warriors are the hardiest and the bravest upon all battle-fields. Their race has never yet fled before the Lochlannaigh; and it is as certain that it will not now flee before us.' Upon these grounds they came to the determination of demanding from Malachy the one-half of Meath, together with the district around Tara, for a possession for themselves and their posterity after them, as the reward of their going with him upon the present expedition." This resolve was made known to the monarch, who was seized with great anger, and forthwith returned home exceedingly indignant and dissatisfied at the result of his visit.

We are not surprised that the indignant and disgusted Ard-Righ should reject the services of allies who coolly demanded the better part of his patrimony of Meath as the price of their assistance. Better was the open enmity of Brian than *such* friendly aid.

Malachy took his resolution. Attended by two hundred and forty horsemen only, he rode to Tara, and without condition, surety, or hostage for his personal safety, entered the presence of Brian. He openly told him of his perplexity and dilemma; announced that he would have done battle for his crown if he could, but that, not being in a position to fight, he had come to submit himself to his rival.

Brian was not to be outdone in generous confidence. "As thou hast come thus to my dwelling," he said to Malachy, "without surety or safeguard from me, I now grant thee a further respite of one year, during which time I shall demand neither homage nor hostages at thy hands. And in the meantime I shall pay a personal visit to these northern people, both Aedh O'Neill and Eochy, son of Ardgal, king of Ulidia, in order that I may learn what kind of answer they will make to me. And then, should they give me battle, thou mayest help them against me if thou wilt."

The year elapsed; Brian collected his forces; demanded hostages from the provincial kings, and from Malachy himself: they were given: the deposed monarch acknowledged his rival as his sovereign, and Brian Boru became king of all Ireland, A. D. 1002.

He was an able administrator. Roads, bridges, and other works of public utility,—schools, churches, monasteries, sprang up under his fostering care. He loved learning, and encouraged it in others. He sent "professors and masters to teach wisdom and knowledge; and to buy books beyond the sea." He compelled the submission of the Ulster chieftains, and carried some of them as hostages to Kincora. He visited Armagh, and offered, on the altar of its church, twenty ounces of gold. His name, inscribed in his presence, may yet be read in its venerable manuscript, the *Book of Armagh*. He made his temporary encampment, while in that neighbourhood, on the rath of Emania. Of the tributes he collected a third part was allotted to "the professors of sciences and arts, and to every one who was most in need of it." His hospitalities at Kincora were unbounded. The tributes of the provinces, which supported these entertainments, consisted annually of 800 cows and 800 hogs, from

Connaught; 300 cows, 300 hogs, and 300 loads of iron, and certain duty-timber, from Leinster; from Ulster, 500 cows, 500 hogs, and 60 loads of iron; while the Danes of Dublin contributed 154 pipes of wine, and the Danes of Limerick 365 pipes of red wine. The southern clans were exempted from all tribute. All his subjects were freed from the galling yoke of slavery; and the laws were so well administered that the lady " rich and rare " in gems and beauty did not fear to stray, secure that, though "lone and lovely," she might pass through the length and the breadth of the land unharmed and unmolested. From the time of Brian Boru we may date the common use of surnames. The sept of O'Brien, who are descended from this great king, have many distinguished representatives at the present day.

It was not to be expected that the Northmen, whose sway in Ireland had been so greatly curtailed by Brian, should acquiesce without a struggle in this loss of prestige. Their race had at this period achieved great successes in England, France, and the islands of Man, the Hebrides, and Orkneys. A Danish dynasty was impending in England. The followers of Rollo were firmly settled in Normandy; the Lord of the Isles was a powerful ruler. The spark which kindled the flames of war among this combustible material came, we grieve to say, from an Irish hand. Maelmurra, king of Leinster, had received a fancied insult at Kincora, at the hands of Murrogh, son of Brian, who was playing chess. Maelmurra counselled a move, which nettled the prince, who remarked that it was no wonder that the Danes had been beaten at Glen Mama, since they followed the advice of so bad a strategist. "If I did give them counsel which caused their defeat in that conflict," said Maelmurra, "I shall now give them another counsel, whereby, in their turn, they shall defeat you."—"Have the yew tree made ready, then, for yourself," rejoined Murrogh, in taunting allusion to Maelmurra's place of concealment, out of which he had himself plucked the king of Leinster after the rout consequent on that battle. Maelmurra's sister Gormley had also previously reproached him for being Brian's vassal, when he sought her aid in replacing a silver button on a gold broidered silken tunic which Brian had given him. The Leinster prince in conveying three pine-masts to Kincora, had, on the ascent of a boggy mountain, given his personal assistance in moving the timber, and in so doing had wrenched the button from his tunic. Gormley, instead of repairing it, threw the garment into the fire, uttering, as she did so, expressions of disdain at the subserviency of Maelmurra. Stung by these accumulated insults, Maelmurra hastily left Kincora, proclaiming his determination to seek redress in arms. Thus the reproaches of a woman, and the thoughtless pleasantry of a chess-player, kindled the flame of war throughout Ireland. The Leinster chieftain, who had all his life intrigued with the foreigner, recommenced his machinations, and, in obedience to his invitation, a host of northern foes assembled in the Bay of Dublin, to contend for the soil of Erin on the battle-field of Clontarf. Earl Sigurd of the Orkneys, with a formidable fleet, Carl

Canuteson, prince of Denmark, with an array of chosen warriors clad in armour; Brodar, a redoubted champion, with levies from the Isle of Man; contingents from Scandinavia—all leagued with the treacherous Maelmurra in this last and most terrible struggle of Northman and Gael, of Pagan and Christian, on Irish soil.

Brian, now an aged man, once more assembled the Dal Gais, and marched on Dublin. The main army rested on the wood, which at that time clothed the bank of the little River Tolka where it empties its waters into Dublin Bay. A detachment had been sent off under command of his son Donogh, to ravage Leinster. With wonderful fidelity, the deposed King Malachy had joined Brian, with the forces of Meath; Teige O'Kelly, chief of Hy Many, was also present with the Connaught contingent; while the Munster troops, which formed the flower of his army, were under the command of his eldest son, the heroic Murrogh. The arrival of the Hy-Manians was a welcome spectacle.

"Brian looked out behind him, and beheld the battle phalanx, compact, huge, disciplined, moving in silence, mutely, bravely, haughtily, unitedly, with one mind, traversing the plain towards them, and threescore and ten banners over them, of red, and of yellow, and of green, and of all kinds of colours." It was a proud moment. Great issues hung in the balance. It was sure to be a conflict to the death, for the foes were "valiant, active, fierce-moving, dangerous," and were armed with "heavy, hard-striking, strong, powerful, stout swords."

The northern reach of the Bay of Dublin, from the estuary of the Tolka, where at that time stood the Fishing-weir of Clontarf, extending towards the Hill of Howth, washes the crescent-shaped sands which formed one boundary of the battle-field. It is a gently-sloping plain. On the landward side came the army of Brian in three divisions.

On the shore were drawn up the Danish army, protected by their ships. They also were in three divisions.

Good Friday, the 23rd of April, 1014, was the eventful day. Brian would gladly have postponed the conflict, unwilling to make that solemn anniversary a day of carnage and strife. But the Danes, inspired by a prediction that on any other day but Friday they would all assuredly perish—influenced also by the fact that the king's son Donogh was absent with a large detachment of the Irish army, determined to force on the engagement. The Danish and Leinster forces mustered about 20,000 men. The Irish army under Brian is also estimated at 20,000. The first division of the foreigners consisted of the Danes of Dublin, under Sitric and Dolat and Conmael, with a band of foreign auxiliaries commanded by Carl and Anrud. Of these Northmen one thousand were in complete suits of armour. These were opposed to the first division of the Irish army, consisting of the Dalcassian troops under the command of Murrogh, eldest son of Brian. Turlogh, the young son of Murrogh, though only in his fifteenth year, fought bravely, and died in battle, as became one of his heroic race; and Teige, Donall, Conor, and Flan, other sons of

Brian, followed the standard of Murrogh. In this first division, also, were the troops of Meath commanded by Malachy. The discrowned king rallied his forces to the banner of his successful rival. In the sacred cause of country he forgot private animosities and personal wrongs.

> " 'Twas a holy time when the kings, long foemen,
>   Fought, side by side, to uplift the serf;
> Never triumphed in old time Greek or Roman
>   As Brian and Malachi at Clontarf.
>
> * * * *
>
> Praise to the king of ninety years
>   Who rode round the battle-field, cross in hand;
> But the blessing of Eire and grateful tears
>   To him who fought under Brian's command!
> A crown in heaven for the king who brake,
>   To staunch old discords, his royal wand;
> Who spurn'd his throne for his people's sake—
>   Who served a rival and saved the land!" *

The second division of the Irish army was led by Brian's son-in-law, Kian, King of Desmond. He was as remarkable for his person as for his courage and bravery. Kian "exceeded in stature and beauty all the other men of Erinn." The Eugenian clans of South Munster followed his banner, and found themselves opposed to the men of Leinster, led by the recreant Maelmurra, and aided by a band of Northmen.

The remaining Scandinavian contingents, principally from the Orkney Islands, the Hebrides, Isle of Man, Wales and Britain, Norway and Denmark, composed the third division of the foreign army. They were led

* From *Inisfail*, by AUBREY DE VERE.

by the renowned Brodar, and by Sigurd, son of Lodar, the Orkney chief. They were opposed by the third division of the Irish army, comprising the Connaught levies under the leadership of Teige O'Kelly, Prince of Hy-Many, and Maelruiné O'Heyne, Lord of Hy-Fiachra-Aidhne. With these were some of the Munster clans and a contingent from Scotland led by Domnall, Maormor, or High-steward of Mar. Thus it was that the ancestor of the Royal Stuarts and the Gael of Alba fought at Clontarf, in aid of their Irish kindred, under the standard of Brian Boru.

At daybreak on that memorable Friday the aged and devout Brian appeared on horseback—his golden-hilted sword in one hand, a crucifix in the other—at the head of his troops to cheer and animate his army on the eve of conflict. He reminded them of the cruel ravages of the Northmen; of their desecration of churches and monasteries; of the tyranny under which they had groaned, and appealed to them as he raised the crucifix aloft, "Was not Christ on this day crucified for you?" He desired to lead them himself to the conflict, but, mindful of his great age, his people implored of him to abandon the idea, and leave to younger men the brunt of battle. Brian retired to his tent. From thence he watched the struggle: a series of hand-to-hand fights: a determined contest between brave and daring champions, enduring from the time of high water in the morning until high water in the evening. Though attended by fearful loss of life on both sides, the combat was redeemed by heroic deeds of individual bravery and daring and indomitable

T

courage. Certainly it was a more noble form of war than the distant carnage of our own times, when a great engagement is decided by artillery almost before the opposing forces have sight of one another. The battle of Clontarf was a series of duels. The first personal encounter was between Plait, a Scandinavian warrior clothed in armour, and Domhnall, the High-steward of Mar. They had challenged each other the night before, and on the morning of the battle Plait came forth "from the battalion of the men in armour, and said three times, 'Faras Domhnall?' that is, 'Where is Domhnall?' Domhnall answered, and said, 'Here, thou reptile,' said he. They fought then, and each of them endeavoured to slaughter the other; and they fell by each other, and the way that they fell was with the sword of each through the heart of the other, and the hair of each in the clenched hand of the other; and the combat of that pair was the first of the battle."

Murrogh, son of Brian, led the van of the Irish army. As the battalions were forming he "looked to one side, and beheld approaching him, on his right side, alone, the heroical, championlike, beautiful, strong, bounding, graceful, erect, impetuous young hero, Dunlang O'Hartigan; and he recognized him, and made three springs to meet him, and he kissed him, and welcomed him; and, 'O youth,' said he, 'it is long until thou comest unto us; and great must be the love and attachment of some woman to thee which has induced thee to abandon me; and to abandon Brian, and Conaing, and Donnchadh; and the nobles of Dal Gais in like manner, and the delights of

Erinn until this day.'—' Alas, O king,' said Dunlang, 'the delight that I have abandoned for thee is greater, if thou didst but know it, namely, life without death, without cold, without thirst, without hunger, without decay; beyond any delight of the delights of the earth to me until the judgment, and heaven after the judgment; and if I had not pledged my word to thee I would not have come here; and, moreover, it is fated to me to die on the day thou shalt die.'—'Shall I receive death this day, then?' said Murchadh. 'Thou shalt receive it, indeed,' said Dunlang, 'and Brian and Conaing shall receive it, and almost all the nobles of Erinn, and Toirdhelbhach (Turlogh), thy son.'" Dunlang O'Hartigan had learned this gloomy intelligence from the guardian sprite of the O'Briens. This Banshee—Aibhell of Craig Liath—had prepared King Brian also to meet his doom.

Murrogh, though he doubtless shared in the superstition of his age—and this particular form of superstition is not yet extinct in Ireland—was in no wise depressed or discouraged. He was prepared to meet his mysterious doom, and was not appalled at death in any aspect. He had cut down successively two Danish standard-bearers, when he encountered the Norwegian leader, Anrud. His right arm was well-nigh powerless from fatigue, but he seized the prince in the grasp of his yet vigorous left hand. He shook him so violently that his armour of mail fell from him as Murrogh hurled him to the earth, and, placing the point of his sword on the prostrate Northman, he stooped over Anrud to bring home the death-wound by the weight of his body on his sword-hilt. As Anrud writhed in the agonies of death, he seized the dagger which hung by his foeman's side and buried it in the heart of Murrogh. Thus died the eldest son of King Brian, the chief captain of the Irish in the battle of Clontarf. His young gallant son, Turlogh, was found drowned in the rising waters of the Tolka, impaled on one of the weir-stakes, his hands grasping the locks of two Danes, with whom he had grappled in deadly conflict.

The Connaught chieftains, too, won the renown of many acts of valour. Teige of Hy-Many, and Maelruiné of Hy-Fiachra-Aidhne, both perished on the battle-field, and their gallant clansmen were decimated, though victorious. Ere nightfall the Danes were in full retreat, closely pursued by the remnant of the Irish forces. The tent of the king was thus left undefended, and, indeed, unthought of. Here Brian had passed many anxious hours, watching the ever-varying tide of battle, or engaged in prayer.

While this "spirited, fierce, violent, vengeful, and furious" battle was waging, the aged king, kneeling on his cushion in his tent, asked his attendant what was then the condition of Murrogh's standard. "It is standing," was the reply, "and many of the banners of the Dal Gais are around it; and many heads are falling around it, and a multitude of trophies and spoils, with heads of foreigners, are along with it."

Brian resumed his prayers, and then again asked his attendant for tidings of the battalions. "There is not living on earth one who could distinguish one of them from the other. For the greater part of the hosts at either side are fallen, and those who are alive are so covered with spatterings of the crimson blood—head, body, and vesture—that a father could not know his son from any other of them, so confounded are they."

Brian's cushion was again spread for him; and again, after another interval of prayer, he demands, "How goes it with the battalions?"—"They appear to me," said the attendant, "the same as if the wood of Coil Tomar (the wood along the banks of the Tolka) were on fire, and that seven companies had been hewing away its underwood and its young shoots for a month, leaving its stately trees and its immense oaks standing. In such manner are the armies on either side, after the greater part of them have fallen, leaving a few brave men and valiant heroes only standing. And their further condition (he said) is, that they are wounded and dismembered, and disorganized all around, like the grindings of a mill turning the wrong way; and the foreigners are now defeated, and the standard of Murrogh has fallen."—"Sad is this news," said Brian; "the honour and valour of Erin fell when that standard fell."

While Brian and his attendant held this colloquy, a party of the foe, in their retreat, passed by the tent thus deserted and unprotected. They were led by the Viking Brodar, who is described in the Norse Saga as one "who had been a Christian man, and a mass-deacon by consecration, but he had thrown off his faith and become God's dastard, and now worshipped heathen fiends, and he was of all men most skilled in sorcery. He had that coat of mail on which no steel would bite.

He was both tall and strong, and had such long locks that he tucked them under his belt. His hair was black." Such was the man who entered the tent of Brian. Its only occupants were the aged king and his youthful attendant. The monarch had time to grasp his arms ere he fell in conflict. Brodar issued from the tent. He waved aloft his reeking double-headed battle-axe. "Let man tell man," he exclaimed, "that Brodar felled Brian."

So died Brian Boru. Of his six gallant sons but two survived Clontarf. On that glorious, but to them fatal battle field, the noblest blood of his clan was freely shed "for the love of fatherland."

> "Long his loss shall Erin weep,
>   Ne'er again his likeness see;
> Long her strains in sorrow steep,
>   Strains of immortality."*

So sang, in the Norse tongue, even the foes of Brian.

* From GRAY's version of *The Fatal Sisters*, from the Norse Saga of *Burnt Nial*.

CHAPTER X.

THE EVE OF THE CONQUEST.

THE mortal remains of Brian and his son Murrogh were conveyed by the monks of Swords to Armagh, and interred with much pomp in the cathedral of that city. The shattered remnant of his tribe, under the leadership of the hero's son, Donogh, retired towards Munster. On the march Kian, king of Desmond, demanded hostages—equivalent to homage—from the Dal-Gais, in conformity with that law of Ollioll Olum, which conferred the chieftainship alternately on the Eugenian and Dalcassian tribes. Donogh O'Brien refused; and the Desmond contingent separated from the remnant of the warriors of Kincora.

Thus reduced in number, and encumbered by their wounded, the gallant tribe who had borne the brunt of battle at Clontarf, found themselves opposed on their homeward march by the men of Ossory, who took this opportunity of freeing themselves from the galling yoke of subjection imposed on them by Brian Boru. The envoys of Ossory demanded hostages, or battle.

" A battle he shall have," said Donogh; " but it is a sad thing that I did not meet with a death like that which my father found, before I suffered the insult of having hostages demanded from me by the son of Gilla-Padraig." He was no less indignant when reminded of his powerlessness to resist.

"Were it ever lawful to punish any ambassadors for the purport of the message they conveyed," exclaimed the angry prince, "I would now have had your tongues plucked out of your heads for this present insolence. For though I had but one solitary camp-follower to stand by me, I should never think of refusing to contend in battle with the son of Gilla-Padraig, and the men of Ossory."

He at once prepared for action. One third of his available force was set apart to guard the wounded, and the remainder ranged in order of battle. But when the wounded men heard of this emergency, they implored of Donogh to have stakes thrust into the ground to which they might be tied, with their weapons in their hands. "Let our sons and our kinsmen," they continued, "be stationed by our sides, and let two warriors who are unwounded be placed near each one of us wounded; for it is thus that we will help one another with truer zeal, because shame will not allow the sound man to leave his position until his wounded and bound comrade can leave it likewise."

The gallant front which the remnant of Dalcassian warriors thus showed to their ungenerous assailants of Ossory, secured their ultimate safety. So noble a display of courage dismayed their enemies and averted the attack. The men of Leinster and Ossory refused to follow their leaders to the assault. "It is not of marching off, or of running away, or of breaking their ranks, or of yielding to panic," they exclaimed, " that yonder men are thinking, but of doing their utmost to defend themselves by making a firm, obstinate, and hand-to-hand fight. For this reason, we will not now contend with them in battle, for to them life and death are alike indifferent. Not one man of them can be slain until five or six of us have first fallen by his hands. And then, what advantage will result to us from dying in their company?"

And so " in want and hardship," the harassed remnant of the Dal-Gais continued their march towards their own country. When Donogh O'Brien reached Kincora, but eight hundred and fifty remained of the warriors who had marched under the banner of Murrogh to the victory which had cost them so dear.

Brian Boru, who had raised his tribe from comparative obscurity; who had compelled all Ireland to receive their supreme monarch from Lea Moha, and not, as heretofore, from Lea Con; who had set aside, by his vigorous individuality, the claim, which long prescription had almost made law, of the descendants of Niall to give kings to Ireland—had died in the moment of achieving a victory—all-important for his country, but ruinous to his house. The astute, unscrupulous, ambitious, but patriotic monarch, had risked too much of the O'Brien blood, and too many members of an infant dynasty to the chances of a battle exceptionally bloody, even in that age of carnage. Yet, before Clontarf, few founders of dynasties could look forward with more reasonable hope of transmitting a secure authority to his descendants. He had asserted that supremacy which his personal qualities justified. He had allayed factions, and triumphed over all opposition. He had ruled wisely and well. He was surrounded by a numerous family. His sons were grown to manhood. His daughters by their marriages had strengthened his alliances. His eldest son Murrogh was himself the father of a son of hopeful promise. He might well believe that a dynasty supported by such princes would bear sway, and give a stability hitherto unknown to Irish political government. No other man had been so successful as he had been in combining the whole people in one national object. He lived late enough into the afternoon of that Friday at Clontarf to see the power of the Northmen in Ireland for ever broken. But the results of his own sagacity and valour, of the ability and bravery of his son Murrogh, of the youthful heroism and gallantry of his grandson Turlogh, were so ordered as to prove ultimately fatal to his family and clan—and, it may be added, to the independence of his country also. The example which he set of successful revolt against the central authority, was followed by others, who emulated his ambition without possessing his abilities. Other tribes and families aspired to raise themselves as the O'Briens had done. Prescriptive rights were set aside, and from the battle of Clontarf to the period of the Conquest—

"The good old rule, the simple plan,
That they should take who have the power,
And they should keep who can—"

became the general law—the right of the strong hand the

sole appeal. Kings " with opposition " *go fresabhradh*, that is, kings whose authority is questioned, opposed, disregarded, are the principal royal personages who from henceforth appear on the scene.

Malachy II. on the death of Brian reassumed the position which that powerful rival had wrested from him. He followed up the victory at Clontarf, captured Dublin, and broke the power of Maelmurra of Leinster, the Irish ally of the Danes. He died in the odour of sanctity on an island of Lough Ennell, the last king of Irish blood that was indisputably Ard-Righ of Ireland— "the pillar of dignity and nobility of the western world."

It has been already mentioned that two sons only, of the numerous progeny of Brian, survived the battle of Clontarf. Teige and Donogh contended for the chieftainship of the Dal-Gais. The former fell in conflict with a neighbouring clan, not without suspicion of foul play on the part of Donogh—who now claimed not merely the Munster chieftainship, but the sovereignty left vacant by the death of Malachy.

Donogh O'Brien was the son of Gormley, that wife of Brian who was sister of Maelmurra, king of Leinster, and who had instigated her brother by her reproaches to take part with the Danes in the alliance which was broken at Clontarf. By her former husband she was the mother of Sitric, the Danish ruler in Dublin. She had also been the wife of Malachy, and the mother of his son Conor.

Donogh O'Brien had married for his second wife a daughter of Godwin, earl of Kent. When her brother

Harold—afterwards the last Saxon king of England—had to seek an asylum during the reign of Edward the Confessor, he found welcome and protection at the court of Donogh. But the sway of Donogh was recognised in Munster and Connaught only. Flaherty O'Neill ruled the northern districts from his fort at Aileach. This prince made a pilgrimage to Rome A.D. 1030, whence his *soubriquet* "*an Trostain*," that is, Flaherty "Pilgrim-staff."

The central districts of the island during this period obeyed the injunctions of Cuan O'Loghan, an eminent poet, and Corcran Claircach, a devout anchorite of Lismore, recalling in some degree the government of the Jews under judges. Meantime a formidable competitor for the supreme place assumed the provincial throne of Leinster. Dermid, son of Mael-na-mbo, was the immediate ancestor of the MacMurroghs. He married a granddaughter of King Brian, and became the powerful protector of Turlogh, son of Teige, son of Brian, to whom he stood in the further relation of foster-father.

Turlogh O'Brien thus became a rival to his uncle Donogh. After many contests and skirmishes Turlogh, aided by Dermid of Leinster, defeated the troops of Donogh, led by his son Murrogh "Short-shield," and compelled Donogh to resign his crown of Munster.

The deposed king, following the example of Flaherty O'Neill, made a pilgrimage to Rome, where he died. He is said to have carried with him the insignia of royalty, and to have resigned the Irish regalia into the hands of the then pope, Alexander II.

We shall not further dwell on the disputed rule of Dermid "of the white teeth, laughing in danger," or of his friend and foster-son, Turlogh, king of Munster, from whom William Rufus obtained the Irish oak which he used for the roofing of one of his great edifices, or of the greater son of Turlogh, Murkertach Mór O'Brien, except to mention a characteristic anecdote told of this prince in connection with William Rufus, but proceed to glance rapidly at the rise of a new family, hitherto unacquainted with sovereign power. The story of the Irish ruler and Red William is this:— It had been reported to Murkertach that the English king, standing on a high rock, and looking towards Ireland, had said, "I will bring hither my ships, and pass over and conquer that land;" on which the Irish monarch inquired: "Hath the king in his great threatening said, *if it please God?*" Then, learning that Rufus had planned the expedition in his own strength only, had rejoined, "I fear him not."

To proceed with the rise of the O'Conors.—The O'Conors of Connaught traced their descent from Eremon, and ruled from Rath Cruachan, the ancient capital of Queen Maev, in Roscommon. Turlogh O'Conor made many hostings into Munster, and in the battle of Moanmore inflicted a signal defeat on the southern clans. Seven thousand of the "defeated and slaughtered" men of Munster are said to have fallen in this engagement; and many Septs had to lament the loss of both Chief and Tanist. On the side of the victorious O'Conor fought Dermid MacMurrogh, second of the name, afterwards distinguished as

Diarmaid na n'Gall, "Dermid of the Foreigners," the king of Leinster who invited the English invasion. Turlogh O'Conor died A.D. 1156, and was buried beside the altar of Kieran at Clonmacnoise, "a man full of charity, mercy, hospitality, and chivalry." How far this eulogy may be the reward of his gifts to the church we shall not pause to discuss.

"Great indeed were the legacies which this prince left to the clergy for the repose of his soul, namely, four hundred and forty ounces of gold and forty marks of silver, and all the other valuable treasures he possessed, both cups and precious stones, both steeds, and cattle, and robes, chess-boards, bows, quivers, arrows, equipments, weapons, armour, and utensils. And he himself pointed out the manner in which its particular portion thereof should be distributed to each church, according to its rank and order."

At this period piety and devotion were still rife among the Irish princes and persons of distinction; but ecclesiastical government and discipline were at a low ebb. The ravages of the Danes had struck the first blow at her seminaries of sacred learning. The turbulent and lawless times which succeeded, were not favourable to the systematic observance of religion. The very isolation and independence of the Irish church permitted its adoption of practices inconsistent with ecclesiastical discipline. A desire for reformation and closer communion with Rome sprang up, as a natural consequence, in the minds of her leading ecclesiastics. Synods with this view were held early in the twelfth century, under the auspices of Celsus, archbishop of Armagh, and Gillibert, bishop of Limerick. But a greater reformer was yet to arise in the person of Malachy O'Morgair, better known as St. Malachy, afterwards archbishop of Armagh, and appointed by Pope Innocent II. his legate in Ireland. On the occasion of a visit made by him to Rome, A.D. 1139, the pope "often and attentively inquired of him, and of those who were with him, concerning the state of their country, the habits of the people, the condition of the churches, and the great things which God had wrought by his means in his native land." On his answers probably were grounded some of the censures of which the Irish people soon after became the objects.

Malachy, like other Irish saints, has been happy in his biographer. His life has been written by his friend St. Bernard, in whose arms he expired while on a visit at Clairvaux, on the 2nd of November, 1148. He was the introducer of the Cistercian order of monks into Ireland. Their first foundation, the abbey of Mellifont, near Drogheda, bears date A.D. 1142.

We are now on the threshold of the English invasion. In 1154, two years before the death of King Turlogh O'Conor, Nicholas Breakspere, an Englishman, ascended the papal chair. No other Englishman, before or since, has ever worn the triple tiara. In the same year Henry Plantagenet ascended the throne of England. Pope Adrian IV., for such was the new pontiff's title, was naturally disposed to gratify the English king, and in his celebrated bull authorised

King Henry II. to invade and conquer Ireland. We give this remarkable document *in extenso*.

"Adrian, the bishop, a servant of the servants of God, to his dearest son in Christ Jesus, the illustrious king of England, sends greeting and apostolical benediction. The desire your magnificence expresses to extend your glory upon earth, and to lay up for yourself in heaven a great reward of eternal happiness, is very laudable and profitable for you, while, as a good Catholic prince, you endeavour to enlarge the bounds of the church, to declare the true Christian faith to ignorant and barbarous nations, and to extirpate all evil from the field of the Lord; which the better to perform, you ask the advice and encouragement of the apostolical see. In the accomplishment of this work we trust you will have, by the assistance of God, a success proportioned to the depth of counsel and discretion with which you shall proceed; forasmuch as everything which takes its rise from the ardour of faith and love of religion is most likely to come to a good and happy end. There is, indeed, no doubt that (as you yourself acknowledge) Ireland, and all other islands which Christ the Sun of Righteousness has illuminated, and which have received the doctrines of the Christian faith, belong of right to the jurisdiction of St. Peter and the most holy Roman Church; wherefore we more gladly sow in them the seed of faith, which is good and agreeable to God, as we know that it will be more strictly required of our conscience not to neglect it. Since, then, you have signified to us, most dear son in

Christ, that you desire to enter into the island of Ireland, in order to subdue the people to the obedience of laws, and extirpate the vices which have there taken root, and that you are also willing to pay an annual pension to St. Peter of one penny from every house therein, and to preserve the rights of the church in that land inviolate and entire, we, seconding your pious and commendable intention with the favour it deserves, and granting a benignant assent to your petition, are well pleased that, for the enlargement of the bounds of the church—for the restraint of vice—the correction of evil manners—the culture of all virtues, and the advancement of the Christian religion, you should enter into that island, and effect what will conduce to the salvation thereof, and to the honour of God. It is likewise our desire that the people of that country should receive you with honour, and venerate you as their master: provided always that the ecclesiastical rights therein remain inviolate and entire, and reserving to St. Peter and the most holy Roman Church the annual pension of a penny from every house. If, therefore, you think fit to put your design in execution, endeavour studiously to instruct that nation in good morals, and do your utmost, as well personally as by others whom you know from their faith, doctrine, and course of life to be fit for such a work, that the church may there be adorned, the Christian religion planted and made to grow, and whatsoever appertains to the honour of God and the salvation of souls so ordered, as may entitle you to an eternal reward from God, and a glorious name upon earth."

King Henry, after receiving this authorisation, held a parliament at Winchester, A.D. 1155, "in which he treated with his nobles concerning the conquest of Ireland: but because the thing was opposed to the wishes of his mother, the empress, that expedition was put off till another time."

The project thus deferred was not forgotten. Henry had solicited the grant in order that he might bestow an inheritance on his younger brother, who had been inadequately provided for by their father's will. His own domestic troubles, the complications in which his quarrel with Thomas-à-Becket involved him, and other reasons, might have caused the bull of Pope Adrian to remain a dead letter. Events, however, gave a new stimulus to the enterprise.

Dervorgilla, the wife of O'Ruarc, lord of Breffny, had been carried off by Dermid MacMurrogh, king of Leinster. The abduction, it is said, had been planned by the lady, between whom and Dermid an old attachment had existed. The lovers were at this time of mature age—Dervorgilla in her forty-fourth year, and Dermid some years older. King Turlogh O'Conor, and, at a later period, his son Roderic, avenged the wrongs of O'Ruarc: Dermid was dispossessed of his territory and driven into exile; while the faithless Dervorgilla sought to atone for her guilt, where her past munificence had prepared for her a reception, in the monastic seclusion of Mellifont.

The discomfited prince sought the presence of King Henry II., who was at that time in France, but so engrossed by his affairs there, and in England, that he was unable to avail himself of the opportunity which the appeal of Dermid presented. Yet he listened with a ready and gracious ear to his representations; and although declining himself to take up his quarrel, received his homage, and gave him his letters of aid.

"Henry, king of England, duke of Normandy and Aquitaine, and earl of Anjou," so the letters ran by which he authorized Dermid to seek for aid in Britain, "to all his liegemen, English, Norman, Welsh, and Scotch, and to all other nations under his dominion, sends greeting. As soon as the present letters shall come to your hands, know that Dermid, prince of Leinster, has been received into the bosom of our grace and benevolence. Wherefore, whosoever within the ample extent of our territories shall be willing to lend aid towards the restoration of this prince, as our faithful and liege subject, let such person know that we do hereby grant to him, for said purpose, our licence and favour."

Thus accredited, Dermid found no difficulty in procuring auxiliary aid. The promise of the hand in marriage of his daughter Eva, with the reversion of the crown of Leinster at his death, as her portion, secured him the alliance of Richard De Clare, earl of Pembroke and Strigul, better known by his pseudonym of "Strongbow." Round the banner of this noble and daring adventurer flocked his kinsmen, the sons and other near connections of the beautiful Nesta, daughter of the Welsh prince, Rhys ap Tudor.

This fairest woman of her day was the mother, by King Henry I., of Robert Fitz Roy, who, as earl of

Gloucester, is distinguished in English history during the war of succession between his sister, the Empress Maud, and Stephen of Blois; she also bore to this King, Henry Fitz Henry—the parent of Meyler Fitz Henry, who played so prominent a part in Irish affairs—and, by a subsequent marriage, was the mother of Fitz Gerald, the progenitor of the Geraldines, that princely race whose representatives, both of the Kildare and Desmond branches, fill so eminent a place, even to the present time, in Irish history. By a yet subsequent marriage, Nesta was the mother of another leader in the conquest of Ireland, Robert Fitz Stephen; while from her daughters sprang the families of De Barri, and Fitz Bernard. Gerald De Barri, better known as Giraldus Cambrensis, to whose "Topography" and "Conquest" of Ireland, we owe so much of our information touching this period, was grandson of the same Nesta. He was tutor of Prince John; was an able, energetic, and learned man, but one animated, as might be expected from his near relationship with the conquerors, by a strong spirit of hostility against the native Irish.

Such were the men by whose aid Dermid, for the brief remnant of his life, was enabled to return to his patrimony. He died A.D. 1171, according to the Irish chroniclers, "as his evil deeds deserved." He has been thus described by Cambrensis:—

"This Dermicius was a man of tall stature and large frame, warlike and daring among his nation, and of hoarse voice, by reason of his frequent and continuous shouting in battle. He desired to be feared rather than to be loved; he oppressed the noble and elevated the lowly; he was the enemy of his countrymen; he was hated by strangers. The hand of all men was against him, and his hand was against all."

On the great event which was now impending, long designed and ultimately precipitated by the reckless selfishness of this too famous personage, it is not the intention of the writer here to enter. The historian of the Conquest, and of the ages which have since elapsed, may have to regret the rough and tedious process of transition through which the country was now destined to begin its passage; but it will always be a satisfactory reflection that amongst its results has been our admission to a larger sphere of civilization, to a share in many peaceful as well as warlike glories, and to the general use of that noble language in which all the gains of science and all the highest utterances of modern poetry and philosophy have found a worthy expression.

NOTE ON THE SOURCES AND NOMENCLATURE.

THE Sources from which the material of this volume has been extracted are, to some extent, in manuscript, and hitherto unpublished. Of these the principal are—

O'Curry's Translation of the Tain-bo-Cuailgné, with its "Pre-Tales," comprising the "Boy-Feats" of Cuchullin; for the perusal of which, and liberty to use the extracts in the text, the author is indebted to the liberal kindness of the Right Reverend CHARLES GRAVES, Lord Bishop of Limerick; and of the Rev. JAMES HENTHORNE TODD, D.D., and J. T. GILBERT, Esq., Secretaries of the Irish Archæological and Celtic Society.

Extract from the " Talland Etair," or Siege of Howth, translated from the Tract in the Book of Leinster, and kindly placed at the author's disposal by WILLIAM M. HENNESSY, Esq., M.R.I.A.

Collections for the Ordnance Survey of Ireland, deposited in the Library of the Royal Irish Academy.

With these exceptions, the sources are all accessible to the English reader in published translations from the Irish and Latin of the original works. From the dates mentioned below, it will be seen that these aids to the modern student have all, save one, been furnished since the first great stimulus to the study of Irish history and antiquities was given by the project for an Ordnance Survey Memoir of Ireland, about thirty years ago. The Irish story is no longer a sealed book; but, to select material for a volume reasonably likely to attract a general interest still requires a considerable range of study. The translated and other works which have been principally used by the author are—

Account of the Danes and Norwegians in England, Scotland, and Ireland. By J. J. A. WORSAAE, For. F.S.A. London; a Royal Commissioner for the Preservation of the National Monuments of Denmark, &c., &c. London, 1852.

Account of the Tribes and Customs of the District of Hy-Many, commonly called O'Kelly's Country, in the Counties of Galway and Roscommon. Edited from the Book of Lecan in the Library of the Royal Irish Academy, in the original Irish; with a Translation and Notes, and a Map of Hy-Many. By JOHN O'DONOVAN, LL.D. Published for the Irish Archæological Society. Dublin, 1843.

Annala Rioghachta Eireann. Annals of the Kingdom of Ireland. By the Four Masters. From the earliest period to the year 1616. Edited from MSS. in the Library of the Royal Irish Academy and of Trinity College, Dublin, with a Translation and copious Notes, by JOHN O'DONOVAN, Esq., M.R.I.A., Barrister-at-Law. Dublin: Hodges and Smith, 1851.

Cath Muighi Rath. The Battle of Magh Rath: from an ancient MS. in the Library of Trinity College, Dublin. Edited in the original Irish, with a Translation and Notes, by JOHN O'DONOVAN, LL.D. Published for the Irish Archæological Society, Dublin, 1842.

Circuit of Ireland, by Muircheartach MacNeill, Prince of Aileach; a Poem written in the year 942 by Cormacan Eigeas, Chief Poet of the North of Ireland. Edited, with a Translation and Notes, and a Map of the Circuit, by JOHN O'DONOVAN, LL.D., M.R.I.A. Published by the Irish Archæological Society. Dublin, 1841.

Cogadh Gaedhil re Gallaibh. The War of the Gaedhil with the Gaill; or the Invasions of Ireland by the Danes and other Norsemen. The original Irish text, edited with Translation and Introduction, by JAMES HENTHORNE TODD, D.D., M.R.I.A., F.S.A., &c. Published by the authority of the

Lords Commissioners of Her Majesty's Treasury, under the direction of the Master of the Rolls. London, 1867. *In the series of the Chronicles and Memorials of Great Britain and Ireland during the Middle Ages, or Rerum Britannicarum Medievi Scriptores.*

Columba (Life of Saint). By Adamnan, ninth Abbot of Hy (or Iona). The Latin text taken from a MS. of the early part of the eighth century, preserved at Schaffhausen; with various readings, illustrated by copious Notes and Dissertations. By the Rev. WILLIAM REEVES, D.D., M.B., V.P.R.I.A. With Maps and coloured Facsimiles of the MSS. Published for the Irish Archæological and Celtic Society, 1857.

Ecclesiastical Antiquities of Down, Connor, and Dromore. Consisting of a taxation of those Dioceses compiled in the year 1306. With Notes and Illustrations by the Rev. WILLIAM REEVES, M.B., M.R.I.A. Dublin, 1847.

Ecclesiastical Architecture of Ireland, anterior to the Anglo-Norman Invasion. Comprising an Essay on the origin and uses of the Round Towers of Ireland. By GEORGE PETRIE, R.H.A., V.P.R.I.A., &c. Transactions of the Royal Irish Academy, vol. 20. Dublin, 1845.

Foras Feasa Ar Eirinn. The History of Ireland from the earliest period to the English Invasion. By the Rev. GEOFFREY KEATING, D.D. Translated from the original Gaelic, and copiously annotated by JOHN O'MAHONY. New York: P. M. Haverty, 1857.

Genealogies, Tribes, and Customs of the District of Hy-Fiachrach, commonly called O'Dowda's Country. Edited from the Book of Lecan, in the Library of the Royal Irish Academy; and from a copy of the MacFirbis MS., in the possession of the Earl of Roden. With a Translation and Notes, and a Map of Hy-Fiachrach. By JOHN O'DONOVAN, LL.D. Published for the Irish Archæological Society, 1844.

History and Antiquities of Tara Hill. By GEORGE PETRIE, Esq. Transactions of the Royal Irish Academy, vol. 18, part 2. Dublin, 1839.

Imtheacht na Tromdhaimhe. Proceedings of the Great

Bardic Institution. Edited by Professor CONNELLAN. Ossianic Society. O'Daly: Dublin, 1860.

Laoithe Fiannuigheachta; or Fenian Poems. Edited by JOHN O'DALY. Published by the Ossianic Society. Dublin, 1841.

Lectures on the Manuscript Materials of Ancient Irish History. Delivered in the Catholic University of Ireland during the sessions of 1855 and 1856. By EUGENE O'CURRY, M.R.I.A.; Professor of Irish History and Archæology in the Catholic University of Ireland; Corresponding Member of the Society of Antiquaries of Scotland, &c. Dublin: Duffy, 1861.

Nennius (The Irish version of the Historia Britonum of). Edited with a Translation and Notes by JAMES HENTHORNE TODD, D.D., M.R.I.A.; Fellow of Trinity College, &c. The Introduction and Additional Notes by the Hon. ALGERNON HERBERT. Published for the Irish Archæological Society. Dublin, 1848.

Primer of the History of the Holy Catholic Church in Ireland. By ROBERT KING, A.B. Dublin: McGlashan, 1851.

Saint Patrick, Apostle of Ireland. A Memoir of his Life and Mission. With an Introductory Dissertation on some early usages of the Church in Ireland, and its historical position from the establishment of the English Colony to the present day. By JAMES HENTHORNE TODD, D.D., &c. Dublin, 1864.

Senchus Mor. Introduction to Senchus Mor and Athgabail; or Law of Distress as contained in the Harleian MSS. Published under direction of the Commissioners for publishing the Ancient Laws and Institutes of Ireland, vol. 1. Hodges and Smith, Dublin: Longmans, London, 1865.

Toruigheacht Dhiarmuda ui Dhuibhne agus Ghrainne inghion Chormuic mheic Airt: or an account of the Pursuit of Diarmiud O'Duibhne and Grace, the daughter of Cormac MacAirt. Edited by STANDISH HAYES O'GRADY, Esq. Published for the Ossianic Society. Dublin, 1857.

Transactions of the Iberno-Celtic Society. Dublin, 1806.

With respect to the Nomenclature, the author has endeavoured to present the names of persons in a guise as little repellent as possible to the eye of the English reader. Their strangeness, their want of association with anything previously known, and their singular difficulty of pronunciation, constitute, in truth, a very great obstacle to any popular treatment of the subject. It would seem as if, in primitive times, when men were sparing of their words, they thought to give increased consideration to all they uttered, and specially to the names of individuals, by magnifying the forms of expression. In more modern times, men have had more to say, and seem to have studied how best to abbreviate and smooth down the old stately but cumbrous forms of expression. This has been notably the case in the old Irish proper names. Thus *Concobar* has been shortened and softened into *Conor*; *Toirdealbach* into *Turlogh*; *Flathbeartac* into *Flaherty*; and so with almost all the longer and more high-sounding names of persons. To mark this process of softening, the writers of the names have everywhere introduced the letter *h* as the sign of aspiration, or "breathing-over," of the slurred consonants. Hence a new feature of very repulsive aspect to eyes unaccustomed to Irish-written texts. Under this process, we have the original sharply-defined names presented in the guise, *Conchobhar*; *Toirdhealbhach*; *Flathbheartuch*. In the endeavour to avoid these awkwardnesses, different writers have resorted to different compromises between the sound and the spelling. Thus has arisen that perplexing variety of forms in which the same name is presented by different authorities. Thus, O'Kearney, the oldest translator of Keating, gives the name *Conchuvar*; O'Mahony, *Concobar*; MacGeoghegan, *Conquovar*; and others, *Connogher*, *Cnogher*, *Connor*, and *Conor*, which last form has been here adopted from O'Curry. To lay down any other than an empirical rule of orthography in such a case seems hardly practicable. What has been here deemed the least objectionable course is, to adhere to whatever form of spelling best indicates the sound to the English-educated eye. In some cases this orthography coincides with the Irish, in others it departs considerably from it. A list of the latter, and much larger, class of names is subjoined, from which the reader, whose curiosity may be sufficiently attracted to the subject, will be able to see the authentic forms of such proper names as have been adapted to English eyes in the text. Amongst these will be found a few names of places. But the topographical names in the Celtic dialects are usually as simple and easy of pronunciation as they are expressive, and, to use the words of an able English critic, full of " a penetrating and lofty beauty." In the process of adapting both classes of names to the rapid and careless modes of utterance of modern times, and among a depressed race, a great degradation is apparent, and many names at present esteemed the most vulgar, are found, in their original forms, lofty and significant of noble qualities.

Ængus	*Aenghus.*
Armagh	*Ard-Macha.*
Awley	*Amhalghaidh.*
Bangor	*Beannchair.*
Barrow	*Bearbha.*
Breffny	*Breifne.*
Brian Boru	*Brian Borumha.*
Burrisoole	*Burgeis Ui Mhaile.*
Callaghan	*Ceallachan.*
Carbre Lificar	*Cairbre Liffeachar.*
Cashel	*Caiseal.*
Clannaboy	*Clann-Aodha-bhuidhe.*
Clonmacnois	*Cluain-mic-Nois.*
Clontarf	*Cluain-tarbh.*
Conari	*Conaire.*
Connaught	*Connacht.*
Conor	*Conchobhar.*
Cong	*Cunga-Feichin.*
Cova	*Cobhthach.*

Creeve Roe	*Craobh Ruaidh.*
Criffan	*Crimthann.*
Cruthne	*Cruithnigh.*
Cuchullin	*Cuchullain.*
Cucongelt	*Cuchoingealt.*
Culinan	*Cuileanan.*
Dalcassians	*Dal-g'Cais.*
Dermid Mac Kervil.	*Diarmaid Mac Cearbhaill.*
Derry	*Doire-Chalgaigh.*
Dervorgilla	*Dearbhforgaill.*
Devenish	*Daimh-Inis.*
Disert Diarmada	*Diseart Diarmada.*
Dodder	*Dothair.*
Donall	*Domhnall.*
Donogh	*Donnchadh.*
Donovan	*Donnabhan.*
Drumceat	*Druimcета.*
Drumcliff	*Druim-cliabh.*
Dundelgan	*Dun-Dealgan.*
Dunnascaith	*Dun-na-sgiath.*
Durrow	*Dearmhagh.*
Eochy	*Eochaidh.*
Eochy Felia	*Eochaidh Feidhleach.*
Eugenians	*Eoganacht.*
Falvy	*Failbhe.*
Fathna	*Fachtna.*
Felemy	*Feidhlimidh.*
Ferns	*Fearna-mor-Maedhoig.*
Flaherty	*Flaithbheartach.*
Fola	*Fodhla.*
Fore	*Fobhar Feichin.*
Gael	*Gaeidhel.*
Gormley	*Gormfhlaith.*
Gowanree	*Gamhanruidhe.*

Note on the Sources and Nomenclature. 301

Inishowen	*Inis-Eoghain.*
Kennedy	*Cenneulligh.*
Kevin	*Caemhghen.*
Kildare	*Cill-dara.*
Kimbay	*Cimbaeth.*
Kincora	*Ceann-coradh.*
Kinel Owen	*Cinel-Eoghain.*
Kenfalla	*Cennfaeladh.*
Lavra	*Labhradh.*
Lea Con	*Leath Cuinn.*
Lea Moha	*Leath Mogha.*
Leary	*Laoghaire.*
Leix	*Laoighis.*
Leinster	*Laighin.*
Lough Foyle	*Loch-Febhail.*
Lough Corrib	*Loch-Oirbsean.*
Maelcova	*Maelcobha.*
Maelmurra	*Maelmordha*
Maev	*Medhbh.*
Mahon	*Mathghamhain.*
Malachy	*Maelseachlainn.*
Malodar	*Maelodhar.*
Moh Nuad	*Mogh Nuadhat.*
Molaise	*Molaisi.*
Mourne	*Mughdhorna.*
Moville	*Magh-bhile.*
Moy Lena	*Magh Leana.*
Moy Mucrivé	*Magh Mucruimhe.*
Moynalty	*Magh-n-ealta.*
Moyrath	*Magh-rath.*
Moy Slaght	*Mugh-sleacht.*
Moyturé	*Magh-Tuireadh.*
Mulloy	*Maelmhuaidh.*
Munster	*Mumha.*

Murkertach	Muircheartach.
Murrogh	Muireadhach.
Murthevné	Muirtheimhne.
O'Conor	Ua Conchobair.
O'Hartigan	Uah'-Artagain.
O'Heyne	Uah'-Eidhin.
Olav Fola	Ollamh Fodhla.
O'Rafferty	Ua Robhartaigh.
Oran	Odhran.
O'Shaughnessy	Ua Seachnasaigh.
Orgiall	Oirghiall.
Owen	Eoghan.
Raphoe	Rathbhoth.
Roderick	Ruaidhri.
Roy	Roigh.
Rury	Ruaidhri.
Sancan	Senchan.
Saul	Sabhall Padraig.
Scoti	Scuit.
Slangé	Slainge.
Sletty	Sleibhte.
Slewen	Slemhain.
Slieve Fuad	Sliabh Fuaid.
Sligo	Sligech.
Soive	Sadhbh.
Sulcoit	Sulchoid.
Sweeny	Suibhne.
Swords	Sord-Choluim-chille.
Tailti	Tailten.
Tara	Teamhair.
Teige	Tadhg.
Thomond	Tuathmhumha.

Tiernmas	. . . . .	*Tighearnmas.*
Tirera	. . . . .	*Tir Fhiachrach.*
Tolka	. . . . .	*Tulcan.*
Turlogh	. . . . .	*Toirdhealbhach.*
Tyrone	. . . . .	*Tir Eoghain.*
Ulster	. . . . .	*Uladh.*
Umor	. . . . .	*Uathmor.*

S. F.

THE END.

LONDON: PRINTED BY WILLIAM CLOWES AND SONS, STAMFORD STREET
AND CHARING CROSS.

www.ingramcontent.com/pod-product-compliance
Lightning Source LLC
Chambersburg PA
CBHW030811230426
43667CB00008B/1158